Textiles: A History

To Fiona Shoop who set me on my way

Textiles: A History

By Fiona McDonald

REMEMBER WHEN

First published in Great Britain in 2011 by
Remember When
An imprint of
Pen & Sword Books Ltd
47 Church Street
Barnsley
South Yorkshire
S70 2AS

ISBN 978 1 84884 509 1

A CIP catalogue record for this book is
available from the British Library.

Typeset in 10pt Palatino by Mac Style, Beverley, East Yorkshire
Printed and bound in India by Replika Press Pvt. Ltd.

Pen & Sword Books Ltd incorporates the imprints of Pen & Sword Aviation,
Pen & Sword Maritime, Pen & Sword Military, Wharncliffe Local History, Pen &
Sword Select, Pen & Sword Military Classics, Leo Cooper, Seaforth Publishing and
Frontline Publishing.

For a complete list of Pen & Sword titles please contact
PEN & SWORD BOOKS LIMITED
47 Church Street, Barnsley, South Yorkshire, S70 2AS, England
E-mail: enquiries@pen-and-sword.co.uk
Website: www.pen-and-sword.co.uk

Contents

Adam and Eve cover their shame
with the first clothes.

Introduction

Into the thickest wood, there soon they chose
The fig-tree, not that kind for fruit renowned,
But such as at this day to Indians known
In Malabar...
... those leaves they gathered, broad as Amazonian targe,
And with what skill they had, together sewed,
To gird their waist, vain covering if to hide
Their guilt and dreaded shame...

John Milton's *Paradise Lost*, Book IX, 1100–1114

Was it really fig leaves mankind made its first clothes from? Stitched together with what? Perhaps vines or reeds even strands of Eve's hair? Archaeologists would find the evidence for this earliest of textiles a bit insubstantial. Instead they have dug up fragments of spun thread, felted clothes, spinning and weaving tools, and pottery bearing the imprints of twisted threads. These artefacts can tell us many things about the history of the fabric we make and the clothes we wear.

Science has advanced to a stage where plant types can be identified from the indentation they have left in soft clay baked hard and buried for thousands of years.

Ancient trade routes have been traced to mark the comings and goings of goods and cultures across the world telling us that China traded silk fabric earlier than the official date given. We know that certain plants were unknown to Europeans although they readily wore clothes made from the cloth spun from the plant.

Textiles are an integral part of life. Terms used for the making of textiles, like weaving and spinning, are used for other aspects of our lives: we weave webs of intrigue and spin lies, cloak ourselves in mystery, knit our brows with worry and tie up loose ends of business. There are blankets of silence, sheets of rain and veils of mist. Textiles define who we are historically and culturally. Whether we live in a high rise city and wear the latest Paris fashions or we subscribe to older traditions away from the hustle and bustle of technology, we are still bound by certain taboos and beliefs about clothing. At funerals we don't wear bright colours; traditionally it is black. Weddings are usually done in yards and yards of white silk, satin and lace but in some Asian countries you are married in red as a symbol of good luck and prosperity.

Boys are still dressed in blue, girls in pink. Red is still seen as a sexy and seductive colour (unless you are getting married in it). Blue and green should never be seen,

The Greek Fates by Walter Crane.

though as it is the word green that rhymes with 'seen' then it could be any colour and green should never be seen.

The creation of textiles is so significant that they have infiltrated our myths and legends. The Ancient Greeks had a trio of goddesses called the Fates. Hesiod (ancient Greek poet) firstly called them the daughters of Night but then amended that to the daughters of Zeus and Themis and sisters of the Horae (goddesses of the seasons). Clotho was the spinner of the thread of human life. Lachesis measured the thread out into the person's allotted life span and the third sister, Atropos would cut it at the moment of death.

Weaving was considered the proper skill for a woman and great pride was taken in it. Arachne, a mortal girl was an excellent weaver by human standards but she foolishly challenged the goddess Athena to a weaving contest. Arachne's tapestry, for it was a woven picture, showed the gods in their disguises and trickery, dishonesty and unfaithfulness. The skill may have been there but it was not a diplomatic picture. Athena wove a picture of herself and Poseidon each striving for the domination of Athens and of course, pictures of stupid mortals who had challenged gods in the past – and lost. Arachne's work was wonderful and had really challenged the goddess's for skill and beauty. Athena destroyed it and assailed Arachne, beating her with her weaving shuttle. Arachne tried to hang herself but Athena, in a fit of remorse, turned her into a spider instead.

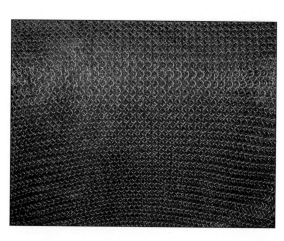

A chain mail shirt made of interlinked metal rings, but is it a textile?

Odysseus's wife, the faithful Penelope used the weaving of her father-in-law's shroud as an excuse to put off choosing a suitor and buying her husband more time to return home. Every day she would weave away and every night she would undo it all.

In China, silk and its production is wrapped in legend and secrecy. The wife of the mythical Yellow Emperor discovered silk when a cocoon fell into her cup of tea. From then on she became the goddess of silk cultivation, spinning and weaving.

Spinning and weaving have been dominated by women everywhere for domestic goods but in some places men had the job of weaving professionally. Knitting too was once undertaken by men: sailors and shepherds and men who knitted professionally. Knitting for home and children's wear was women's work.

The history of fabric is long and complicated. It is not just the history of the discovery of spinning and weaving thread out of different raw materials but it involves politics, travel, trade and war and society.

While I have tried to be thorough in my research there will, inevitably, be things missed from this book's contents. For that I apologise and can only hope that what is within these pages stimulates the reader to digging further into this fascinating subject.

Timeline

BC

38,000:   Earliest textile art made in the form of twisted thread made from gut, sinew and vines
Beads made of stone and teeth used as decoration

34,000:   Impression of twisted flax yarn found in clay vessel found in Republic of Georgia

28,000:   Czech Republic

26,000–20,000:   Needles made in Eastern Europe and Russia

25,000:   Clay figurines of Venus type shown with clothing

18,000:   Lascaux caves *bast* fibres found

Mesolithic Age

9,000:   Evidence of domestication of sheep

8,000:   Evidence in Finland of use of 2 ply willow *bast*
Flax is being cultivated

Neolithic Age

6,500:   Flax used for linen in Middle East
First evidence of warp weighted looms in Hungary

6,000:   Evidence of Naalebinding technique being used in Israel
Textiles used for wrapping the dead at Catalhoyuk (modern day Turkey)

5,000–4000   Sheep developed woolly coat

5,000:   Linen being woven in Egypt

4,200:   Evidence of Naalebinding technique being used in Denmark

4,000–3000:   In many parts of the world thread making had been long established and the
 • distaff in use
 • Swiss Lake dwellers use native flax for making yarn and cloth
 • Sheep brought to Britain by Neolithic settlers

3,500:   Early wool industry underway
Cotton cultivation begins in Mexico, Peru and the Indus valley region (modern Pakistan)
Egypt and Mesopotamia produce pictures showing horizontal ground looms

3,000:   Flax cultivated in the area that is now modern day Iran and Iraq
Use of wool spreads to Germany and Switzerland

Bronze Age

2,500:   Sheep being farmed in Britain, mainly a variety called Soay
         In Europe nettle (*bast* fibre) is used for making cloth
2,430:   Egyptian wall painting in tomb of Khnumhotep shows the cycle of
         flax processing from harvesting to weaving cloth

Iron Age

200:   Evidence of needleknitting, based on a form of naalebinding, in
         Peru

AD

43:   Romans bring a white-faced, short wool sheep to Britain and breed
         it with the Soay
247:   Naalebinding fabric in Dura Eropas, a Roman outpost
298:   Earliest known foot powered loom
500:   Spinning wheel used in India
800:   Danes introduce a black-face short wool sheep to Britain
1000:   A pair of elaborately decorated knitted socks, earliest example of
         'true' knitting, found in Egypt
1077:   Bayeux tapestry completed, quite possibly embroidered with yarn
         made from English wool
1154:   Flax main textile fibre in Europe
         Medieval short-wool (Ryeland) and medieval long-wools (Cotswold
         and Lincoln) become the most common breeds in England
1180:   Fulling mill introduced to England
1250:   Buttons come into use as fasteners for clothing
1300:   Spinning wheel (great wheel) replaced distaff as main spinning tool
         in this century in England
1331:   Seventy Flemish textile craftsmen and women invited to live in
         England by Edward III
1347:   The Black Death invades every country in Europe
1485:   Henry VIII begins dissolution of monasteries
1495:   First paper mill is built in England
1555:   Steel needles replaced drawn wire ones. The new needles are easier
         to work with and produce finer work
1560:   Introduction into England of worsteds and other 'new draperies'
         by protestant immigrants fleeing persecution on the continent
1562:   Evidence of purl stitch, found in a burial chamber in Toledo, Spain
1589:   William Lee invents the knitting machine
1600:   Modern type of spinning wheel, the Saxon wheel, comes into
         frequent use
1607:   First English colony established in North America
1611:   Cotton planted in Virginia as an experiment
1714:   Lustre long-wool developed from medieval long-wool and Downs
         sheep breeds developed from the black-face short-wools
1733:   John Kay patents his flying shuttle
1738:   Lewis Paul patents the draw roller

1758:	Jedediah Strutt adds a second set of needles to William Lee's stocking frame to create the rib frame
1764:	James Hargreaves invents the spinning jenny which is then patented in 1770
1767:	Spinning frame invented by John Kay
1768:	The hand-operated warp knitting machine is invented by Josiah Crane
1769:	Richard Arkwright invents the water frame Problems involving William Lee's stocking frame are solved by Samuel Wise
1770:	Hargreaves patent his spinning jenny
1779:	The spinning mule is invented by Samuel Crompton
1783:	Arkwright uses Watt's rotary steam engine to power a cotton mill; this is the first instance of it being put to such a use
1784:	The power loom is invented by Edward Cartwright
1785:	Boulton–Watt apply their rotary spinning operation to cotton Cartwright patents basic power weaving mill
1789:	Textile machinery design taken to the US by Samuel Slater
1790:	Arkwright builds the first steam powered textile mill in Nottingham, England
1791:	The mechanisation of the warp knitting machine is finalised by Dawson
1793:	The USA sees its first successful cotton spinning mill set up in Pawtucket by Samuel Slater
1794:	Eli Whitney patents his cotton gin
1798:	Boulton-Watt rotary steam engine applied to spinning mule The circular bearded needle knitting machine is patented by Decroix of France
1799:	Bleaching powder is invented and patented by Charles Tennant
1801:	The Jacquard punched card loom is invented by Joseph Marie Jacquard
1806:	Manchester cotton mill is fitted with gas lights The first latch needle for knitting machines is patented by Pierre Jeandeau
1808:	Weavers strike in Manchester
1809:	England introduces its first Factory act
1810:	Crompton's mule
1813:	Improvements made to the power loom by William Horrocks
1814:	The first power loom is set up in the USA by Paul Moody of the Boston Manufacturing Company
1823:	In England the second factory act is brought in
1826:	East Lancashire weavers' riot
1828:	The leather belt and pulley power transmission system is developed by Paul Moody (see above) which will become the standard fixture for US mills
1829:	Manchester weavers' riot
1833:	England brings in another factory act

1842:	A semi automatic power loom, the Lancashire Loom, is developed by Bullough and Kenworthy
1846:	Elias Howe patents his lockstitch sewing machine
1847:	The 'Mason self-acting' mule is patented by William Mason
1849:	A variant of the latch needle for weft knitting machines is patented by Matthew Townsend
1856:	First ever synthetic dye invented by William Henry Perkin
1857:	A multi-head knitting machine is patented by Arthur Pagent and named after him
1859:	The 'Raschel' warp knitting machine invented by Redgate
1864:	William Cotton patents his straight bar knitting machine, the 'Cotton'
1865:	Elias Howe establishes the Howe Machine company to make his sewing machine designs
	Isaac Singer renames his company Singer Manufacturing Company
	Flat bed knitting machine using latch needles patented by America Isaac Wixom Lamb
	The double-headed latch needle applied to knitting machine by Clay in order to knit purl stitch
1900:	The flat bed purl knitting machine invented by Heinrich Stoll
1910:	The circular bed purl knitting machine invented by Spiers
1911:	11,000 workers at Singer's largest factory in Clydebank, US, went on strike in support of 12 female workers. As a result of their actions four hundred workers were sacked
1920:	George Hattersley and Sons develop their Hattersley loom
1949:	A sewing / knitting machine brought out by Heinrich Mauersberger called the 'Malimo'
1953:	DuPont Company brings out first polyester fabric
1954:	Fibre reactive dyes invented
1963:	Czechoslovakia develops open ended spinning

PART I

The Raw Materials

How much do we really think about the origins of our clothes? Like so much of everything around us we probably take it for granted. The cotton shirt, linen trousers, the environmentally sound shopping bag, the carpets we walk on, the curtains we draw to keep out the dark, the woollen blankets, the lace doilies, the rags used for polishing the car. Textiles surround us and yet do we ever stop to think where they all came from?

In the first part of this book we will look at the raw materials from which some of those everyday items are made. We will discover that flax is a *bast* fibre which means the inner core of the stem of the plant is used to make thread. Cotton behaves more like wool, and silk is something that stands alone in the textile world. Wool was the backbone of the English economy for centuries and two separate continents made fabric out of similar products using similar techniques without the knowledge of each other.

Whether or not Adam and Eve covered their newly discovered shame with fig leaves is highly debatable. It is far more likely that they and the other early ancestors used first animal hides and then *bast* fibres before they got down to the nitty-gritty of spinning and weaving.

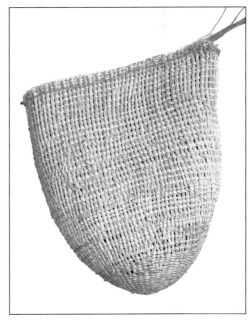

An example of basketry made by a contemporary Indigenous Australian craft person whose work can be compared with some of the earliest textile finds.

CHAPTER ONE

Plant Fibres

Flax, Hemp and Other *Bast* Fibres

Flax and hemp are probably the oldest known plant fibres in the world used for making textiles. They are still in use today. Linen, a fabric synonymous with good quality, makes the best Manchester and its characteristic crispness in classic clothing speaks volumes of good taste. Yet flax and hemp are humble plants whose appearances belie the silken fibre hidden inside them; it is a wonder that mankind ever discovered how to turn them into yarn. These fibres are known as *bast* and are found within the stems of certain plants, for instance: flax, jute, hemp, willow, ramie and certain other nettles. The fibres are held together in bundles of 30 to 40 fibres. Each stem has approximately 30 bundles.

There have been traces of processed flax fibres found within a cave in the Republic of Georgia. The thread survived as an imprint in a piece of baked clay and has been dated to 34,000 years ago. Of course, a finding this old sparks heated debate as to the accuracy of the date given to it but the archaeologists are adamant that the methods they have used for both identifying the fibre and telling how old it is are dependable. Such a find is rare but it doesn't stand alone. A few years before the Georgian Republic find another imprint of a fibre was discovered in the Czech Republic and was dated to 28,000 years old. The hypothesis about these most ancient of textile fibres is that the plants from which they were processed were wild, not cultivated and that they were harvested from the surrounding area.

Other ancient textile finds include *bast* fibres unearthed in the famous Lascaux Caves in France dating to 18,000 years ago. Nets made from two-ply willow *bast* have been found in Finland and have been carbon dated to 8000 BC. Flax or hemp *bast* nets from Lithuania and Estonia have been found which date to between 6000–4000 BC.

The flax plant.

Bast fibre plants like willow were probably used for their excellent basket weaving properties. The long, flexible young branches could be woven and twisted into shape. The discovery of using the even more pliable inner fibre may have occurred when such branches were left out in the wet. The outer fibre rotted exposing the bundles of inner fibre.

The most popular of *bast* fibres and one that became the most widespread is flax, followed closely by hemp, from which linen is made. Flax (*Linum usitatissimum*) is known to have been cultivated about 5,000 years ago in areas that are now modern day Iran and Iraq. Its versatility to grow in different climates and soil types meant that its popularity as a crop spread quickly and within 2,000 years it was to be found growing in Syria, Egypt, Switzerland and Germany.

Although it is tough, flax is the more temperamental of the two plants. It doesn't like heavy clay soil or dry gravelly soil very much whereas hemp will grow almost anywhere.

Flax and hemp produce fibres that make beautiful and strong textiles but their appeal as a crop is also because both of them have other properties. They both produce edible and medicinal seeds; these can be further processed for oil which can be put to various uses. Linseed oil was a long-time favourite medium for oil painters who used to it thin paint and facilitate glazes, and linen or hemp sails were often treated with oil from the seeds to make them waterproof (hemp is known to be resistant to the rotting effects of salt water). The same seed can be used for human consumption or as a supplementary food for animals.

With such versatility of purpose and its ready adaptation to different environments flax is one of the oldest agricultural plants of any kind.

Flax is an annual crop that grows to approximately 1.2 metres tall. The leaves are a dull green and the flowers a pale blue (sometimes red) each with five petals. Flax plants also bear fruit, round dry cases containing several glossy brown seeds. Originally flax grew wild from the East Mediterranean all the way to India and in some parts of South America. Other varieties of flax include *Silene Lineold* which grows well in the colder parts of Europe and *Silene Linicola* identified as the variety grown in ancient Egypt and Mesopotamia.

Flax in China

In China the first plant fibre to be cultivated for its use as a textile product was not flax but hemp, predating the use of silk (which was always kept for more luxurious costly items). Hemp fibres imprinted in pottery shards are estimated to be over 10,000 years old. Hemp linen was the main source of fabric fibre, even over flax, until the introduction of another *bast* fibre, ramie, and then the introduction of a completely different kind of fibre, cotton.

Pottery shards with fibre texture imprinted on it.

Linen, either from flax, hemp or ramie fibre would have been grown, harvested and turned into cloth by most family groups to make into their own clothing and home adornments. However, it would not have taken long before its marketable dimension was realised and it was produced on a commercial scale to be traded for more exotic or not so easily obtainable goods.

Egyptian linen

Egypt presents us with some of the earliest visual records of flax in the form of murals on tomb walls. The paintings depict its growing, spinning and weaving as an industry. In other documentation linen is referred to it as 'woven beauty' or 'woven moonlight'. Linen was the most important textile of the Egyptians. The Pharoah Ramses II, whose mummified body was discovered in the late Nineteenth Century, was wrapped in perfectly preserved linen bandages, as was the body of the daughter of a priest serving the god Ammon, 2,500 years ago. Linen curtains provided for Tutankhamen's tomb were reportedly in a good state of preservation. It is also in Egypt that records survive of linen being an industry.

Pliny the Elder

Pliny the Elder, 23–79 AD, was a Roman administrator historian who, amongst other things, wrote about flax, its cultivation and uses and made social comments about the various people who worked it and wore it. He begins the chapter on flax in his *Natural History* by upbraiding certain countries for growing flax in order to turn it into sails and rigging for ships. He says:

> What audacity of man! What criminal perverseness! Thus to sow a thing in the ground for the purpose of catching the winds and tempests, it being not enough for him … to be borne upon the waves alone'. *Natural History*, Book XIX.1

According to Pliny the excellent properties of flax and its usefulness for making sails, as well as fine clothing for ladies, had led to the bridging of geographical distances, bringing Egypt into close proximity with Italy: and all down to one humble plant. It seems, therefore, rather churlish of the women of the Serrani family to make a habit of never wearing linen as Pliny further informs us (it probably was more due to the fact that it creases dreadfully).

Pliny's work is entertaining as well as informative. He goes on to talk about the different properties of linen made in different parts of the world. Egypt's linen is not as strong as others but is of a particular fineness. In Germany, apparently, they wove their flax inside deep caves and this gives it certain highly desirable attributes. Flax is used for making everything from sails to hunting nets to dresses for men and women. Pliny describes different types of linen, comparing a fabric with a distinct downy nap with one that is smooth and lustrous and so underlining the plant's numerous potential.

In the second chapter of *Natural History* Pliny discusses how to grow flax, noting that it damages the soil considerably by sucking all the goodness from it. It is therefore, he states, an excellent crop to be grown along the banks of the Nile where it is subject to annual flooding. Flax does in fact deplete the soil of nutrients so the flood plains of the great river would have the ability to renew the soil's rich minerals in the annual floods.

Processing flax

Pliny not only provides a commentary on the who and where of linen but gives a detailed description of how it is cultivated, harvested and processed.

> In our part of the world the ripeness of flax is usually ascertained by two signs, the swelling of the seed, and its assuming a yellowish tint. It is then pulled up by the roots, made into small sheaves that will just fill the hand, and hung to dry in the sun.
>
> It is suspended with the roots upwards the first day, and then for five following days the heads of the sheaves are placed, reclining one against the other, in such a way that the seed which drops out may fall into the middle.
>
> Linseed is employed for various medicinal purposes and it is used by the country people of Italy beyond the Padus in a certain kind of food, which is remarkable for its sweetness: for this long time past, however, it has been in general use for sacrifices offered to the divinities.
>
> After the wheat harvest is over, the stalks of flax are plunged in water that has been warmed in the sun, and are then submitted to pressure with a weight…
>
> When the outer coat is loosened, it is a sign that the stalks have been sufficiently steeped; after which they are again turned with the head downwards, and left to dry as before in the sun: when thoroughly dried, they are beaten with a tow-mallett on a stone.[1]

Pliny's description goes on to include what happens to the *stuppa* the part of the inner fibre closest to the outer coat. The flax here is inferior to the innermost fibres and is used mostly for candle wicks. The outer coat of the flax is used as fuel for fires. The spinning of flax, says Pliny, is an honourable employment, even for men. Once the flax has been spun it can be beaten to make it suppler and after it is woven it will improve with further beating. Pliny estimates that for 50 pounds of harvested flax 15 pounds of flax will be combed out ready for spinning.

Flax on the move

From Egypt the art of spinning flax spread first to the Hebrews, then to the Assyrians and Phoenicians who were renowned for their sea journeying. Pliny bemoans, somewhat tongue-in-cheek that linen led men to take to the seas, so the Phoenicians proved his point. They installed enormous woven linen sails on their ships. It was Charlemagne who first fostered the linen industry in Flanders during his reign in the Ninth Century. The Flemish were already

A comb for flax fibres.

becoming established as accomplished makers of woollen cloth. It was not long before they dominated the market in linen as well.

Flax in the home was hand spun just as wool fibre was but with the use of flax jelly to keep the fibres under control. Later, when the Saxon wheel was well in use in domestic situations, flax was also being spun on a wheel modified especially for flax. It was still a common characteristic for the thread to be somewhat uneven in texture.

Flax and wool were the textiles most people wore and used in their homes for centuries. Silk was only for the wealthy and cotton was not well known in the west for a long time and when first introduced it was considered a luxury in the way silk was.

With the rise of cotton in the late Eighteenth Century in Britain and the subsequent mechanisation, the processing of flax into fabric became less of a viable option. It was time consuming to produce and cotton was being supplied by America under slave labour and in India under conditions not much better so that the material was available to most people in the Nineteenth Century. The once common linen became a quality luxury item, a status it has retained into the Twenty-first Century although hemp and ramie are making a huge comeback in popularity because of their environmentally friendly qualities and through programmes that aim to help people in developing nations earn a fair wage.

Flax these days is retted mechanically and often in a chemical bath.

Flax and hemp facts at a glance
- The short fibres are called tow and the long ones are called line
- Line fibres are already to spin, no other processing is necessary whereas the tow have to be combed and carded
- Flax and hemp fibres are strong, twice as strong as cotton, but have low resiliency and no elasticity
- Flax fibres are different colours when retted in different ways: dew retted (lying in the field) gives a greyish hue and water retted (lying in a prepared bath of water) gives a yellow hue
- Flax is annually sewn in spring. It is harvested by pulling up by the root in autumn. It can easily sew itself just by letting the seeds fall naturally. The flowers will follow the path of the sun during the day
- Hemp is more productive than flax producing more fibre per crop and the fibres can be up to eight feet tall
- Hemp is a great source of fibre to make paper with as it does not require the addition of toxic dioxins to help break down the cellulose

Hemp has many useful properties and it appears to be friendly to the environment on more than one level, however, because of its relation to the hemp plant grown for the production of cannabis-based drugs it has been banned from growing in the USA since the mid 1940s.

Flax fibre was also being cultivated and used as a textile in an almost identical manner in Peru in a similar time frame. Flax ready for spinning has a natural tendency to twist in a clockwise direction; this has led to it traditionally being spun in that direction.

Sisal

Agave sisalana is the scientific name for sisal which uses the *bast* fibres of the leaves of the plant. The individual fibres, at 10cm, are nowhere near as long as those of flax, so the thread produced will not be as smooth as linen.

Jute

Corchorus capsularis, commonly known as jute, and like hemp, makes a coarser yarn and fabric. The retting process takes up to twice as long as that of flax. It can't be bleached which makes it less versatile than hemp. It is used for carpets, sacks and, when mixed with flax and or wool, has been used for the weaving of tapestries.

A modern jute shopping bag.

Hemp

Hemp is part of the nettle family; its scientific name is *Cannabis sativa* and because it is part of the cannabis group the growing of it has been limited in certain countries. Hemp fibre is processed in the same way as flax but it is not as fine. It has a history of making rougher, tougher fabric used for things like sails, bags, and rug backing. Hemp is making a comeback in the modern world with a trend in linen type clothing being made from it.

A t-shirt made of hemp fibre.

Nettle

Who would have thought that such an unfriendly plant would be so useful: it can eaten and spun into cloth. One of the plant's attractions is that it does not exhaust the soil of its nutrients in the way flax does. The procedure for obtaining the *bast* fibres differs from flax and hemp too. Firstly the outer stem is removed through cutting and scraping not beating. Then it is boiled in water to remove the sticky gum that binds the fibres together. The fibres are very long, have little elasticity but great strength.

The whiteness and fineness of the thread is sometimes mistaken for cultivated silk. It has been grown and harvested in China, Japan, where it was one of the first fibres to be used and other neighbouring countries for over 5,000 years. It is now coming into worldwide favour as a sustainable textile material.

Note

1. From *The Natural History*, Pliny the Elder, John Bostock, London, Taylor and Francis Fleet Street, 1855.

- The plant called flax native to New Zealand is, in fact, not related to *Linum usitatissium* or its family at all although the seed head bears a resemblance to it
- Flax flowers are one of the few real blue flowers. Most other blue looking flowers are strictly a shade of purple
- In Seventeenth Century Saxony and Bohemia spinning schools were set up to teach poor girls a way to earn an honest living. Children as young as six years attended these schools
- The flax plant is the emblem for Northern Ireland. It appeared on the British two-pound coin minted from 1986–1991, it represented Northern Ireland
- Flax it the national flower of Belarus
- Flax grew in the Garden of Eden
- Linen was considered the finest cloth in the world and was therefore chosen as the desired textile of the gods
- One tablespoon of ground flax seeds plus three tablespoons of water can be used instead of an egg in recipes for baking
- A decree in 827 England forbade women to shear sheep, card wool or beat hemp on Sundays. Presumable they were still allowed to spin the fibres though

CHAPTER TWO

Plant Fibres

Cotton

The cotton plant, of the genus *Gossypium* (named by Carl Linnaeus in his *Species Plantarum in* 1753), first appeared in the warm and moist corners of the world seven million years ago or thereabouts.

Cotton in two continents

The seeds of the different wild varieties blew hither and thither across the globe on their tiny filaments and cross-fertilised with other cotton plants to create new types. Although there are more than 50 kinds of cotton plants in the world today, only four varieties bear fibres suitable for spinning into thread.

Interestingly, these four varieties, all belonging to the swamp mallow family *Gossypium malavaceae*, can be split into two groups, two of which evolved in Africa and Asia and the other two in Central and Southern America. One theory explaining this split is that when Gondwanaland separated and drifted into distinct continents the cotton species thrived and developed in the two hemispheres. While this may explain the initial division of the same plant developing on different continents, it has also been found that there has been a long history of cross-fertilisation of the different species, evolving into the four distinct varieties suitable for spinning. Hybridisation, through natural and man-made interference, has worked in harmony to produce a textile that forms one of the world's largest industries.

Gossypium arboretum is native to the Indus Valley region (modern day Pakistan) spreading to Nubia (where it was cultivated by the Meroe people who were the first African civilisation to weave textiles), and Nigeria in Africa and *Gossypium herbaceum* was found in sub-Saharan Africa then eventually made its way to China. On the other side of the world *Gossypium barbadense* first grew in Chile and Peru while *Gossypium hirsutum* flourished in Central America and Mexico.

The history of the cultivation of the cotton plant and its use as a fibre for spinning into thread and weaving into cloth appears to have as close a parallel history in both eastern and western hemispheres as the evolution of the cotton plant itself. However, the archaeological evidence is by far the most prevalent in Asia, Europe and Africa than it is in the Americas.

The Indus Valley

There is strong proof in the findings of the remains of cotton thread that the cultivation of cotton as a textile fibre began in the Indus River Valley (the site of modern Pakistan) about 5,500 years ago. This date is approximately the same for the cotton fibres found in Mexican Caves in the Tehaucan Valley, evidence supported by fossil findings in other parts of South America that date to 2,900 BC. Remains of cotton thread, dated to 2,500 BC, show that Peruvians were using cotton thread to make fishing nets.

Cotton was being cultivated in India and the Indus Valley and traded with other countries as long ago as 5,000 BC. For the Harappan civilisation of the Indus Valley, cotton textiles were a major industry and even though they were domesticating sheep and cattle at the same time as they were refining their cotton, it was the latter, not animal wool that was the more successful export. After the decline of the Harappan people, around 1000–900 BC the area they had inhabited and its neighbouring surrounds continued to produce much of the cotton products in the Old World.

Cotton in Egypt

From the Indus valley the growing and use of cotton for making fabric spread to Mesopotamia and Egypt. A statue excavated in one of the Indus Valley sites wore a sculpted stole over its shoulders with a detailed pattern etched into its stony surface. Apparently it was the spitting image of an actual textile found in the tomb of Tutankhamen in Egypt. This evidence would then suggest that the Harappan people traded in cotton textiles from a very early time.

Egypt's fertile Nile flood plain was an excellent location for growing cotton. The annual flooding brought essential nutrients to the soils that were quickly depleted from them by the ever hungry cotton crop. While Egypt did produce large quantities of cotton and cotton fabric, their own people tended to wear linen clothing, keeping the fine cotton for special occasions only. The Egyptian priests would don cotton robes to undertake special ceremonies. The quality of the finished material was similar, or even superior to that produced by India.

The Greeks

While the fabric was known to the ancient Greeks, it was an import and not produced locally. Herodotus, in the Fifth Century BC says of the cotton plant, 'there are trees which grow wild there, the fruit thereof is a wool exceeding in beauty and goodness that of a sheep. The natives make their clothes of this tree-wool' (Book 111, ch. 103–107). The fact that Herodotus claims the cotton plants grew wild shows that countries relying on imported fabric remained highly ignorant of its cultivation, not unlike the ignorance surrounding the farming and processing of silk. The first written evidence of cotton is from Herodotus and the first mention of trade in the fabric was in Periplus on the Erythrean Sea.

When Alexander the Great, King of Macedon, took his troops to India in 326 BC they were all intrigued by this lightweight fabric resembling the finest of fine linen but which grew in a fleecy down on shrubs.

Sir John Mandeville claimed to have seen cotton growing as lambs on trees.

A block printed cotton fabric from India, picture courtesy of the Anokhi Hand Printing Museum, Jaipur.

They stuffed the wool-like substance into their saddles as wadding, marvelling at the 'tree-wool', and introduced it to Macedonia and Greece. From Greece it found its way to Rome where it was considered a luxurious fabric.

One of Alexander the Great's generals, Nearchus, founded a Macedonian colony in the Indus Valley. He was in great admiration of a flowery printed, lightweight cotton fabric called 'chintz' which hundreds of years later caused such a big sensation in Europe in the Eighteenth Century.

In the Seventh and Eighth Centuries AD, Hebrew and Phoenician merchants traded in cotton fabric across the known world outside Europe.

Cotton arrives in Europe

Before the introduction of cotton fabric into Europe, the main textiles were made from wool or linen, or a mixture of the two. The Moors took cotton and the secrets of its spinning and weaving to Spain in the early Middle Ages.

Vasco da Gamma, the Portuguese explorer, loaded his ship with calico on his return exploratory trip from Lisbon, around the Cape of Good Hope to Calcutta. The opening of this new trade route meant that Spain and Portugal became leading traders in cotton.

Meanwhile, across the Atlantic ...

Cotton bolls were being carded, spun and woven into fabric by the native people of the West Indies. Captain Gonzalo Fernandez De Oviedo wrote of Christopher Columbus's first encounter with some of the indigenous people in his log book of 1492–3. When they saw the European ship the natives swam out to meet it carrying gifts for those on board which included parrots and balls of string. Despite the technology to spin thread they did not appear to wear clothes.

In exchange for the equivalent of a farthing, one native gave a sailor, 16 balls of cotton which would fetch about 25 pounds back in Europe. Gonzalo says he would have liked to forbid such goings on and trade with the Indians himself on behalf of his Majesties. He does not say he would offer a better exchange rate for it.

A few days later the sailors arrived at an island where cotton cloth was woven. On the 5th November,

The cotton plant.

two members of the crew went off exploring and when they returned told of what they had seen.

> They had a great abundance of cotton spun into balls, so much that a single house contained more than 12,500lb of yarn. They do not plant it by hand, for it grows naturally in the fields like roses, and the plants open spontaneously when ripe, though not all at the same season. For one plant they saw a half-formed pod, an open one, and another so ripe that it was falling. The Indians afterwards brought a great quantity of these plants to the ships, and would exchange a whole basket for a leather tag. Strangely enough, none of the Indians made use of this cotton for clothing, but only for making their nets and beds – which they call hammocks –and for weaving the little skirts or cloths which the women wore to cover their private parts.[1]

During the second voyage, 1493–6, Dr Chanca, court physician who accompanied Columbus, writes of their travels in a letter made to the City of Seville. Firstly he talks about their stay on the island of Guadalupe. The people there, he says, were of a gentle and industrious disposition.

> These people seem to us more civilised than those elsewhere. All have straw houses, but these people build them much better, and have larger stocks of provisions, and show more signs of industry practised by both men and women. They have much cotton, spun and ready for spinning, and much cotton cloth so well woven that it is in no way inferior to the cloth of our own country.[2]

In marked contrast, Chanca writes, with the wild Carib people (who have cannibalistic tendencies, and their custom of wearing two woven cotton braids, one just below the knee and the other at the ankle). On the island, christened Isabela, in honour of the Spanish queen, Chanca goes on land himself. He sees marvellous trees, not with animals hanging out of the pods but which:

> … bear very fine wool, so fine that those who understand weaving say that good cloth could be woven from it. These trees are so numerous that the caravels could be fully laden with the wool, though it is hard to gather, since they are very thorny, but some means of doing so could easily be devised. There is also an infinite amount of cotton growing on trees the size of peach trees …[3]

The wool bearing trees have since been identified as the ceiba or silk cotton tree.

South America
Columbus had discovered cotton growing wild in the Caribbean that was spun by the natives into thread, and sometimes woven into fabric. Later Cortez, Pizarro and other Spanish Conquistadors, were astounded to find that the inhabitants of New World Peru not only could spin and weave cotton into high quality fabric but that they wore it as well.

Cotton in Britain

Cotton cannot grow in the English climate. Britain has always had to rely on imported raw material in order to feed its thriving cotton textile industry. In the past it imported cotton from India, America, Egypt and Australia.

The art of making fabric out of cotton came from the Netherlands during the Sixteenth Century. Within a century mills for spinning and weaving cotton had sprung up. Cotton overtook the traditional spinning and weaving of flax as a popular textile, though it was never seen as a rival to wool cloth.

Cotton in America

When England claimed parts of America as British territory it took advantage of the new land's climate to establish cotton plantations. The first of these was in Virginia in 1607. The seeds were brought from the West Indies. The first crops were experimental but the plants grew so well and were so prolific that cotton plantations sprang up across the south.

By 1640 the growers of cotton, linen and wool were being offered cash incentives to get the textile industry up and running as an economic success. Wool and cotton were commonly woven together into a fabric known as fustian.

Within two years West Indian cotton growers were exporting their raw cotton product and the increasing demand for it meant more workers were needed to grow and harvest it. Slave trading boomed and many African people were stolen from their native land and transported in appalling conditions to the West Indies to work their lives away for someone else's profit.

By Washington's time it was not an idle thought that textile production, largely from home-grown cotton could become a United States mainstay, not only as an export but for the use of its own, growing population.

Interestingly, the new inventions that were revolutionising the textile industry in Britain were being exported to the States and hand production remained the main method of spinning and weaving long after the English had adapted to their new factory system.

Eli Whitney's Cotton Gin

One of the most important inventions to be made in America was the cotton gin: the brain child of one Eli Whitney. It enabled cotton to be cleaned of extraneous material in a simple process by a machine that was so easily copied that Whitney's patent was inefficient to cover it from plagiarism.

The overarching effect of Whitney's invention was to speed up the cotton cleaning process to such an extent that the exports of raw cotton from America to Europe multiplied 700 times. Before the implementation of the cotton gin in 1791, 400 bales of cotton went to Europe from the American docks, by 1800 more than 30,000 bales annually crossed the ocean. Ten years later than this it had risen to some 180,000 bales.

Eli Whitney's cotton gin.

Slave labour leads to American Civil War
By the time the cotton gin was in constant use consciences were turning against slavery but because the gin made it so much easier to clean the bolles it meant that more could be processed in a shorter time. It seemed impossible for the plantation owners to get rid of their labour just as the whole industry was going to make the economy boom.

One of the biggest problems with the American cotton product was the fact that it relied solely on slave labour. The plantation owners argued that they were providing a civic duty to a people who were incapable of making adult decisions. They were given clothing, food and shelter in return for their labour in the cotton fields. And the arduous task of thinking for themselves was also removed.

The ethics behind such self justifying arguments did not win everyone over and ultimately it led to civil war in America. The northern and southern states more or less divided, the former wanting to abolish slavery and the latter advocating it as a legitimate way of life and business.

Going back in time to the English Invasion of India ...
Before the emergence of the cotton gin, England, in 1757, decided to invade India and take over its natural resources, including cotton.

When the act of invasion was complete and India became a colony of Britain, the Indian people virtually became slaves within their own country. They were not allowed to produce cotton fabric from their own raw product but had to cultivate and harvest it so that British textile mills could turn it into material and sell it back to the Indians at an inflated price. To make the whole matter worse, Britain used the sale of Indian cotton to supplement its slave trade to the West Indies.

England buys American cotton
By 1840 the cotton industry in India was not efficient enough to supply the mills in Britain and so England looked to America to supply extra material. American cotton by this time was of a very high quality.

Cotton mills of England
The Industrial Revolution and the rise in cotton textile manufacture in England were by and large reliant on each other. The mechanisation of the spinning and weaving of fabric was already burgeoning for wool and silk when Eli Whitney's cotton gin revolutionised the cleaning of cotton making it far quicker to process.

Before Whitney in America, James Hargreaves, Richard Arkwright and Samuel Crompton were three of the major names in the Industrial Revolution, known for their services to the textile industry.

Arkwright put his own meagre funds, plus those of investors he managed to convince of his competence, into a cotton spinning mill in Lancashire in 1771. It was already a success with its water driven wheel before either the cotton gin or James Watt's steam engine.

By 1778 cotton had over taken the making of woollen and linen fabrics in England: cotton reigned supreme.

Back in America

The issue over slave labour finally came to a head and civil war broke out between the northern and southern states of America.

The civil war took a heavy toll on America's population, industry and morale. Slavery was abolished and slaves were officially made free people. However, it did not necessarily turn out happily ever after for everyone. Suddenly people who had been dependent all their lives were thrust into fending for themselves. The cotton magnates found they couldn't work their plantations with paid labour and many former slaves were left homeless and jobless.

It took a huge effort for America to turn this economic disaster around. A business man from the south, William Gregg motivated others to set up their cotton businesses anew. Americans invented their own spinning and weaving machines and in 1881 the International Cotton Exposition in Atlanta was the perfect place to showcase them. As a consequence cotton mills sprang up everywhere and thrived. For the rest of the century and even up until World War II the industry flourished in America.

The second half of the Twentieth Century saw other factors emerge that changed cotton production. The main one of these was the invention of synthetic fabrics with their easy care qualities and inexpensive prices.

Back in Britain ...

England had been more than happy to purchase American slave-produced cotton, even though they abhorred the use of slave labour. When civil war broke out American cotton was prevented from leaving the country's shores by Union blockades, the northern Confederates thinking this move would initiate action by Britain to support their cause in the war. It did not.

Egyptian Cotton

The British and French left America to fight its own war and turned to Egypt instead. The Egyptians, encouraged by the interest from these two countries invested heavily in cotton plantations, borrowing heavily to set them up. The trade lasted only until the end of the American Civil War and then, without further thought to Egypt's position, France and England dropped the Egyptian product and resumed trade with America. It was disastrous for Egypt which was declared bankrupt in 1876. It was no surprise then that in 1882 Egypt became an extension of the British Empire.

What happened to cotton in India?

Britain withdrew from India after the Second World War, declaring it would transfer rule back to India at the end of June 1948. It was a time of turbulence in India with fighting breaking out between the Hindu and

The charkha spinning wheel.

A hand printed cotton fabric from India, image courtesy of the Anokhi Hand Printing Museum, Jaipur, India.

Muslim population. The outcome was a partition of the country into a smaller India and the New Dominion of Pakistan.

A political and spiritual leader of the time, Mahatma Gandhi (as he is known in the west) played an enormous part in the process of Indian independence. He proscribed satyagraha, civil disobedience as a means of fighting domination. It was a philosophy that advocated non violent methods of protest.

One of the important policies he introduced to the Indian National congress in 1921 was the practise of *Swarja*, the boycott of foreign, particularly British products. He urged his fellow Indians to go back to making and wearing khadi, homespun cloth and suggested that all citizens regardless of caste, gender, age or financial status to spend a period of time each day spinning thread to support solidarity in the movement against the British occupation.

The use of spinning and weaving as a tool to unify the people against oppression was to link India back to its ancient cultural past. Spinning and weaving were integrally linked to the Hindu belief in a balanced and unified existence, compared to a piece of fabric that goes on forever.

The Rig Veda, 1500 BC is the earliest known religious text to mention weaving. In the Artharva Veda there is a story involving two sisters, day and night, who weave warp and weft. Besides the metaphor for the continuation for life, weaving and spinning were, and still are, considered the perfect activities to accompany meditation; repetitive movement with a definite rhythm. Gandhi used his own portable spinning wheel, the charkha, to spin on everyday to accompany his meditation.

Cotton in the Twentieth Century

After the American Civil War and slave emancipation the solution to working the cotton fields came in the form of sharecropping. Freed slaves and white men without their own farms were able to work for cotton plantation owners with a view to sharing the profits from the sale of the raw material. It was a system that worked reasonably well until the introduction of machinery in the early part of the Twentieth Century. Workers were laid off then two world wars came along to occupy them all.

By 1950 new machinery was invented to facilitate the harvesting of cotton and the trade picked up so that cotton was again a major export product of the United States.

Since then the biggest competitor for cotton has been the increase in popularity of synthetic fibres. Cotton has been in and out of fashion since the sixties and now many fabrics are a mix of cotton and synthetics.

But what is cotton?
Unlike the *bast* fibres of flax and hemp, whose fibre comes from inside the stem of the plant, cotton fibre forms inside the seed head, called the boll, and looks like fluffy cotton wool, its appearance giving rise to the aforementioned stories.

Originally cotton grew as a perennial bush or small tree but through its domestication it is cultivated as an annual. The cultivated cotton plant grows into a bush approximately one metre high. It produces small white flowers (that turn red overnight) and later green seed pods after the petals have fallen from the flowers. Six to eight weeks after their emergence, these pods burst open revealing a mass of light, white downy stuff with small seeds attached. Left to its own devices, the cotton seeds will disperse on the wind, each carried on its own little cloud of fluff.

Properties of Cotton
The tensile strength of cotton fabric is far greater when the material is wet than when it is dry. It can withstand pressure of 30,000 to 60,000 pounds per square inch when it is wet and depending on the quality of the cotton and its processing. Another of cotton's versatile properties is its absorbency. Cotton fibre can suck up to 27 times its own weight in water. It does not have the same fire resistant qualities of wool but it can be boiled for sterilisation purposes. A piece of woven cotton can be folded 50,000 times without damage. It is a good fabric to wear in hot and humid climates as it will absorb the excess moisture of perspiration and will dry quickly.

Processing of Cotton
To process the vegetable wool into fibre for spinning it must first be picked. This was done by hand for centuries. It was then beaten to release the seeds from the fibres and also to remove bits of dirt and other extraneous matter.

Each *boll* produces 20,000 or so fibres which range in size from 10 to 60 mm long, the longer the better for spinning. After the *bolls* have been cleaned they are pressed into bales. The bales are then sent to the cotton mill where the bales are reopened, the fibre further cleaned, dried and spread out. They are then rolled together to form a *lap*. It is carded to straighten the fibres out and to be pulled into a sliver from which the shorter fibres are removed. Slivers are then drawn through a roller to thin them down further and to twist them. The final strands are called roves.

Before the industrial revolution these process were all done by hand and it was very labour intensive.

Cotton's worst nightmare
Cotton's biggest natural fear may well be the cotton boll weevil. This insect attacks cotton crops in the spring and summer. Eggs are laid at a rate of 200 per adult female over 10 to 12 days. Each egg hatches within three days and feasts on the emerging cotton buds.

They multiply at an alarming rate, the life cycle of larvae to adult only taking three weeks. It is possible for 10 generations to exist in one season. The loss to crops is devastating.

It was at the end of the Nineteenth Century that the cotton boll weevil migrated from Mexico into the southern states of the US and from there to every cotton growing district in America. It meant huge losses in the early part of the Twentieth Century and did nothing to help the economic difficulties of the Great Depression.

In 1978 America implemented its Boll Weevil Eradication Programme which has been very successful in cotton growing areas of the world.

Another major disease is a fungus that attacks the plants via the root system and extracts all the moisture from the stem of the plant giving it the characteristic wilt which gives the fungus its name: 'cotton wilt' or 'fusarium wilt'. In 1901 it did great damage to the cotton fields in Peru. It took 10 years for an enterprising Puerto Rican agriculturist, Fermin Tanguis, to come up with a viable solution. He cross-germinated various cotton plants and finally came up with a hybrid that was strong enough to resist the fungus. The cotton type took the name of its inventor, Tanguis and has been the preferred crop for Peru ever since.

The cotton boll weevil.

The modern German word for cotton is *baumwolle* which translates as 'tree-wool.'

Notes
1. Cohen, J.M (ed. And trans.), *The Four Voyages of Christopher Columbus*, The Cresset Library, London, 1988 (1969) p. 79.
2. Columbus p. 135.
3. Ibid. p. 155.

CHAPTER THREE

Animal Fibres

Wool

Wool, the warm, insulating coat grown by members of the *Caprinae* family, is a protein fibre. Each single hair is made up of a medulla, cortex and cuticle.

- The medulla is the core of the hair and is fundamental to wool's famous insulating properties
- The cortex is the component of the fibre that creates a crimp effect when it is subjected to heat and moisture. This is because the cortex is made up of two separate parts that work differently under these conditions
- The cuticle is covered in scales, situated around the base of the fibre's core. When the fleece is growing on the sheep's back the lanolin covered scales on each fibre deflect rain from the skin. When the greasy lanolin is washed from the fleece the scales are able to mesh together to make felt, especially when aided by heat, moisture and pressure

Wool can be left on the skin and used as a furry rug, shorn from the living animal and carded into soft rolls ready for massaging into felt or spinning into yarn to be woven, knitted, embroidered or knotted into myriad different things. It is soft, it is warm, it can deflect water, it is difficult to burn and it is used in many aspects of our lives today. It is also one of the oldest fibres manipulated by mankind and there are uses and processes that really haven't changed dramatically in thousands of years.

Prehistoric wool

Sheep were domesticated at least 9,000 years ago. They were not necessarily bred for their fleece or even their hides. These early farmed sheep would have produced meat and milk first and then the skins would have been used for making clothing, shelter and bedding.

Sheep in their woolly coats.

It wasn't until about 5,000 BC that sheep began to show their potential for growing wool. The amount and quality of wool that a sheep produces depends on the breed, just as with cattle, some types are bred primarily for meat, others for their milk.

It is largely the breed of sheep that determines the wool quality and amount of wool produced. How and where they are raised can affect the quality. The same type may produce extra fine or extra long fleece in one country and in another it may be considerably shorter and coarser. The fleece from one individual sheep may vary from season to season depending on the food source available, the overall health of the animal and its age. Human hair can show symptoms of disease or lack of nutrition too.

Selective breeding over centuries has produced a number of types of sheep that are well known for the particular attributes of their fleece. The earliest sheep breeding, with an idea to industry, was undertaken in south-eastern Sumeria about 5,500 years ago. By 3,000 BC there is evidence that wool was being used as a clothing textile in a broad geographical area reaching as far as Germany and Switzerland. Implements for shearing sheep have been found that date to 2,300 BC.

The wool industry in England
In Australia we talk about the economy having ridden on the sheep's back but it would be even more relevant to apply this saying to England, which has had a flourishing wool production industry since early medieval times, possibly even earlier (wool was being woven in Britain from about 1900 BC). Wool was certainly one of the most commonly used fibres from which the native population and the subsequent invaders and settlers fashioned textiles to clothe themselves. The Romans found a thriving industry in spun and woven wool, comparing its fineness to spider's web.

The green and pleasant land was conducive to raising sheep and not only did the animals provide meat and milk for cheese but their fleece was soft, long fibred and strong: ideal for spinning into thread.

Textiles made somewhere between the Ninth and Eleventh Centuries have been found in York. They seem to be made from the long-haired fleece of a sheep native to northern Europe. The spun thread is somewhat coarse and heavy. It contrasts dramatically with the type of fleece being produced centuries before, during the Roman occupation of Britain when sheep were brought over from the Mediterranean. At some point the different types of sheep were interbred to produce other qualities of fleece. English wool even at this early stage took dye extremely well which was an attractive characteristic.

In the Middle Ages two distinct breeds of sheep emerged from several that grazed the fields. One was a small animal with a short fleece but was very hardy and prospered on rocky mountainsides with sparse grazing and relatively poor pasture. The other type was much larger, had a longer fleece and was raised on the fenlands with its rich grass and easier living conditions.

Flanders enters the field
We might note here that across the English Channel at a similar time another country was busy raising sheep for wool. This potential rival was Flanders. It too offered excellent grazing for sheep with its low lying coastal plains that were not

particularly good for general agriculture such as the growing of crops. However, even with such good pasture it was generally accepted that Flanders didn't produce such fine fleeces as the English did.

For some time the two countries developed a largely parallel industry. In Flanders wool was so easily grown that it wasn't long before the country had more fleece than it could use in its domestic market. Processing, spinning and weaving into cloth, was an ideal way to occupy a rapidly expanding population: lots of unemployed meant cheap labour. Cloth as a finished product became a major export for the Flemish.

Indisputably the English were able to produce a finer quality fleece than their counterparts across the water, and as the people of Flanders were putting more effort into turning their raw wool into cloth, the two countries, instead of competing with each other, decided it would make more sense for the Flemish to import fine fleece from England, weave it into fabric, dye, finish it and sell it, not only back to the English, but to many other countries in Europe and the East as well. The major centres of cloth making in Flanders were: Ypres, Ghent, Douai, St Omer, Arras and Bruges.

To keep ahead of any possible rivals in the cloth-making trade the Flemish were constantly improving techniques and developing machinery to spin and weave wool. For many years Flanders and England were content to support each other

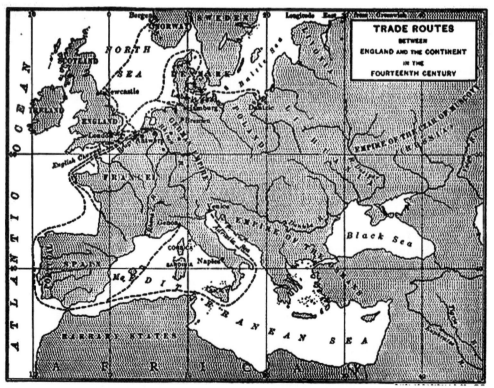

A map of trade routes in the Fourteenth Century between England and the Continent.

in this way: one, supplying the wool, the other turning it into exemplary cloth. In 1113 a contemporary reference suggests that the mutual trade between England and Flanders was already well established. It has been further suggested that it began as early as the Tenth Century.

With an interdependent trade relationship between Flanders and England it would seem that everything was smooth sailing. But, instead of it being a rock steady one, it was fraught with problems. Perhaps it was the very nature of the interdependence that helped fan the fires of discord because, although Flanders needed English wool, they were geographically aligned with France and therefore often obliged to show support for the rulers of that country. This meant that when relationships between England and France grew unsteady, Flanders would be caught up in it, being pulled in both directions for its allegiance. Two main camps arose in Flanders: the 'Leiliaards' who supported the French and the 'Klauwaarts' who supported the English. Troubles would flair and subside countless times over the centuries and always affected trade in some way. For centuries the English wool trade and politics were inextricably linked.

For instance, King John made an enemy of Philip Augustus of France and consequently lost not only his own fiefdoms in France but also those belonging to many English barons. Then, after virtually splitting England from France, John antagonised Pope Innocent III and more trouble ensued from both outside England and within its own ruling classes as English noblemen found themselves stripped of ancient ties to France. The eventual outcome was John's signing of the Magna Carter Treaty under order of the English barons. This caused yet another rift with the Flemish.

Here come the Italians
It was during this turmoil that John ordered goods belonging to Flemish merchants in London be seized; in the case of one unfortunate trader it meant the loss of about 18 stone (114.305 kg) of wool. To make matters worse a decree was issued that made it illegal for Englishmen to trade with Flemings unless the seller had a special license. Trading with Flanders didn't cease, it was still one of the major importers of English wool during the Twelfth and Thirteenth Centuries, but hostile behaviour, as exhibited by King John, meant that England needed to find other outlets for their product and as the Italians were also fine cloth makers it was natural that Italian centres like Florence offered a ready market for English wool.

Italian merchants were in an excellent position to trade with England. They were able to borrow money at lower rates of interest and therefore could pay for wool in advance, making trade with them a very attractive option.

As the demand for raw wool grew, both for the overseas and the domestic markets, different groups of people in England began to raise sheep. Cistercian monasteries were one example who, through slow and careful breeding managed to accumulate a sizeable amount of wealth. But sheep farming wasn't just for large scale groups like monasteries or the landed gentry, anyone could graze a sheep or two on the common, shear the wool and use it for family clothing and bedding and then sell any surplus for a small but welcome profit.

It was the merchants who were making the real profit, growing so wealthy from selling wool that when Edward I imposed a tax of seven shillings sixpence per sack, they didn't raise a murmur of protest. It must be noted, however, that when he tried to raise it a couple of decades later to 40 odd shillings a sack, the merchants were not nearly so complacent in accepting it.

In the late Thirteenth Century wool was such a profitable export for the city of York that a large amount of revenue was raised by charging a toll of one shilling per sack that was brought into or sold out of the town. Many of the merchants on whom this toll was imposed came from overseas, though there were a certain number of English merchants trading in wool too. Flemish and Italian traders were joined by German and French.

Flanders is squeezed out of the market

1270 saw the culmination of more strife with Flanders and Edward I had all Flemish merchants in England arrested. This meant that the other European merchants were given the opportunity to gain ground in the wool business. While the Flemish had been prepared to travel around the countryside to buy wool the Germans and Italians preferred to stay in London and leave the gathering of the raw product to London merchants.

In 1287 when the English lifted their ban on trade with Flanders, the Flemish merchants found that their position as number one wool buyers had been superseded by other Europeans and were eventually eased out altogether as exporters of English wool.

Florence as master cloth makers

In the meantime Florence had emerged as another great centre of cloth manufacture and the Italian ships sailed to London ports full of exotic wares for the English (and particularly the London) market then loaded up with fine English wool to carry home. The Fourteenth Century historian and financier, Giovanni Villani, commented on the shape of the city of Florence. It was shaped like a cross and the Arte della Lana, the guild centre for woollen cloth manufacturers, lay at its centre. This was symbolic of the importance of spinning and weaving cloth to the local economy. Approximately a third of the population depended on the cloth industry for its livelihood, one way or another. It was estimated that in the 1330s, Florence sold more than 80,000 rolls of finished cloth and that it brought in about 1,200,000 florins: the worth of two kings' ransoms.

Merchants, merchants everywhere: foreign merchants in England

In fact, the growth in numbers of merchants from outside England coming to English cities to buy wool (and other goods) became a perceived threat to the local population. In York, in the early part of the Fourteenth Century, citizens put together a petition requesting that a law be made forbidding foreigners to stay more than 40 days in their city on a single visit.

While English merchants despised and distrusted the foreign counterparts and wanted strict measures put in place to keep them under control while on English soil, the king and his government tended quite often to lean in favour of the outsiders.

In 1303 Edward I issued a charter called the Carta Mercatoria. It virtually threw open trade within England to traders from Germany, France, Spain, Italy and the Netherlands by exempting them from paying the usual tolls and tariffs imposed by the staple towns. It also gave the foreigners licence to stay where and when they liked within England, not compelling them to stay with native merchants and lifting the restrictions on how long they stayed. It overturned nearly all the strategies formally put in place to keep trade fair and regulated for the English merchants.

In 1311 under the newly appointed King Edward II, the following ordinances were made:

> Item, it is ordained that the customs of the kingdom shall be received and kept by men of the kingdom itself, and not by aliens; and that the issues and profits of the same customs, together will all other issues and profits pertaining to the kingdom from any source, shall in their entirety come to the king's exchequer and be paid to the treasurer …
>
> Also new customs have been levied and the old have been increased upon wool, cloth … and other things – whereby [our] merchants come more rarely and bring fewer goods into the country, while alien merchants reside longer than they used to, and by such residence things become dearer than they used to be, to the damage of the king and his people – we ordain that all manner of customs and maltotes levied since the coronation of King Edward [that is Edward I], son of king Henry, are to be entirely removed and utterly abolished forever …[1]

Even though ordnances of this sort were put in place the trend for trade within England to be carried out by foreign merchants continued until the end of the Fourteenth Century. It has been suggested that this may be attributed to the English merchants' lack of economic wiles and capital to travel outside their own country in order to find customers for their wool. Of course, this was already changing. The Merchants of the Staple, for whom a patent roll was made in 1313 by Edward III, were indeed such traders who based themselves eventually in Calais. Besides, England was free of the kind of civil strife that afflicted other countries and the general peace was conducive to the raising of fat, woolly sheep without fear of raids by marauding neighbours.

England traded with many European countries, including parts of Scandinavia, Germany, the Netherlands, France, Spain and Italy. Flanders, Germany and Italy were the principal ones.

Italian finance

England in the Middle Ages was somewhat behind its continental neighbours in its comprehension of the detailed matters of economics. The English were neither as experienced, nor as wealthy as some other countries and the government, even though it taxed goods for export, did not have ready cash available to fund military expeditions and the like.

The Italians were accomplished bankers and were able to offer ready money to the king in the form of a loan against the taxes when the revenue became available. It was Florentine money that sponsored the early part of the Hundred Years' War, to be paid against taxes placed on sacks of wool (and other export items).

Even kings can run up debts that cannot be paid. In 1348, Edward III became so indebted (to the tune of $3m in modern money) to Italian bankers that he was unable to pay the loan back, even when the taxes came in and consequently the financiers that had backed him were left wanting. England's monarch was not the only defaulter at the time and some of the banks failed under the strain of unpaid debt.

Guilds

> An Haberdasshere and a Carpenter,
> A Webbe, a Dyer, and a Tapycer—
> And they were clothed alle in o lyveree
> Of a solmpne and a greet fraternitee

Prologue from the *Canterbury Tales* by Chaucer[2]

A major aspect of the wool trade was the rise of institutions called guilds. These were the formal gatherings of craftsmen (craft guilds) who participated in the same craft, for example, weaving, spinning or making gloves and merchants (mercantile guilds) who wanted to keep control of the quality and price of the goods they sold. To come together in this way, as an organised body of people with the same interest and livelihood meant that there was opportunity for conditions and pay to be

The interior of the Hall of Merchants Company in York.

regulated, to provide larger purchasing power and to build a social network which could, in theory, also provide support for those workers who found themselves in difficulties.

The rise of wool-related guilds in England grew out of the increasing interest in the production of cloth itself. Carding, spinning and weaving had been practised for centuries by women in the household in order to clothe the family and make comfortable, draught reducing furnishings such as bed hangings and curtains, blankets and quilts.

Often the textiles made in these domestic situations were fairly unrefined. The people who had crafted them were doing it out of necessity and had not been trained or given the opportunities to use innovative techniques brought over from the continent. Besides which it was time consuming and had to fit in with other household chores and baby rearing. Children would grow and require new clothes, old ones would be worn out: an endless task of spinning, weaving and sewing.

The professional production of cloth was left to the men. Processing wool and making it into cloth and striving to perfect it became the focus of professional craftsmen situated in the larger towns and cities, rather than rural backwaters or villages.

Guilds were emerging as a force to be reckoned with from early in the Middle Ages. The weaver's guild, for instance had been given Royal approval in Henry I's

The Hall of Merchants Company in York.

reign, and was still chartered in the mid to late Twelfth Century under Henry II. It was forbidden for non guild members to ply their trade in London, Southwark or other places where London did business in the wool or cloth making industry. Business had to be conducted in the place and at the time stipulated by the guild controlling that trade. Non guild members were required to pay hefty tolls for the privilege of trading in guild towns, whereas members were exempt from these.

An example of this can be found in documents relating to trade in Southampton:

> And no one in the city of Southampton shall buy anything to sell again in the same city unless he is of the gild merchant or of the franchise.

Of course charters were not granted out of the goodness of the reigning king's heart. It meant money. To receive a royal charter for a guild to practice it had to pay a yearly fee. For the weavers in Henry II's time this was: two gold marks (1,400 silver pennies). It was not a trifling sum by any means.

Guilds were supposed to be given royal approval before setting themselves up in practice; besides giving the king an opportunity to make money from them, it gave the guild a legitimacy to have a royal charter. However, in reality, many guilds, particularly those in rural centres, away from London and the seat of power, just set themselves up without a charter.

There were distinct advantages to belonging to a guild:

- Solidarity could present before the King or to some other authoritarian body in order to have wrongs righted
- Prices for buying and selling could be regulated
- Buying power was strengthened
- Guild members enjoyed certain privileges in the manufacturing, or processing of their wool; such as in Leicester where only guild members could have their fleece washed in the town water or packed by local packers
- The guild had power to fix wages: in 1281 in Leicester it was decided that wool wrappers would be given a penny a day for labour plus food but flock pullers would get three halfpence and no food. Any guild member who was found to pay more than this would be fined by the community of Leicester
- Guild members didn't have to pay tolls whereas non members had to
- Only guild members could sell particular produce at a retail level
- It was the guild members who made sure that middle men did not profit at the expense of the public or the guild members themselves
- Guilds offered a support network for fellow guild members when things got bad

While there was a certain amount of safety to be found in numbers being a guild member brought burdens and obligations. For a start, there was a fee to be paid in order to become a member. There were rules to be obeyed, such as a member was not allowed to go into partnership with a non member. To be a guild member meant municipal duty and members tended to become the upstanding leaders of the towns, adopting positions of power such as the mayor. As Chaucer says of his Haberdasshere, Webbe and Dyer, 'Wel semes ech of hem a fair burgeys, to sitten in a yeldehalle on a deys', that they were comfortably off, suggests that they were all fit to be aldermen, and that their wives would have themselves called 'madame' and have the train of their gowns lifted by a servant. Members of guilds were an up and coming class.

Other aspects of life became embedded in the guild traditions, which had not even the most tenuous of connections with their business. An important one was the putting on of public performances of 'miracle' plays with guild members strutting their thespian skills (or lack thereof, if we take Shakespeare's' 'rude mechanicals' as exemplars).

Though guilds as institutions of master craftsmanship remained for centuries (some are still around today) they did not retain the power they had enjoyed in the Middle Ages. The interest in English cloth making overtook the previous passion for exporting raw wool and the demand for cloth became so urgent that manufacturing was being undertaken by all and sundry, skilled or not.

Organisation of medieval mercantile guilds

The guilds organised themselves into sophisticated committees. The officiating member was called the alderman who was supported by a number of official staff: stewards, bailiffs, skevins, ushers, deans and chaplains.

Meetings were held regularly and the agenda for discussion would include items such as required new laws to protect their livelihood, the election of officers, and admittance of new members. Sometimes these meetings were held in conjunction with a guild feast which meant that it was not just a matter of business but also of pleasure. An example of another of the guild's fraternal nature was the support in which it gave its members when they found themselves in trouble or if one of them had died:

> If a gildsman be imprisoned in England in time of peace, the alderman, with the steward and with one of the skevins, shall go, at the cost of the gild, to procure the deliverance of the one who is in prison ... If any of the brethren shall fall into poverty or misery, all the brethren are to assist him by common consent out of the chattels of the house or fraternity, or of their proper own ... And when a gildsman dies, all those who are of the gild and are in the city shall attend the service for the dead, and gildsmen shall bear the body and bring it to the place of burial.[3]

It can be seen how the guilds were forerunners of municipal government with the offices still bearing familiar names, like alderman.

The craft guilds also regulated the apprenticeship system. One of these was that after an apprentice had served his time under a master craftsman, often a period of seven years, he was free to work at his craft under his own direction. These men were called journeymen after the French word *journée* meaning by the day, the term could also have come from the fact that such free craftsmen were often required to travel, journey, to different places everyday in order to secure work.

From being a journeyman, the craftsman would try to make enough money to set himself up in a set place, perhaps a shop and then take on apprentices of his own.

An apprentice at work in his master's workshop.

Decay of the guilds
- When manufactured cloth took over from raw wool as England's major export the demand for cloth meant that it was being made by people everywhere, particularly in rural areas where extra money was always welcome and where there was time and space to do it: spinning could be done in the main room of a cottage by candle light
- The government took over many of the guilds' fiscal operations
- As the guilds became stripped of their duties and purpose their numbers declined

By the Sixteenth Century the power and influence of the guilds had waned to such an extent that dire measures were often taken by those remaining in them to keep them going. One idea was to amalgamate guilds, such as the guild of goldsmiths in Hull in 1598, where it is documented as including not only goldsmiths but also smiths in general, pewterers, plumbers, glaziers, painters, cutlers, and incongruously musicians, stationers, bookbinders and basket makers.

In Ipswich there were The Mercers who included such diverse crafts and trades as: mariners, shipwrights, bookbinders, printers, fishmongers, sword-setters, cooks, fletchers, arrowhead-makers, physicians, hatters, cappers, mercers, merchants, and several others. The Drapers did not merge with the tailors or even the shoemakers but joined with carpenters, publicans, freemasons, bricklayers, tilers, carriers, casket-makers, surgeons and clothiers. The Tailors aligned themselves with the cutlers, smiths, barbers, chandlers, pewterers, minstrels, peddlers, plumbers, pinners, millers, millwrights, coopers, shearmen, glaziers, turners and tinkers.

The disparity in the types of trades represented in the new guilds could perhaps be explained that they were not organised within trade related groups but rather within the town geography so that the occupants of certain streets belonged to the one guild.

In an attempt to retain some power at local government level, the guilds would appoint an alderman and a couple of wardens. Craftsmen or traders wishing to set up business in a town would be placed in a seemingly appropriate guild regardless of their occupation. By the early Seventeenth Century guilds had changed completely from their medieval forms.

Merchants of the Staple

The trade in raw wool between England and the Netherlands needed some kind of national organisation. In England this system was called the 'staple'. Particular towns were selected, known as 'staple' towns, to be collection centres for wool that would then be taken to a staple port for export. The staple towns would eventually be places where exports would be registered, weighed and duly taxed before being shipped abroad, keeping the bulk of the business on home turf.

To facilitate trade at the overseas end, the government nominated a town in the Netherlands to which the goods could be sent for processing, sale and dispersal but under a watchful English eye.

From 1354, in the dozen or so staple towns in England, a Mayor of the Staple and two Constables were appointed by the merchants of the staple to oversee the king's financial interest by way of tax collection, ensure foreign merchants were kept happy and also just for the general keeping of civil peace within in the town.

Merchants of the Staple was a trading group that formed out of the guild of merchants called 'the Brotherhood of St. Thomas Beckett'.[4] It is not known for certain when they were first founded but the earliest charter still in existence dates to 1296.

The Staple was the official body that purchased and sold raw wool. One of its purposes was to make it easier to collect tax on the goods and another was to observe the amount of trade going on. A foreign city, or collection of towns was chosen to be the place of business and all exports had to go through it and be handled by the Merchants of the Staple, appointed to the position by Royal charter.

If the Merchants of the Staple were the men involved in organising the export of wool, staple towns were the specially designated towns through which they did it and through which foreign merchants could buy and sell wool from the official traders. To trade outside this system was illegal.

The arms of the Merchants of the Staple in London.

The King to all to whom, etc., greeting. Know ye that whereas before these times divers damages and grievances in many ways have befallen the merchants of our realm, not without damage to our progenitors, sometimes Kings of England, and to us, because merchants, as well denizen as alien, buying wools and woolfells within the realm aforesaid and our power, have gone at their pleasure with the same wools and fells, to sell them, to divers places within the lands of Brabant, Flanders and Artois: We, wishing to prevent such damages and grievances and to provide as well as we may for the advantage of us and our merchants of the realm aforesaid, do will and by our council ordain, to endure for ever, that merchants denizen and alien , buying such wools and fells or cause them to be taken to a fixed staple to be ordained and assigned within any of the same lands by the mayor and community of the said merchants of our realm, and to be changed as and when they deem expedient, and not to other places in those lands in any wise.[5]

Organisation of the Staple [Patent Roll, 6, Edward II, p.2, m.5], 1313

However, it was never plain sailing for the Merchants of the Staple and at various times the government policy on the staples and export would change, sometimes in favour of the English merchants and at other times in favour of foreign merchants. At another stage the whole system was done away with and trade thrown open to all and sundry.

After decades of moving from city to city (even though official arguments were put to the king in 1319 for the establishment of a Home Staple), including Bruges and Antwerp, the Staple was settled at Calais in 1363. Twenty-six merchants formed the company at Calais and became known as the Company of the Staple at Calais.

Edward I was the instigator of a regulated national customs duty on exported goods, including wool and leather. Because he needed regular finance for the war against France he knew he needed a means of exacting tax from merchants on a systematic basis.

To start with, Edward I organised merchants to centralise their business dealings overseas so that export could be monitored and so that no potential taxes could slip by unnoticed.

The word staple comes from the old French word for market, *staple*.

In return for their diligent work for the Crown they were granted the sole right of trading in English raw wool.

It was the Merchants of the Staple who became financiers to the king, lending him funds to wage war against the French. In the first third of the Fourteenth Century the Hundred Years War began. Several factors played a part in starting the war; one was conflict over the French throne (Edward the III claimed his right to it because he was the son of the late French king's sister), another was over control of the English Channel as a line of defence for the English, and thirdly there was the need to keep open the lucrative trade market with Flanders (as we have already seen, Flanders was under French rule which made trade with England in times of conflict difficult).

During the long series of battles the Merchants of the Staple not only continued business as usual but fought for their English King against the French. However, they were also the king's creditors and although he might be able to rely on them to fight beside him in war, he couldn't take them for granted when it came to asking for finance for military campaigns.

> Edward, by the grace of God king of England and France and lord of Ireland, to all our sheriffs, mayors, bailiffs, ministers, and other faithful men to whom these present letters may come, greeting. Whereas good deliberation has been held with the prelates, dukes, earls, barons, knights of the shires – that is to say, one from each for the whole shire- and commons of cities and boroughs of our kingdom of England, summoned to our great council held at Westminster …, concerning damages which have been notoriously incurred by us and by the lords, as well as by the people of our kingdom of England and our lands of Wales and Ireland, because the staple of wool, leather, and wool-fells for our said kingdom and lands has been kept outside the said kingdom and lands; and also concerning the great profits that would accrue to our said kingdom and lands it the staple should be held within them and nowhere else: so, for the honour of God and the relief of our kingdom and lands aforesaid, and for the sake of avoiding the perils that otherwise may arise in times to come, by the counsel and common assent of the said prelates, dukes, earls, barons, knights, and commons aforesaid, we have ordained and established the measures hereinunder written, to wit:-
>
> First, that the staples of wool, leather, wool-fells and lead grown or produced within our kingdom and lands aforesaid shall be perpetually held in the following places: namely, for England at Newcastle-upon-Tyne, York, Lincoln, Norwich, Westminster, Canterbury, Chichester, Winchester, Exeter, and Bristol; for Wales at Carmarthen; and for Ireland at Dublin, Waterford, cork, and Drogheda, and nowhere else …[6]
>
> Excerpts from the Ordinance and Statute of the Staple (1353)

The Merchants of the Staple were able to make their way up the social ladder by acquiring lands in wool growing districts, largely in the West Country, and managing to establish distinguished families whose names are still revered.

The export of raw wool was at its height in the middle of the Fourteenth Century but over the next fifty years it began a steep decline until by 1500 or thereabouts it constituted a fraction of England's overseas trade. The Merchants of the Staple who had held a monopoly on the export of raw wool found that their own livelihoods were under such a strain with the disappearance of the demand for their product that they could no longer keep up the civic responsibilities that they had been in the habit of maintaining. One of the casualties was the English garrison at Calais.

The Merchants of the Staple enjoyed many long years of monopoly of the wool trade in England. Members grew prosperous and often ended up with influential positions in government. It was not to last. Even after their demise as a functioning business group, the Merchants of the Staple still exist.

Hanseatic League

Across the Channel, Europe was developing its own guilds and trading laws commensurate with the craft guilds of England and particularly the Merchants of the Staple. It is thought to have originated in the town of Lübeck in Northern Germany after 1159. The term *Hansa* was first documented in 1267 but the organisation was already well established by then. Members of the Hansa tried to improve trade conditions for themselves and were successful in getting Henry II to lift trade embargos and fees so they could trade throughout England without restraint. Henry's compliance did not please the English traders.

Flemish traders who bought and sold goods with England also organised themselves into a formal group: the Flemish Hanse of London. The rules under which the league worked were similar to those of the Merchants of the Staple and forbade trade by non members except under special licence or through paying tolls.

The German Hanse consisted of traders from the towns of Lübeck, Hamburg, Bremen, Dantzig, and Brunswick as well as up to 80 more unspecified ones. These Hanse cities had bargained with the English government for all sorts of special trade privileges and concessions.

Not only did the Hanse end up trading under the same terms and conditions in England as the English merchants, they were even more privileged outside of England. This meant that they were able to offer much more competitive prices to potential customers than the English.

While the English merchants were busy petitioning their king to get tough on foreign merchants in England, the town of Hamburg was doing a similar thing to the Merchant Adventurers. The English tried to establish a base, first in Emden, then Hamburg and then Emden again. The second attempt at Emden, in 1579, proved successful although the Hanseatic League tried to have the Count of East Friesland expel them. The Merchant Adventurers used Emden as their European

staple until 1587. Surprisingly, in 1586, the Senate of Hamburg issued an invitation back to Hamburg but it did not eventuate until much later. By 1611 the staple was established in Hamburg.

The Hanseatic League suffered its own decline and by the late Sixteenth Century was in deep distress through its inability to deal with organisational issues as well as the political and international trade changes that were happening. The Hanse's last formal meeting was held in 1669, which only nine members attended. The Hanse struggled to survive in to the Nineteenth Century, just as its English counterparts the Merchants of the Staple and the Merchant Adventurers, but had become not much more than a social club.

Wool in the Time of Chaucer

> A Marchant was ther with forked berd,
> In mottelee, and hye on horse he sat;
> Upon his heed a Flaunderyssh bever hat[7]
>
> Prologue from *The Canterbury Tales* by Chaucer

At the beginning of the Fourteenth Century raw wool was still the major export product of England. Everybody was raising sheep, from peasants with a single animal to large landholders with hundreds of them. Wool exports in the early years of the century amounted to 30,000 sacks a year. Cloth was also exported but was a marginal industry; 5,000 pieces of cloth was a sixth of the raw wool export.

The English were producing cloth for their own use, though still importing the finished fabric back from Flanders. The home-made, coarse textile was made for many years to come but the guilds in the towns were working hard to refine their techniques to make a fabric comparable to the Flemish. Even before the start of the Hundred Years War, Stamford cloth was renowned for its fineness as far away as Venice.

In the Fourteenth Century the industry changed, slowly but surely. The guilds had monopolised the manufacture of cloth and they had made it into an art form for which one had to be apprenticed for a set term in order to learn all there was to know about spinning and weaving. The making of cloth itself, rather than the growing of wool, was on the rise and people everywhere were beginning to take it up, just as they had embraced the raising of sheep. To be sure, quality suffered because the guilds were no longer the major producers. Any peasant in the middle of nowhere could spin a bit of extra thread and the merchants found that the cost was a lot less than when manufactured by master craftsman, therefore profit could be larger.

Edwards I and II oversaw action that banned the import of finished cloth into England. This meant Flanders no longer had a ready market to sell their cloth to. Craftsmen from abroad were brought to England to teach the native population their innovative techniques and trade secrets. English craftsmen strongly resented the intrusion by the foreigners, at the crown's expense and request; it could be seen as nothing but insulting. The visiting craftsmen were given government protection from attacks by the outraged Englishmen.

During the century the manufacture and export of finished cloth continued to grow. Broadcloth was a popular, densely woven woollen fabric which was made on a broad loom (the width measuring 1.75 yards) was made from the short staples of wool and 'fulled' after weaving. 'Fulling' was a process where water, heat and agitation made the fibres, creep and shrink (felting) to make strong, smooth fabric. The export of this cloth over several generations in the Fourteenth Century multiplied nine-fold. And, correspondingly, the export in raw wool declined. The peak of the raw wool export industry was the mid Fourteenth Century.

Spinning and weaving.

Different areas of England were becoming specialised in certain aspects of wool growing and manufacture. For instance: The West Country, the Pennines in Yorkshire, and the countryside of Lancashire had plenty of luscious pasture for farming sheep, soft water for washing, dyeing and scouring fleece, and running streams which would later supply water power for driving fulling mills.

In Norfolk and its surrounding areas in East Anglia, the sheep grew a long, fine fleece which was made into worsted cloth, named after the village of the same name in Norfolk.

The Merchants of the Staple, who had monopolised the industry so well, also faded into the background as their market fell away; with England using more of its own raw material and making it into a new export product. With less trade they made less money and had less power. They were also less able to perform their municipal duties; such as providing the means for maintain the defence force at Calais.

Increase in exports meant an increase in demand for goods to sell which in turn meant that a highly organised production line was the only realistic way of meeting the demand. This could not be done by the guilds; their system did not encompass the whole process from start to finish but only the crafting of a particular section in it. The need for a general overseer saw the rise of a new kind of merchant, the entrepreneur, the person who linked all the manufacturing steps into a seamless production line. It was he, aided by financial backing, that would make sure wool would get from one stage to the next on time so that orders from afar could be filled and the money roll in.

Wool in Tudor times

The next step in the history of the English cloth trade was an enormous one and it meant that England remained prosperous for centuries. It did, however, also mean the decline of the craft guild. Towns as centres of production were no longer important; much of the cloth making, in its various stages was done in the country in small villages or by rural people.

It was a great opportunity for the poor of the land:

- They could do as much or as little as they could
- They didn't need their own equipment
- Inclement weather meant that there was an opportunity to still make money
- The whole family could help
- Skill was not of the greatest importance

To have the workers working in their own homes like this was the start of what was known as the Domestic System and continued for a long time. Of course, there were as many disadvantages to the system as there were advantages:

- Workers were not independent and relied on the business owners
- Tools had to be hired from the business owner and paid for out of the money made from producing the cloth
- There was no negotiation about prices or conditions
- There was often the possibility that the worker ended up owing more money to the owner than he made

As someone who probably already worked for a landowner these disadvantages would have been nothing new in the experience of the poor. Any work was better than no work.

Extra tax had been added to the export of raw wool in order to encourage the making of finished cloth. By 1420 cloth exports had overtaken those of raw wool: during the 50 years be tween 1350 and 1400, cloth exports multiplied eight-fold to an average of 40,000 pieces a year. Ninety years later this figure itself had quadrupled to 160,000 pieces of finished cloth. Despite the large amount of material going overseas it appears the home market utilised two or three times that.

The cloth industry in England was well established by the end of the Fifteenth Century and would remain its dominant industry until the appearance of cotton in the Eighteenth Century.

Monopolies still existed over the trading of cloth, just as it had done over raw wool; the type of merchant and how he traded changed.

The North Sea became a difficult place to trade with strong opposition from the German Hanse. The Hundred Years War, although long ended had left ongoing problems from the direction of France. This all meant that the Netherlands was the only real option for entering European markets.

The demand for raw wool to be turned into undressed cloth meant that every available piece of land was turned to the raising of sheep, or so the popular theory goes. There is some dispute as to the real cost of sheep versus land for general agriculture. The enclosure of land for sheep was thought to have contributed to a national food shortage, a large body of unemployed rural populous and displaced persons.

The kings of England were still using revenue from wool and cloth export taxes to pay for war against European neighbours.

Henry VIII, and his rejection of the Pope and Catholicism, undertook a massive task in the dissolution of the monasteries. This meant important opportunities for those with money or influence with the king. The monastery at Cirencester had two newly built fulling mills, which the former abbot had ordered at a cost of £500 or more. Such a set up as this was in effect a prototype of the factory; offering a variety of potential processes to be done under the one roof, or at least on the one property.

Enclosure, legislated in 1487, was another topical issue for the people of Henry VIII's time. The cloth trade was again putting pressure on England to increase its product and in order to do so more sheep needed to be farmed for wool. Land that had been traditionally used for crops was marked out for pasture. Food became scarce and prices skyrocketed. Another disastrous consequence was the displacement of agricultural workers whose services in ploughing, harvesting and processing food were no longer in demand. As is the way, those that got the money were the great landowners and merchants.

Like his predecessors, Henry VIII was an expensive war monger; borrowing heavily from foreign financiers to fund his was chests. It consequently led to a debasement of the English currency which meant that English wool and cloth were once more very attractive imports for foreign merchants.

At the time of Henry VIII's demise England was exporting twice as much cloth than when he had ascended the throne. While the increases in exports might look like prosperity, the proceeds from industry generated tax went back into the war coffers or to its financial backers.

Weaver makes good

Men of influence tended to come from the merchant class or the aristocracy but John Winchcombe, known as Jack Newberry in Delony's ballad of 1597, was neither. He had been a humble weaver whose first step to success was to marry the widow of his former master. His business interests never looked back and when he died in 1520 he was extremely rich. His son, John Winchombe II, furthered his father's meteoric social rise by becoming a Member of Parliament.

The Merchant Adventurers of London

The term Merchant Adventurer is undoubtedly romantic and not necessarily a misnomer in this case. There were merchants who would sail the seas in search of goods to buy and of ports in which to sell English merchandise. They were indeed referred to as 'adventurers', 'venturers' or 'merchant adventurers'. The term loosened over time to include the meanings of financial venture, as in economical risk taking rather than physical risk taking.

The hall of the Merchant Adventurers in Bruges.

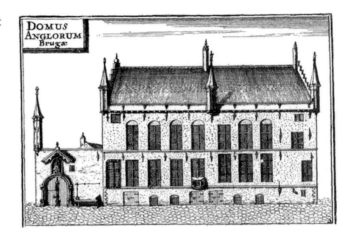

In the early days of the company the Merchant Adventurers mainly exported plain broadcloth (a dense, woollen cloth that was fulled after being woven) and imported all sorts of exotic and luxury goods to England. In its early days it was based at Antwerp in the Netherlands and was able to sell cloth to other Dutch towns as well as to Flemish markets. The company was made up of separate but associated groups, mostly from non London towns including York, Norwich, Exeter, and Hull.

As time went on the fellowship's aims grew similar to those of the Merchants of the Staple before them, that was; to build a monopoly of the trade by making it illegal for anyone to trade without complying with the Adventurers conditions. It was decided to make it harder to become a member. In order to become one you had to either be an apprentice, inherit from your father, or purchase a membership. These conditions did much to ensure that the Adventurers were largely a London based organisation made up of London traders. To be an apprentice to a member or to inherit a position meant residing in London. Traders from other towns and cities in England were welcome to purchase a membership but there were exorbitant fees involved, which were, of course, designed to limit outsiders from the city.

As with the Merchants of the Staple different kings of England put forward different trading rules; some favoured the English merchants, others favoured those from overseas. Also, the bases from which the traders could sell changed continuously; sometimes they were based in England and sometimes abroad.

The Fifteenth Century saw the Adventurers rise as a major rival to the Merchants of the Staple. In 1486 the city of London authorities publically recognised them as a legitimate company and the group became the Fellowship of the Merchant Adventurers of London. They had been formed as a commercial body long before this time and as early as the mid Fourteenth Century they were giving the Staples a run for their money.

The Adventurers enjoyed similar privileges to those of the Merchants of the Staple. They had a base overseas, enjoyed government backing, power and wealth. To become a member of this elite establishment the trader had to pay the exorbitant sum of £20. In 1497, through an act of parliament the fee was dropped to a more manageable £6 13s. 4d.

In 1498 the Merchant Adventurers were distinguished with their own coat of arms. Sixty-six years later they became known as The Merchant Adventurers of England, granted by royal charter. In power and wealth they outstripped the Merchants of the Staple, who had kept their trading interests to the export of raw wool and so limited their potential as financial entrepreneurs.

They carried on the tradition of merchants offering other services to the king, such as providing men to fight on his behalf. Where the Staplers had offered to provide up to a hundred men at arms, the Merchant Adventurers were supposed to have sent two thirds of the ships that made up the battle fleet that would face the Spanish Armada.

The Merchant Adventurers were advocates of exporting only undressed cloth, that is, cloth that is woven but not dyed or finished in any other way. In 1514 the company put forth series of arguments for this.[8] And it was for exactly the opposite reason that a patent roll was issued in 1616–17 to establish a company that would export in dressed cloth because the Merchant Adventurers would not.

> James by the Grace of God, etc.:

> We have often and in divers manners express ourselves … what an earnest desire and constant resolution we have that, as the reducing of wools into clothing was an act of our noble progenitor King Edward the Third, so the reducing of the trade of white cloths, which is but an imperfect thing towards the wealth and good of this our kingdom, unto the trade of dyed and dressed, might be the work of our time.

> To which purpose we did first invite the ancient company of Merchant Adventurers to undertake the same, who upon allegation or pretence of impossibility refused.[9]

The Merchant Adventurers enjoyed a long reign as supreme traders but in the Seventeenth Century they lost their trading privileges following the Glorious Revolution of 1688 (and the overthrow of James II). Parliament opened trade to everyone and the Adventurers, though seriously declining as a trading company, existed into the Nineteenth Century.

Friction between the Staples and the Adventurers

As England became more of a cloth manufacturer and less of an exporter of raw wool, tensions between the two great merchant companies grew in intensity. In 1504 a judgement was made by King and Council in the 'Sterre Chambre' concerning:

> … certain disputes between the said merchant adventurers and the merchants of the staple of Calais, whereby wither party making any use of the privileges of the other, should be subject to all regulations and penalties by which the other is bound.[10]

The decline of the Staples and the rise of the Merchant Adventurers is well illustrated in the following poem by William Forrest in the time of Edward VI. It demonstrates how the Staples, relying on the sale of raw wool, had been steadily finding their countrymen turning to making cloth for export and using the raw wool for their own cloth manufacture. The Merchant Adventurers were all set to exploit this new industry and export the woven textile instead of the fleece.

> No town in England, village or borough
> But thus with clothing be occupied.
> Though not in each place clothing clean thorough,
> But as the town is, their part is applied.
> Here spinners, here weavers, there clothes to be dyed,
> With fullers and shearers as be though best,
> As the clothier may have his cloth drest.
>
> The wool the Staplers do gather and pack
> Out of the Royalme to countries foreign,
> Be it revoked and stayed aback,
> That our clothiers the same may retain,
> All kinds of work folks here to ordain,
> Upon the same exercise their feat
> By tucking, carding, spinning and to beat.[11]

The Domestic System

At the end of the Middle Ages, as raw wool was gradually being replaced by woven cloth as a major export, the domestic system of manufacture was a new and radical system that eventually saw the decline of the guild system. People were able to produce spun yarn and woven cloth in their own homes, earning themselves a little extra money.

While there had always been a percentage of workers producing goods for sale outside the guild system, by the end of the Fifteenth Century it was becoming an increasing trend. A new type of merchant had emerged, known as 'clothiers', or 'merchant clothiers' who were buying wool, not for export, but to have made up as cloth, which they would then export. It was these merchants who were responsible

A household working in the domestic system.

for the rise of the new domestic system of manufacture. They required the work to be done within certain time frames and therefore arranged the collection from one set of workers and delivery to the next to ensure a seamless flow of production. It meant that master craftsmen no longer had control over the market; they couldn't regulate costs, conditions or quality and quite often it was not of a very good standard. Those who undertook work offered by the clothiers were paid in the form of wages.

Placing themselves outside the reputable craft towns meant that the guilds were not in a position to interfere with the new system either. A law made in 1495 saw that authorities were unable to use their power to clamp down on non-guild member activities of manufacture.

The towns that had made a name for themselves as centres of craftsmanship lost their monopoly on the trade and consequently found their previous posterity on the downward slope. Taxes could not be paid and building projects often had to remain unfinished. While the clothiers became wealthy and non guild workers enjoyed some extra wages the urban areas suffered an economic crisis.

As we have seen, England had never been up to the same standard of manufacture of woollen cloth as their Flemish counterparts. To improve the skills needed to upgrade their product, England welcomed the knowledge and techniques brought to them by foreigners. Religious persecution of Protestants in various parts of Europe saw many refugees fleeing to Britain. Many of these immigrants were textile workers and were more than happy to begin plying their trade in England and passing on their skills to the local population.

At first the newcomers were strongly resented and were only supported by the royal authority. However, with time they settled in and as they became immersed in their business and shared their expertise with their new neighbours they were accepted. Not only did they bring technical skill with them, the refugees brought inventions that would eventually revolutionise the cloth industry. In Queen Elizabeth I's time the 'stocking frame' was invented, although it did not fulfil its potential for another hundred years or so.

The domestic system of cloth manufacture grew steadily for the next couple of centuries until it, like its guild worker predecessors, suffered through a new type of manufacture in the rise of the mechanised factory.

Wool in Nineteenth Century

Evidence of Mr. James Ellis, 18 April, 1806 (a clothier of Harmley, near Leeds, working with an apprentice, two hired journeymen and a boy, and giving some work out)

Do you instruct this apprentice in the different branches of the trade?

As far as he has been capable I have done.

Will you enumerate the different branches of the trade which you yourself learnt, and in which you instruct your apprentice?

I learnt to be a spinner before I went apprentice; my apprentice was only eleven years old when I took him; when I went apprentice I was a strong boy, and I was put to weaving first; I never was employed in bobbin winding myself while I was apprentice; I had learnt part of the business with my father-

An engraving of Hogarth's *The Lazy Apprentice*.

in-law before I went; I knew how to wind bobbins and to warp; after that I learnt to weave; we had two apprentices, and after I had been there a little while we used to spin and weave our webs; while one was spinning the other was weaving.

Did you also learn to buy your own wool?

Yes; I had the prospect of being a master when I came out of my time, and therefore my master took care I should learn that.

Does that branch require great skill?

Yes it does; I found myself very deficient when I was loose.

Different sorts of wool are applicable to different dyes and different manufactures?

Yes. I was frequently obliged to resort to my master for information as to the dyeing and buying of wool.

Does it not require great skill to dye according to pattern even when you have bought wool?

Yes.

Were you also instructed in that?

Yes; I kept an account all the time I was apprentice of the principal part of the colours we dyed, and practised dyeing: I always assisted in dyeing; I was not kept constantly to weaving and spinning; my master fitted me rather for a master than a journeyman.

And you instruct your apprentice in the same line?

Yes; we think is a scandal when an apprentice is loose if he is not fit for his business; we take pride in their being fit for their business, and we teach them all they will take.[12]

The Old Apprenticeship System in the Woollen Industry [Report of Committee on the Woollen Industry, 1806 (III), p.5, 1806][13]

Wool in the Twentieth Century

The Merchants of the Staple, the Merchant Adventurers, and craft guilds may, or may not, still exist in some form today but long gone is their power and control over the wool export industry.

The wool industry in the Twentieth Century was given the name The International Wool Textile Organization (IWTO) which also went by the name of the Federation Laniere Internationale (FLI) and it formed out of groups of industry workers. It was initiated in 1928 as an international arbitration body for the wool trade in its various processes. Its purpose has since grown to include the regularising of weights and measures used, to facilitate trade between member countries, to collect statistics and other information, and to support research for many aspects of the industry. The organisation is much more focused on the wool trade with the extra activities that grew from the Merchant groups like civil duties and the putting on of miracle plays are within the reserve of the individual as non-work related practice.

Wool in Australia

In 1788, when the first fleet landed on the shores of the new British colony of Australia, it carried not only convicts and their gaolers but also the first sheep to step onto that land. They were not taken there for their wool but for their meat.

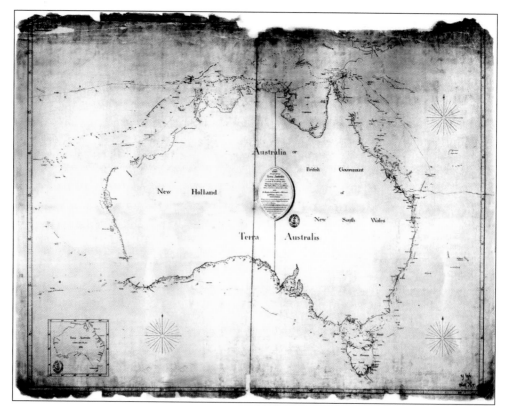

Map of Australia.

Not long after Spanish Merinos were imported and 1796 saw the start of what was to be another long and prosperous industry. These first immigrants were joined by other wool producing sheep from Britain, Europe, and even the USA (Rambouillet and Vermont breeds).

The first samples of commercially viable wool were sent to England in 1801 and the first bale ever to be auctioned of Australian wool was in 1806. From then until about 1870 England was the main consumer of Australian wool; its mills were still churning out yards of woollen cloth. And in response to the demand, Australia began to breed sheep in earnest, just as England had done centuries before.

The main type of wool grown in Australia was Merino. It was graded into three categories: superfine, fine and medium according to the length and fineness of the fibres. And just as in early England, different sheep thrived in different conditions producing different types of wool, so did they in Australia. The superfine Merino wool preferred the colder and wetter climates of NSW, Victoria and Tasmania whereas the dry, harsh landscape of South Australia required a tougher sheep that consequently bore coarser wool.

Wool was transported long distance in bales, apparently invented so that a bale could sit comfortably either side of a camel's hump. They were enormous things, twelve of them weighed about two tonnes. They were not just carried by single animals however, but more often by teams of bullocks pulling large, cumbersome wagons.

Toward the very end of the Nineteenth Century Australia's wool exports moved primarily from England to Europe itself. The mills of England were no longer producing the wool cloth it had been so famous for.

Shearing sheep

Before wool was taken from the live sheep, the hair (similar to goat hair) covered hides would have been used to make clothes, blankets, foot wear and rugs. As the sheep developed wool they would leave lumps of it behind during the moulting season. It was gathered, teased into lengths and twisted into a primitive yarn.

From gathering naturally shed fleece humans devised ways of harvesting wool in larger batches at a time more suited to them than nature had devised. It started with plucking by hand and combing with bone and bronze implements to cutting away from the skin with knives. Shears have been found that are over three thousand years old. Up until the age of electricity hand shears, like large scissors, were used to shear a sheep. Now they are given a 'number 1or 2' haircut with an industrial set of electric razors similar to those a barber uses.

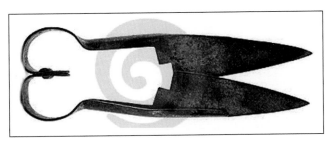

A pair of traditional shears.

The fleece is sheared from the skin of the sheep, a job that has become an art form. It takes dexterity to negotiate the bends and folds of an animal with four legs even with modern technology. The fleece is removed as a whole, unbroken coat.

The coat is picked up and thrown onto a table for the wool classer to skirt it (trimming away the outer edges of the fleece to leave the longer, better quality). The classer categorises the fleece according to colour and fibre length and strength.

With the fleece sorted into bins of similar quality it is then taken and pressed into a bale of wool. One bale comprises about 40 fleeces and weighs up to 200 kg. This wool is unprocessed, that is, it has not been washed or had any of the lanolin (the fleece's natural oil) removed, it is known as greasy wool.

The cleaning process is called scouring and involves washing the fleece to remove, not only dirt and extraneous bits and pieces (twigs, grass seeds etc) but also the lanolin which is separated from the rubbish and made into cosmetic creams such as hand moisturisers. The clean wool is then ready for further processing: combing, carding and spinning.

Worsted processing

Worsted processing uses only virgin wool, that is, unused in anyway previously (some wool is reprocessed after an initial spinning meaning that it not virgin wool). The staples need to be long and fine and scoured to remove any impurities and oil. Any short fibres will be discarded to be reused in a different process. One of the main features in worsted yarns is the fact that the fibres are combed carefully so they lie parallel to each other as much as possible. The fibre is spun into a tight twist.

A tailor's sample book of worsted fabrics.

Worsted wool is a classic textile for making men's suits.

A tailor's sample book of worsted fabrics.

Wool processing
All sorts of wool fibre can be used in the woollen process, even fabric. It will be broken down into fibre before being mixed with other sorts of wool, greasy, scoured, short fibres etc. This means that waste from worsted wool spinning can be used.

Some of the major sheep wool types
There are many more different breeds of sheep than mentioned here but this list comprises the most commonly used ones for wool:

- Blackface – coarse mountain wool
- Bulky low lustre wool
- Cheviot
- Coopworth – coarse long lustre wool
- Corridale – medium fine wool
- Hampshire-short bulky wool and meat
- Leicester – long lustre wool
- Lincoln – long lustre wool
- Merino – fine wool
- Perendale – Long, bulky
- Polwarth – medium fine wool and meat
- Romney – long lustre wool and meat
- Suffolk – short bulky wool and meat

Parasites and other problems
Sheep may be fairly hardy and can live happily in the pastures without too much human intervention; however, there are several problems that can interfere with a sheep's health and well being.

- Common parasites that can infest sheep are: intestinal worms, maggots and lice. Worms can be controlled through good farm management, prevention rather than cure. The grazing paddocks need to be in good shape, not overstocked or bare of grass. Then drenching can be applied once or twice a year. Drenching is a liquid worm medicine squirted into the sheep's mouth. A narrow race is filled with sheep so each can be given its dose and then let out the other end
- Lice are a problem for sheep just as they are for humans. To control the breeding sheep are back-lined (in which the chemical is applied along the backbone) or put through a long trough full of the chemical, this is called dipping
- In Australia sheep can suffer from maggot infestation caused by the larvae of the blowfly. The site of the infestation is usually around the backend where wool gets soaked with urine. Removing the tails of lambs has been a traditional way of helping solve this problem but ethical questions are being raised about the methods used to do this (without anaesthetic). An additional measure is to crutch the sheep before the wool gets too dirty and attractive to flies. This is a quick shearing around the bottom. At the other end, wool can grow too long over a sheep's eyes so they can't see. They are sometimes given a hair cut in a process called wigging

- Footrot is a highly infectious disease which can stay in the ground for a week or more. It cripples the animal. Infected sheep are given a toe nail clip and walked or stood in a chemical bath. If the infection is too bad the sheep are sent to the abattoir to be used as meat

- In medieval times sheep poo was an important fertiliser for crops and just as useful a product as the animals' meat and wool
- When Richard the Lionheart was held for ransom, certain religious orders who were wool growers were able to contribute to the release money through paying taxes in wool
- A decree was issued in 827 that women were to shear the sheep
- William the Conqueror took English textiles back to France with him where it was widely admired for its high quality
- Policy on foreign merchants during the early part of the Fourteenth Century was that they were only supposed to stay in the area for 40 days for the purpose of conducting trade, and furthermore, that they should stay with a native merchant who could watch they didn't get up to mischief. They were not allowed to stay in an inn
- Henry II, in 1163, gave the weavers of York the right to have their own guild. For £10 a year they had the sole right to weaving and dyeing striped cloth. This was paid dutifully for about 40 years but in the very early years of the Thirteenth Century the guild's ability to pay its dues declined until they were not only totally unable to pay their annual subscription but where several years in arrears (by 1309 the weavers' guild of York owed the King £780)
- In 1180 Henry II, probably inspired by the success of the London weavers' guild and their annual contribution to his coffers, tried to seek out all unregistered guilds and fine them. He managed to track down the saddlers' guild in York and they had to pay a sum of 20 shillings; the guild of glove makers had to pay 2 marks, the same as the weavers in London paid for their annual charter, and a guild of hosiers had to pay 1 mark
- The guild of weavers forbade the weaving of cloth at night because candles were insufficient to see well by in order to produce top quality cloth
- The weavers' guild became a powerful force in London in the Middle Ages and at one point the city administrative centre tried, with bribery, to get the king to get rid of it. No action was taken, the bribe never materialised for one thing and the weavers increased their fee to 1,600 silver pennies a year instead. The king could hardly turn away from such a secure source of revenue.
- Astronauts wear wool when in space
- Wool is an ideal insulator, protecting from heat, cold and sound. This is because the crimp of the fibres adds bulk to the textile which traps air
- Wool absorbs moisture well. It can absorb approximately one third of its own weight
- Wool bearing animals were being domesticated and the processes for spinning and weaving it were developing in South America at a similar time to the

developments on the other side of the world. The animals were not sheep but llamas and alpacas whose closest relatives are those of the camel family

- The wool industry was of such importance to England that the wool sack became the symbolic seat for the Chancellor. There were four of them to start with, large red bags of wool, probably introduced in Edward III's reign to symbolise England's major export
- Wool is used as a low fire risk fibre. It needs a higher temperature to make it ignite and the rate of spreading is relatively slow compared to other common fabrics. It will not melt, drip or let off toxic gases when alight. A woollen blanket is a good thing to wrap a burning body in to stifle the flames
- Jackie Howe was an Australian shearer who, in 1892, managed to shear an incredible 321 sheep in a day
- Lucius Columalla was a Roman living in Spain. He is supposed to have first crossed the native Spanish sheep with the Roman Tarrentine and come up with the Merino
- 'Morrowspeches' was the name given to guild meetings in which members might be disciplined or fined or to have grievances aired
- In 1350, in London there were more than 40 craft guilds operating
- The word 'sterling' as in pounds sterling, originally came from the word 'Easterling' which was used to name the traders from Germany and the Netherlands
- One suggested etymology for the word blanket is that the article, made of wool, was invented by a Thomas Blanket in the Fourteenth Century. This turned out to be a humorous suggestion made by a Nineteenth Century Canadian author of fiction
- A parliamentary act of 1666 and 1678 forbade the burial of a corpse in any garment or shroud unless it was made of wool; also the coffin was to be lined with wool. This was yet another effort by the English government to boost its industry. By 1814 so many people had disobeyed the law that it was repealed
- Pope, in his *Moral Essays*, Ep. I, iii (1733),has a funny take on this:

'Odious! In woollen! 'twould a saint provoke!'
(were the last words Narcissa spoke).
'No! Let a charming chintz and Brussels lace
Wrap my cold limbs, and shade my lifeless face.

Notes

1. *Sources of English constitutional History*, (eds) Carl Stephensen and Frederick George Marcham, Harper and Brothers Publishers, New York and London, 1937, pp. 193–4.
2. The Riverside Chaucer, (ed.) Larry D. Benson, Oxford University Press, third edition, 1988.
3. Cheney, Edward Potts, *An Introduction to the Industrial and Social History of England*, Project Gutenburg, 2007, Chapter III: Town Life and Organisation.
4. From *A History of Commerce*.

5. English Economic History, pp. 178–8.
6. Taken from: Stephenson, Carl and Marcham, Frederick George, *Sources of English Constitutional History*, Harper & Brothers Publishers, New York and London, 1937. pp. 228–229.
7. *The Riverside Chaucer* , (ed.) Larry D. Benson, Oxford University Press, third edition, 1988.
8. See English Economic history, pp. 402–404.
9. English Economic History, p. 454.
10. Tanner, J.R. (ed.), Tudor Constitutional Documents AD 1485–1603, Cambridge university Press, Cambridge, 1951, p. 260.
11. Trevelyan, G.M. *Illustrated English Social History vol. I*, Longmans, Green and Co, London, 1958, p. 129.
12. English Economic History, pp. 499–500.
13. From English economic History (eds.) Bland, Brown and Tawney, G. Bell and sons Ltd, London, p. 499.

CHAPTER FOUR

Silk

With time and patience a mulberry leaf becomes a silk gown

Chinese proverb

The Legend

Lady Lei-Tzu, wife of the Yellow Emperor, sat with her attendants under the shady bough of a glorious mulberry tree. Sun filtered through the leaves, dappling the ladies with golden light: the perfect afternoon in which to tell stories and sip tea. Lady Lei-Tzu took a delicate cup of amber liquid, steam gently rising and tickling her nose, and with an elegant hand raised it to her mouth to drink. Plop. A small splash sent drops of hot tea falling onto the pearly skin, scalding it. Lady Lei-Tzu shrugged off the hurt and looked into her cup to see what had interrupted her refreshment. An oval ball floated amidst the jasmine leaves. With two slim fingers she tried to pluck it from the water but as she touched it the ball unwound into one long thread, soft and sticky and intriguing beyond anything she had encountered before.

It was the cocoon of a caterpillar that regularly feasted on the white mulberry leaves growing abundantly in the palace gardens. Lady Lei-Tzu looked up into the branches canopying over head and saw that under many of the leaves cocoons had sprouted like exotic fruit. She pulled one off, and beckoned to a maid to pour another cup. She dropped the swathed bundle into it and watched again as it began to unravel. The strand was finer than hair and felt so smooth and soft. What, luxury, the lady thought, to have a gown made from such a substance. From then on the empress was known as Lady of the Silkworm.

And so it is Lady Lei-Tzu, wife of the great mythical Yellow Emperor, Huang Ti, (traditionally his reign is put at 2677–2597 BC) who is popularly credited with the invention of silk as a textile and presides over silk rituals as its officiating goddess.

Silk! A soft, light, elusive material whose name has become synonymous with refined luxury whether it is referring to the taste of chocolate, an infant's skin or the human voice. As a textile it stands apart from cotton, hemp, flax or wool, being neither a direct product of the soil or grown on an animal's back. It is, instead, a seemingly magical thread produced by a

Lady Lei-Tzu drinking tea.

small, insignificant grub. And the procedure for growing, harvesting and weaving the thread into glorious fabric, is, in the human scheme of things, an ancient one shrouded in mystery.

Discovery and early production of Chinese silk
The legend of Lady Lei-Tzu is unforgettably romantic but archaeological finds of dyed red silk ribbons have placed silk cultivation several hundred years further back in time than the 2700–2600 BC dates in which Lady Lei-Tzu was the consort of the Yellow Emperor. Impressions of woven silk fragments in baked clay, spinning and beating tools and carvings on cups and other implements depicting silkworms have been unearthed along the banks of the Yangzi River, providing further evidence that silk was being produced in China up to 7,000 years ago. One particular find, dating to 2850–2650 BC has been identified as silk from the *Bombyx mori* species. This dates the early cultivation of silk to just before or during the early reign of the emperor Fuxi, the first of the three mythical emperors. Fuxi, who preceded the Yellow Emperor and his lady, has also been accredited with discovering silk and overseeing the beginning of its cultivation. While this story has more archaeological evidence to support it, it does not complement the fact that women were the main silk textile workers.

The predominance of women in the industry of growing and weaving silk might explain why the story of Lady Lei-Tzu discovering silk became more widely accepted than that of the previous emperor's. It may also explain why, in the early days of silk cultivation, Lady Lei-Tzu's main rivals to the title of Lady of the Silkworm, were women. However, by the time of the Shang Dynasty and its many written records, Lady Lei-Tzu was well established as the major goddess of sericulture accompanied by a large cohort of minor silk deities, most of them female. The importance of women to the industry is reflected in the fact that rituals involving the silk goddess were the only ones officiated over by the empress instead of her spouse.

In the early days of sericulture worship it is believed that human sacrifices were sometimes made to ensure the continuing success of silk in all its aspects. This practice didn't persist but the worship of Lady Lei-Tzu presiding over silk production continued right up until the Nineteenth Century by many female factory workers. The true origins of the discovery of making cloth from silkworm cocoons in China will always remain swathed in legend.

Silk, though a strong and resilient fibre, will not stand the stresses of time unless preserved under optimum conditions and therefore most early specimens disintegrated within years of its manufacture. Evidence, then, of the knowledge, use, and cultivation of the silkworm lies mainly with archaeological finds such as sculptures and carvings, tools related to reeling, spinning and weaving. For instance, one of the earliest pieces discovered was a carved ivory bowl with an engraved silkworm on either side.

The discovery of the cocoon as a source of silk was preceded by the use of the intestines of the silk worm itself. Again the proof lies in a depiction of a cocoon cut in half with a thread being pulled from inside the grub. The cocoon was apparently soaked in an acidic solution such as vinegar, sliced open and the gut of the caterpillar drawn out as a sinewy thread. This fibre is very strong and can exceed 100 metres in length. One could easily see how the progression from using the silk

Bombyx Mori.

worm intestine to using the silk forming the cocoon could be made through the initial soaking process.

The biggest development in Chinese silk production and the reason that China tended to dominate the market for silk, was the domestication of a species of moth derived from China's native wild moth, *Bombyx mandarina moore*. This species, through careful breeding and nurturing eventually became the renowned flightless and sightless *Bombyx mori* from which the Chinese were able to make the finest silk in the world. Not only was it the cultivation of this silkworm but the method for harvesting the silk, the reeling off of unbroken filaments from the cocoon, that were responsible for the success of Chinese silk, and it was these methods which they supposedly kept a national secret for so many years.

It has been suggested by some historians that perhaps it was not so much an issue of keeping a secret from the outside world in order to dominate the market that gave China its commercial edge but more the fact that the cultivation of mulberry trees and *Bombyx mori* in other parts of the world were just not successful.

Supporting this theory is the fact that at more than one point in China's early history the demand for silk was so high in its own country that they couldn't keep up the demand from the domestic market, let alone making enough silk to export it.

While mulberry leaves are not the only food that the *Bombyx mori* can eat (it is suggested that children in the western world, keeping them as pets or for school projects, can feed them ordinary lettuce leaves) it is definitely a highly suitable one. As the mulberry trees grow prolifically along the banks of parts of the Yangzi River, it was only natural that they would attract the silkworm moths as a food source for their young once hatched. The climate was right and a food source in abundance, the ideal set up for silkworm farming: more food, more grubs, more cocoons, more silk.

Silk follows the trade routes

Silk became known outside China well before the official recognised date for the start of trade along the Silk Road which has been put at the Second Century BC. The Scythians had trade routes already operating in the Sixth Century BC that went from China to Eastern Europe. A number of quality silk items were unearthed from a frozen Scythian tomb in Siberia (dating to the Fourth to Fifth Century BC), including a delicate silk panel appliquéd onto a felt saddle blanket. These finds support the probability of the existence of earlier trade routes than the Silk Road. The silk panel from the Siberian burial chamber may, or may not have been of Chinese origin but it certainly wasn't from Siberia.

The Chinese frequently used silk textiles as gifts for foreign dignitaries, offerings of peace to potential invaders along its borders and for other diplomatic purposes; it was used in dowries and as tribute. This meant that there was the potential for fine silk from China eventually being dug up from the tombs of ancient Egypt or other faraway places.

By the Fourth Century BC silk textiles, including those from China, were known to both the Greeks and the Romans, though these cultures were ignorant about how the textile was produced. For centuries the Romans believed that silk came from the underside of the mulberry leaf and was therefore a plant fibre. They did know that it was chiefly made in Serica by the Seres: the Latin words for the people and country being the same as for the textile. The silk that found its way to Rome, and caused such a sensation, would have got there via the Silk Road, probably brought by Arab or Parthian traders.

As it has been said, it is thought that not all the silk being traded was made in China. By the Second or Third Century BC silk manufacturing was already being undertaken in Central Asia and India though the fabric was made from the cocoons of wild silkmoths, not domesticated ones. Around 200 BC Korea learnt sericulture through Chinese emigrants who may also have introduced the *Bombyx mori* species of silkworm to that country along with the knowledge of how to raise them and reel off the silk. A couple of hundred years later there is documentation noting that the Japanese emperor was given a gift of silkworm eggs by his counterpart in China, and this was not the first or only gift of its kind between China and its neighbouring countries.

The secret is out

Whatever the facts were about the spread of sericulture beyond China, the fable behind how the carefully kept secret about silk was finally broken, according to the records of a Seventh Century monk, when a young Chinese princess was betrothed to a prince in Khotan, India. The thought of leaving her home, country and family did not bother the young lady nearly as much as the fact that outside China there was no knowledge of making silk. How could life be bearable without ready access to that luxurious of textiles!

The princess hid mulberry tree seeds and silkworms in her elaborate headdress and gave them to her husband as wedding present. He was more than delighted at having been given the means of a lucrative business.

Silk in Rome

However and wherever the silk was made, when it arrived in Rome it sparked a huge desire in the population for owning and wearing it. There were stories told that the demand for this particular luxury import was so strong that it threatened to cripple the Roman economy and in 14AD Emperor Tiberius issued a decree banning the wearing of silk because it was going to lead to decadence. Tiberius's ban did not last because a hundred or so years later Roman envoys were sent directly to China in order to create a sea trade between the two civilisations. Trade between China and the west flourished and by the Tang Dynasty of the Seventh Century AD decorative influences from the west were flowing back to China to be incorporated in their own designs for the aesthetic taste of the Chinese as well as for the export market.

Chinese consumption of silk was heavy during the Tang Dynasty and it is recorded that Lady Yang, the Precious Consort, had seven hundred weavers allocated to making silk cloth for her royal robes.

Chinese silk weavers in Persia

Tang silk weavers were taken prisoner during the Battle of Talas, when China was defeated by the Persians, and were taken to Persia and Mesopotamia in order to teach the local textile workers the craft of silk spinning and weaving. Chinese secrets were slowly being dispersed into the vast world.

All the time, through trade and war, famine and feast, developments in weaving techniques were being made. Different cultures brought different influences and, as sericulture became established in other geographical locations, so novelty weaves such as cut velvet pile were applied to silk.

In the Seventeenth and Eighteenth Centuries China had begun to weave silk rugs based on the technique of the Turkic tribes who had devised it for the use of wool. This coincided with the rise of chinoiserie in the west, the love of all things decorative with a distinctive oriental flavour. Exports from China included beautiful bolts of painted silk with Chinese designs adapted for European taste.

Mechanisation in China

Just as the Industrial Revolution in England had caused problems for the cottage manufacturer, so did the importing of machines to facilitate the reeling process in China. The negative effects of these machines did not last long and the industry settled and grew to such an extent that new areas of manufacture sprang up in China to satisfy world demand. While most factories embraced the new technology there were outposts of traditional practise that continued with the time honoured methods.

The revolution that saw the end of not only the Qing Dynasty but dynastic rule altogether did not halt the production of silk. It still formed a major part of the Chinese export economy and its biggest threat was the rise in popularity of synthetic textiles. The smaller silk producing centres were devastated and some

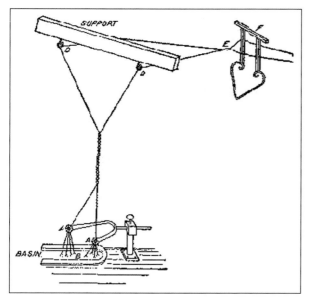

A hand reeling silk machine.

of the social structures that had grown out of female involvement in the industry changed as a result when they had to seek lesser kinds of employment elsewhere. The larger silk producers incorporated synthetic fibres into their textiles to satisfy the new demands of fashion.

With the rise of the Peoples' Republic in 1949, when luxurious goods were seen as evil, silk production managed to stand firm because it was still one of China's major exports. It was not used by the general populace in any form of personal or domestic commodity but did find an artistic outlet in government propaganda. One good to come out of so much strife in a country under the iron thumb of Communism was the preserving of traditional methods of craftsmanship, including all the ways of working silk that were starting to diminish in the Nineteenth Century under mechanisation.

The Twenty-first Century has seen the rise of China as a major manufacturer of everything from plastic toys to motorcars and while silk is no longer a dominant export for China, China still provides a large bulk of the world's silk.

Independent silk development outside of China
According to recent archaeological activity there is evidence that challenges the notion that silk production, perhaps even cultivation of silkworms, was not the sole discovery of the Chinese although it has been noted that the ancestor of the *Bombyx mori* silk moth (the moth used for producing China's best silk thread) was a species unique to China.

Putting this point aside but not out of mind, finds such as the copper wire ornament with fragments of silk fibre still attached to it (dating to approximately 2450 BC) unearthed at an archaeological site of the ancient and prosperous civilisation of Harrapa, in what we now call Pakistan, throw interesting possibilities into the debate. And, on further investigation this thread is found to be made of a type of wild silk and not that of *Bombyx mandarina moore* (*Bombyx mori's* great, great ancestor). The partially processed silk thread fragment (2500–2000 BC) seems to have been reeled in the manner of Chinese silk though the fibres themselves are from a wild species of moth. Silk made from wild moth cocoons is usually formed from spun, shorter threads because the cocoon has been broken when the moth has hatched from it.

Fragments of fabric made from a mixture of spun silk (as opposed to reeled) and cotton from 1500 to 1000 BC were found in India but this is almost all the surviving silk textile to be unearthed at such an early date. Silk fragments have also been found at an archaeological site in Germany dating to 700 BC, well outside the official date for the beginning of silk export from China to the West, though in the light of the evidence found at Harrapa it is possible the silk is from another silk producing area.

Production of silk in the West
Whether it happened through gifts of silkworm eggs and mulberry seeds given to foreign diplomats and emperors or through ancient industrial espionage the secret of sericulture spread to Korea and Japan, from Persia to Byzantium. Chinese silk craftsmen captured in battle found they had to make silk and teach reeling and weaving skills to their captors. In the Eighth Century AD silk was being produced

A silk scarf made for the Western market.

in exportable amounts in central Asia by Chinese prisoners of war taken by Arabs. The silk that was produced by these slaves was of the same high quality as that produced in China.

Silk was traded and sold all over Europe and sericulture followed along with it into Spain, Italy and other parts of Western Europe where the climate was conducive to the growing of mulberry trees and the rearing of silk worms. England, unfortunately, proved too wet and cold for silkworms to survive, let alone thrive, and silk, or at least the raw materials, remained an imported product.

Byzantine silk

Byzantium in the early centuries AD was the jewel of the world and almost everything bright and beautiful either passed through it on the way to somewhere else or it was made there and then sent on its way. The Byzantines learnt all aspects of Chinese sericulture, from the nurturing of precious mulberry trees to the reeling off of the filaments from unbroken cocoons and then weaving it into cloth as light as air using specialised weaving and spinning skills they'd learnt from the Persians and Syrians. The Byzantine craftsmen could also perform the elusive and complicated task of spinning silk 'organzine', a four-strand thread from which the strongest, most lustrous and costly silks could be made.

For centuries Byzantium had a strong hold on the silk trade, not only producing and manufacturing it but also distributing it. By the Tenth Century AD Byzantium was at its peak in the silk world but from the Eleventh Century onwards there was a decline in its power through a succession of wars, not only from outside attack but also from civil discontent. The Byzantine capital, Constantinople finally fell to foreign invaders in the Fifteenth/Sixteenth Century.

Silk production in Europe

Displaced silk workers, fleeing strife in Byzantium, found their way to Europe. Moorish traders had already introduced the silk industry to Spain and established workshops there where Byzantine craftspeople found a welcome home. Italy was another major centre where silk workers settled and resumed their craft. In fact Italy became one of the best known European producers of silk yarn and fabric. The Italians, following the fabled secrecy of the Chinese, subsequently shrouded their own knowledge and inventions for reeling and spinning silk *organzine* with similar zeal.

Lucca was the site of one of the earliest water driven silk throwing (the process of twisting the reeled fibres together to form a strand of yarn) mills enabling the production of the prized *organzine* with ease and speed not possible with the laborious hand throwing method. The reeled silk has to be twisted (thrown), doubled and twisted back on itself to form the four-ply thread and a machine that could be powered by water to turn the spindles for this was an invaluable invention. Over the next hundred years the device was installed at the major Italian silk centres in Florence, Bologna and Venice.

By the end of the Fifteenth Century France wanted to be part of the silk making world. Under Louis the XI, Italian silk specialists were taken to the centres of Lyons and Tours where they were required to teach local people the art of weaving silk. The Italians had not brought with them the secrets of throwing silk or the secrets of how to make *organzine* thread. At this time in Italy it was forbidden to tell these secrets in forfeit of your life: silk spinning was a deadly game.

It was only a matter of time before French weavers were able to produce fabric as beautiful as the Italians, using, of course, imported silk thread. The French specialty was their ability to produce exquisite new designs in fabric every year. By 1667 it was impossible for the Italians to compete with the French in their imaginative and prolific output of designs. The French had not been idle in the matter of inventions either and had adapted the draw loom so that all sorts of woven textures could be achieved. Amongst others there was chenille, crêpe de Chine and chiffon.

Not to be outdone by its ancient rival, France, England too had to be part of the luxury silk industry. James I was instrumental in getting silk weaving established in Britain. He gave incentives to nobles to set up groves of mulberry trees in which to nourish silkworms to get sericulture started in England. Black mulberry trees were used in place of the traditional white mulberries of China, possibly because they were more tolerant of the colder, wetter weather that England was notorious for. Even though several serious attempts were made, including the planting of 2,000 mulberry trees in Chelsea Park, London, sericulture never thrived.

Silk in the colonies
It was also James I who introduced sericulture to the American colonies in 1619. The industry took hold within certain New England communities like the Shakers but remained a cottage industry. In the Eighteenth Century New Jersey became a major silk producer although the US relied on imported Japanese silk for the bulk of its silk fabric.

Silk weaving in Britain
Even though Britain couldn't produce its own silk there was no shortage of skilled labour in the weaving of it and consequently it was able to set up successful weaving factories. The persecuted Huguenots had fled to England, amongst other places, and a fair number of them had been in the weaving trade. Their presence was welcomed and indeed actively sought as early as the reign of Queen Elizabeth the First.

A silk processing mill in Britain.

A century later a wave of some 5,000 refugees settled in Britain and with them they brought the skill of making lustring – a fine, light, glossy silk. This involved stretching and heating the silk thread.

Spitalfields, just outside of London, was chosen as the site of the Royal Lustring Company by Eteienne Seignoret, a silk merchant originally from Lyon. The silk woven in this mill was called 'flowered silk' after one of its most popular designs, though flowers were by no means there only design. English silk hit the export market with huge success.

There was still the matter of *organzine* silk thread to be taken care of. No matter how many skilled craftspeople came from the continent, none of them had brought the secret of the machinery behind its viable production. To make it all by hand was incredibly tedious even with the use of a spinning wheel and an undernourished waif to run the length of the mill in order to wind the thread around a 'gate' at the other end to enable the doubling process.

Espionage and murder
Two brothers, Thomas and John Lombes, both in the textile trade, decided to investigate the Italian secret.

John went to Italy and, pretending to be a worker, bribed his way into a factory where he surreptitiously sketched the water driven mill. He was caught in the act but escaped with his drawings back to England where his brother built a spinning machine to the specifications of the Italian model. Intriguingly, John was later poisoned by an Italian woman, perhaps a hired assassin, for his theft of industrial secrets.

Thomas grew rich on the earnings from his new machine and was further enriched when the government of England paid him £18,000 for the patent on it.

Silk in Ireland

Ireland also saw its share of Huguenot refugees and the silk industry tried to take off in that country too. For various reasons the silk trade did not prove as easy or as successful to run as it was in England. Workers were angry at the introduction of powered machines because it meant workers were laid off and riots ensued. Imported silk did nothing to support the Irish industry even though the Hibernian Silk Warehouse, established in 1765 did what it could to help. Again there were attempts at growing the raw material with the planting of 80 acres of mulberry trees. This attempt failed, but a monastery of Cistercians was able to cultivate silkworms and process the cocoons in order to make silk cloth, though this was much later in the early Twentieth Century. It did prove though that it was physically possible to farm silkworms in that kind of climate.

Silk weaving continued to grow as an industry in Britain. Advances in weaving technology in the Nineteenth Century meant that silk could be produced at a much greater rate and therefore could be sold at a much lower price, bringing it within the range of more of the population. The stress of supplying cheaper silk to the general public meant that there was always the threat of a fall in quality of the finished goods.

Dyeing and printing methods for catering to large quantities of consumers lead to innovations in both these areas and the use of the new aniline dyes broadened the colour spectrum considerably. As the dyes evolved spectacular hues were achieved making the already sumptuous textile even more alluring.

The Queen wears mauve silk and then black

Queen Victoria was instrumental in making mauve silk all the fashion and after Albert's death, she was the instigator of the fashion for black mourning wear, popularly black crepe silk.

Silk remained in demand, just as in China, well into the Twentieth Century, and again, owed its reduced popularity not to war but to the rise of man-made fibres such as nylon.

Twentieth Century attempts at English sericulture were undertaken by Zoe Lady Hart Dyke at Lullington Castle in Kent. England is still one of Western Europe's main producers of silk fabric.

Thai silk

Thailand did have an ancient tradition of sericulture that has been revived in the Twenty-first Century. It produces silk from two main types of wild worm, one cultivated and the other wild: *Bombycidae* and *Saturniidae* respectively. The silk is still often hand reeled and woven in home industries, despite the modern day technologies available. The

Silk weaving in Thailand.

silk is soaked in hot water and bleached in order for it to take dye as wild silk is notoriously resistant to dye.

Cultivated Silk Process

Bombyx mori spins a long, fine, even filament for its cocoon and when it is harvested it produces a much longer thread than that of its wild cousins. The resulting silk is considered finer and more desirable. The process for making this kind of silk involves killing the unhatched pupa in its cocoon. It is killed before it breaks through the cocoon in order to preserve the length of the filaments. Throwing the cocoon with its pupa into hot water serves the double purpose of killing the insect and loosening the sericen, the binding glue, of the cocoon and freeing the threads for reeling off as unbroken thread.

Life cycle of Bombyx mori

The life cycle of the *Bombyx mori* moth begins with the female laying approximately 500 miniscule eggs over a period of four to six days on specially prepared trays. The moth having accomplished its purpose of reproduction and, having no mouth to feed with, will die relatively soon after.

The tiny caterpillars emerge from their eggs about ten days later and are as fine as a human hair and only 3mm long. They will grow to be 10,000 times the weight they were at hatching, outgrow and shed their skins four times and become fully grown at 10cm in their first seven weeks of life. As they grow they are placed on trays of fresh mulberry leaves.

Every two hours a frame with netting covered in leaves is placed over the old one. The caterpillars wriggle through to attack their new food source. When the caterpillars are ready to pupate they are supplied with a different kind of frame from which they can attach and spin their cocoons.

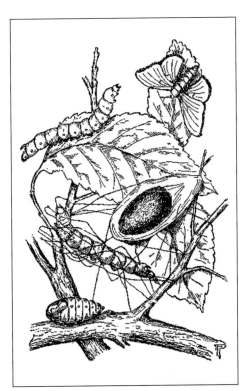

The life cycle of the *bombyx mori* silk moth.

Spinning the cocoon

Silk moth eggs.

From two glands within the head of the grub, but forming into one tube-like outlet, the worm spends three days moving its head back and forth in a figure of eight, an activity which winds the silk around its own body, eventually sealing itself within the cocoon.

Over a period ten days the pupa will metamorphose into a moth.

What happens next
If, as is the case with fine Chinese silk, the object is to get as long and fine a thread as possible it is necessary to kill the pupa before it hatches, this is to keep the filament intact. This is performed through application of heat in the form of boiling, steaming, baking or immersion in a salt bath. The cocoon is then put in a vat of boiling water to release the filament from the gum, sericen, which holds it all together.

The loosened thread is picked up and wound straight onto a reel (the process is called reeling) where a single thread can be as long as 2,000 metres. It is usual to reel the silk from several cocoons at once which also twists them into a single thread. The spun thread is then wound into skeins and collected into books. The silk is then thrown and processed into the type of yarn desired for weaving (for instance, *organzine*).

Cocoons that have broken can have their short fibres spun into thread just as a sheep's fleece is.

In ancient times all this was done by hand. Reeling was performed with a wooden instrument, often formed into a 'H' shape. This was replaced by the spindle wheel, originally used for flax and hemp fibres. The silk was reeled directly onto wooden reels which were then placed on spindles. The thread was cleaned of excess gum, knots etc and thrown into hanks.

Waste silk
As in nearly every kind of processing, silkworm cocoons produce a waste product. The outside of the cocoon, and the threads that attach the cocoon to its frame are not able to be reeled but it doesn't mean they can't be used. These extra bits are gathered together and spun as cotton or wool is. The textile has quite a different texture to that of purely reeled silk but it has its own beauty.

Wild silk
There are many species of silk moth throughout the world, possibly more than 500, although not all of them spin a cocoon from which silk can be made. As has been mentioned earlier, it was probable that locations other than China were producing quality silk for export in ancient times, perhaps even contemporaneously; the Harrapa civilisation in the Indus Valley for instance.

What differentiates these silks from Chinese silk is the fact that they relied upon wild silk moth cocoons from which to make the yarn, whereas China's reputation for fine silk textiles was due to its domestication of the silk moth *Bombyx mori*. China silk was unparalleled in its strength, fineness and smoothness of thread and lustre.

In modern, or at least, relatively modern times, wild silk has been used for making textiles in Africa. In the highlands of Madagascar the silk moth species known as *Borocera Madagascariensis* provides the filaments for weaving a naturally dull brown silk that is of a coarse texture and is used primarily for the making of shrouds. It does not take dye well.

In Northern Nigeria there are a couple of varieties of the species *Anaphe: Anaphe moloneyi* and *Anaphe infracta*. These caterpillars eat the leaves of tamarind trees. The two varieties differ in that *infracta* grubs group together when they spin clusters of cocoons with a common covering. They must be separated before the individual cocoons are processed for their silk. The ensuing silk thread is dull brown and feels as coarse as the *Borocera Madagascariensis* silk. *Anaphe moloneyi* do not form clusters like their cousins but each caterpillar spins its individual cocoon like the *Bombyx mori*. The *moloneyi* cocoons are white but the silk is a light beige colour when spun into yarn.

A wild silk moth type.

Earlier production of silk in Africa can be dated back to the Tenth Century AD where contemporary written evidence points to an already well established trade in silk export from Tunisia.

It was, however, China that held a monopoly on the secrets of sericulture and trade in the finest quality silk threads and woven textiles. Both the domestication of the silk moth and the process for recovering the filaments are the key to the Chinese success in making silk.

Wild silk is the textile made from the cocoons of uncultivated moths. The broken cocoons of hatched moths are gathered from the trees the larvae feed on and then processed in a different manner to that of cultivated silk.

Tussah silk from India is usually made from wild silkworm pupae although it has been semi cultivated in China, it can be de-gummed and reeled like the filaments from *Bombyx mori*.

Wild silk moth types

- *Antheraea pernyi: This moth is* native to China and can be de-gummed as in *Bombyx mori*. The natural colour of the silk is dependent on the climate and the soil
- *Antheraea assamensi*: A wild moth found in Assam, India. It has a natural golden sheen for which it is famous and was reserved only for the use of the Royal family of Assam. It is never dyed or bleached and its natural colour improves with careful ageing
- *Antheraea yamamai*: This is a wild moth though it has been cultivated in Japan for a 1,000 years. It is naturally white but will not take dye well. It is not produced in any great quantities these days
- *Antheraea polyphemus*: is native to North America
- *Ansiota senatoria*: Native to North America called the 'orange-tipped oakworm moth'
- *Gonometa postica*: Native to the Kalahari
- *Gonometa rufobrunnae*: Native to southern Africa and feeds on the Mopane tree
- *Alaskenaras Silkiterious*: silk worm from Alaska
- *Antheraea assamensis*: are terminus feeding and spin cocoon with a convenient exit hole which means the thread can be de gummed and reeled off after the moth has flown

Woven silk scarves by Annamaria Magnus
of Woodbridge Handweaving Studio.

- Early attempts at making aeroplanes often used a lightweight frame covered with stretched silk. Despite its delicate appearance, cultivated, reeled silk is surprisingly strong
- Silk is a poor conductor of electricity and tends to become static with it
- It takes approximately 5,500 silkworms to produce 1 kg of silk
- The eggs are miniscule and a gram comprisea a hundred or so of them. From 28 grams worth of eggs come approximately 30,000 silkworm grubs
- One ounce (28.34 grams) of *Bombyx mori* eggs brings forth 20,000 silkworms, which in turn can eat about a tonne of mulberry leaves during their larvae stage
- Silkworms have prodigious appetites, so it is necessary to have a large supply of fresh food for them. That many tiny mouths can gnaw their way through a tonne of mulberry leaves. Yet the same number of cocoons will only produce five and a half kilos of silk
- In the early days of silk cultivation and production, the cocoons were gathered and killed just after the grub had finished spinning its cocoon
- The dead pupae can be used as food they are high in protein
- Silk is one of the strongest of the world's natural fibres, however, it loses about 20 per cent of that strength when it is wet
- Silk has relatively poor elasticity, once stretched it tends to stay that way
- 'Peace Silk' is a term invented to be applied to silk produced by methods which don't involve killing the un-hatched pupa. The moth is allowed to emerge through the cocoon wall, breaking the filaments in the process. The silk is processed by spinning, not reeling and typically has a rougher, less even finish. Peace silk is not necessarily derived from wild silk moths but rather cultivated moths left to their natural life cycle
- The exportation of information about sericulture from China to the outside world was, for a long time, punishable by death
- The fineness of the filament from the pupae's cocoon is shaped by the grub's orifice from which the thread emerges. *Bombyx mori* produces the best shaped fibre
- Leonardo da Vinci tinkered with the idea of a water powered silk machine

- Over the thousands of years of its domestication *Bombyx mori* evolved to become blind and flightless; adapting, it would seem, to its sole purpose of breeding more silkworms and spinning silk cocoons for the benefit of making silk fabric
- Silk has been used to make parachutes, bicycle tyres, artillery gunpowder bags and even bulletproof vests

Glossary specifically for silk, including imitation silk

Barathea: brightly coloured, striped silk originating in India as the distinctive dress of the Bajadere dancing girls whose lives are dedicated to dancing.

Bengaline: originally a pure silk product from Bengal in India, now often made of wool, cotton and synthetic fibres. It has a ribbed texture.

Brocade: originally a luxury and decorative silk weave but no made in a variety of fibres. The pattern is woven against a twill ground or vice versa.

Brocatelle: originally a silk fabric but now made in other fibres. It is supposed to have been inspired by the craft works of Italian tooled leather. It features a twill pattern on satin ground or vice versa. The main effect is of embossing.

Camocas: a luxurious fabric that was very popular during the Renaissance. It featured gold or silver thread and was composed of silk and linen.

Cendal: silk fabric that looks like taffeta that was in use in medieval times. **Charmeuse:** is divided into two types, satin charmeuse and crepe charmeuse depending on the weave. It has a particular lustre and lends itself well to draping.

Chiffon: comes from the French word meaning rag. Originally made of silk but now made of a variety of fibres. Its characteristics are of a sheer, lightweight fabric composed of tightly twisted yarn.

China Silk: the original Chinese made *Bombyx mori*, reeled silk fabric.

Crepe de chine: a sheer, textured fabric with a raw silk warp and a twisted silk filling.

Crepon: was originally a wool fabric but now often made of silk or rayon. Has a wavy texture.

Cultivated Silk: is the silk made from domesticated silk worms killed before they can emerge from their cocoons in order to keep the filaments whole. This kind of silk is of the highest and finest quality. It is very strong because the threads are not composed of short, spun fibres.

De-gummed silk: silk fibre which has undergone a process, usually of boiling in water, to remove the sticky sericin (glue-like substance) that coats the fibres.

Duppoini Silk: has a distinctive texture which feels coarse to the touch. It is a strong fabric with a lustrous sheen.

Faconne: from the French word for fancy weave. The patterns on the fabric are made of a denser weave than the background.

Faille: a fine material that resembles grograin in its weave and has a lustrous finish.

Foulard: originally an Indian silk, a fine, light fabric with a small printed pattern on a dark or light background.

Frise: this is a looped fabric with a background of cotton or other sturdy fibre. The loops may be cut to form a pattern or uncut or a mixture of both.

Glove silk: made on a warp knitting frame with a fine knit. Used for gloves and underwear.

Habutai Silk: also known as china silk. It is not as fine as cultivated or mulberry silk but is a much cheaper option.

Honan: a top quality wild silk, similar to Pongee silk, made from silkworms found in the Honan region of China. It is the only wild silk that will dye evenly.

Illusion: a very fine silk gauze that was a product of France, it has an open mesh weave.

Lamé: a fabric with silk thread running through it, not limited to silk but often used with it for a luxury fabric.

Marquisette: an open weave, mesh-like weave with a swivel dot or clip spot, which gives it its name.

Matelasse: a fabric with a quilted appearance produced on a jacquard or double loom in a double cloth weave. The quilted look is made by the use of crepe yarn in double weave which shrinks and gives it its distinctive texture.

Messaline: a soft and lustrous silk fabric named after the third wife of the Roman Emperor, Claudius.

Moire: a stiffish fabric with a watermark design imprinted onto the fabric by inserting it between engraved rollers. The effect is not permanent.

Momme Weight: is the standard measurement for a piece of silk measuring 100 yards long and 45 inches wide.

Mousseline de soie: is basically a silk muslin, light, open and sheer.

Mulberry Silk: is not only a cultivated silk made from unhatched cocoons but is a silk made from the *Bombyx mori* silk moth larvae that have been fed exclusively on mulberry leaves. Mulberry silk is considered to be the best in the world.

Net: this fabric is made by knotting on a lace machine and is used as the basis for lace.

Noil: is sometimes called raw silk but this is a misnomer. It is actually a fabric made from the waste silk of the cultivated silk moth. It is of an inferior quality to other types of silk being not as strong and not able to accept dyeing as well.

Organza: is a fine, light and crisp finish with a silvery sheen. Has a springy feel to it.

Ottoman: has very definite flat ribs and is sometimes called Ottoman cord or Ottoman rib. It is a very stiff and heavy fabric.

Panne: from the French word for plush. It looks like lustrous velvet but with a longer pile.

Peau de cygnet: from the French for 'swan skin'. It is a textured lustrous fabric made of crepe yarns.

Peau de peche: from the French for 'skin of peach'. The fabric is given a soft nap finish after weaving, resembling the down on a peach.

Peau de soi: from the French for 'skin of silk'. A satin type finish with a dull lustre.

Pompadour taffeta: a silk taffeta with floral designs in a velvet pile on the taffeta ground.

Pongee: a wild silk fabric from China that was made on hand looms. It is light weight and has a natural tan or ecru colour.

Satin: conjures up a smooth, glossy fabric that is synonymous with luxury. However, satin refers to the type of weave rather than the material from which it is made. It is often made from man-made fibres such as acetate, polyester and rayon, though it has of course been made from silk as well.

Silk Velvet: velvet is again the type of weave used not the raw fibre from which it is made. It is possible to get cotton velvets and these days, man-made fibre velvets. True silk velvet costs a fortune.

Shantung: a silk made from Tussah wild silk or silk waste. Similar to Pongee but is usually heavier and coarser.

Spun or Cut Silk: this is made by spinning the shorter fibres of the silk cocoon, a bit like the waste silk used in Noil silk. The filaments are sometimes taken from the inside area of the cocoon which is not as strong as the outer, longer filaments. Spun or cut silk is also made from the short fibres of the wild silk moth. .

Taffeta: from the Persian word for 'fine silk fabric'. It is smooth with a sheen and a crisp finish.

Thrown or Reeled Silk: the cultivated silk moth is killed before the filaments are removed, which they are by a process known as reeling, or throwing. This means that the end of the filament is secured and then carefully wound onto a bobbin in one continuous length.

Tricot: is a knitted fabric with a thin texture.

Tulle: a knotted mesh made on a lace machine. It gets its name from its place of origin, Tulle, in France. It is a stiff open mesh fabric, traditionally used in the underskirts of ballet tutus.

Tussah Silk: is made from the wild silk moths of India and China.

Velvet: has a pile weave with extra warp yarn. The word velvet comes from the Latin *vellus* which means fleece or tufted hair. Silk velvet is a very expensive fabric.

Wild Silk: silk made from the cocoons of moths that have already hatched and therefore broken the filaments of their cocoons. The shorter threads are spun after de-gumming and the silk has a quite different appearance and feel to that of cultivated silk but has its own beauty.

PART TWO

Processing

W e have seen how some of our raw materials are grown and harvested, the history of their use and some of their properties and characteristics. In those discussions spinning and weaving have been mentioned with the assumption that all readers will have some kind of knowledge of what is being talked about. But, in truth, what do we, the lay people, know about these processes? We can probably tell each other that spun thread is the twisting of a raw material into a long thin string that is then wound into a ball. We probably know a little more about weaving and knitting, able to tell at a glance whether a fabric was produced by one or the other method. And that may well be the sum total of our knowledge.

The use of weaving and spinning vocabulary in our everyday lives must tell us that the crafts of spinning and weaving are so deeply ingrained in our history that we use the terms as metaphors for many different aspects of life.

A lady spinning with a distaff and spindle.

We spin a yarn, meaning to tell a story, and similarly weave a tale. We knit our brows in worry and contemplate the very fabric of our being.

Mythology also uses textile imagery: the Greek fates spun out mortal lives in thread and cut them at their appointed time of death. Foolish humans challenged immortal wisdom to weaving competitions, lost and were turned into spiders.

It is perhaps time then that we looked at the origins of these sayings and beliefs; our cultural heritage to find out where it all began.

CHAPTER FIVE

Spinning

The first twisted thread

The idea that twisting a length of gut or sinew would make it stronger was an early discovery of mankind. Plying such strands together made the cord stronger still. Early applications of twisted cord were to bind an axe head to a wooden shaft, stitch pieces of leather hide together, and to knot nets for fishing and hunting.

When did humans first notice that other fibres could be twisted in this way? Was it the earliest handfuls of wool that pulled out of the sheep's back showing the fibres lined up against each other and pulling into a thinner and thinner thread as it was pulled out further?

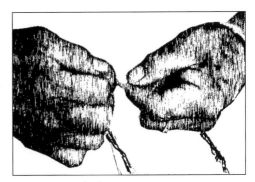

Spinning with the fingers.

Did people fiddle with fleece still on the hide as they lay around the fire at night, twisting the fibre into thread as they told stories or sang? On discovering the *bast* fibre inside reeds and other plants, did the process of twisting leap to mind because the silken looking fibres looked like fine, fine sinew?

Whichever of these came first, and it is highly likely that more than one was discovered simultaneously in different parts of the world with different fibres, the result was ultimately life changing.

All the fibres presented in this book undergo a process to make them into thread which in turn can be woven, knitted or tied to make into an expanse of flat cloth: from silk to flax to wool or man-made nylon, it all undergoes a spinning process.

Before the spindle, thread was hand rolled, often along the thigh. This process is still used among certain people today. Plant fibre is sometimes chewed to make it pliable and then the string of fibre can be rolled with the palm of the hand to twist it to make it stronger.

The spindle

Who and how they began spinning with a spindle is not known, archaeological evidence shows that many cultures used a spindle of some type to facilitate the spinning of various fibres. Hand spinning using only your hands, pulling the fleece or other fibre into teased out pieces and then rolling them into a twist is very time consuming.

Inventing a tool to make it quicker, more efficient and to make a finer and more even thread would have followed not long after the first hand twisted efforts.

The remnants of spindles and other fibre processing equipment have been found dating back thousands and thousands of years. It may not be actual spun fibre that has survived, it is a delicate and easily decomposed substance, but other evidence provides us with the fact that spinning technology was used a long time ago. Remains of stone spindles, impressions left by twisted cord in clay, pictures of spinning.

True spinning, called draft spinning, was more than twisting long fibres together. To use short fibres for making textiles they had to be felted or spun. The fibres had to be combed to rid them of twigs and dirt and to arrange them so that they would slip into a thread easily. The ideal format for fibres that are to be spun is to have them all facing in one direction. Combing will facilitate this.

Spindle whorls

Spindle whorls have been found that date back to the 7,000 years ago. The earliest spun woollen thread dates to 4000 BC. Spindles developed independently in various parts of the world including Peru.

The spindle, in its most primitive form is nothing more than a weighted stick. Sometimes the weight is a smaller stick bound across the bottom end of the spindle. The carded (combed until resembling candyfloss) fibre is held in one hand. The spindle, with a notch or hook at the top, is held in the other. Fibres are drawn out and fixed to the hook. The spindle is given a

A Peruvian woman spinning with a spindle, photo courtesy of Annamaria Magnus.

twist as it is dropped and more fibres are pulled from the bunch and automatically drawn into the twist of the spinning spindle. When the spindle reaches the ground, the spun thread is wound around it and the process begun again until all the carded fibre is spun and wound onto the spindle.

Make it yourself

One of the delights of spinning with a spindle is the fact that you can easily make the basic tools yourself at very little cost. It is a fun activity to do with children too.

You will need:

- A piece of dowelling approximately 12 inches long (30cm) and about 3/8inch (1cm) in diameter
- A lump of plasticine

Make a cut or notch in top end of dowel. Roll plasticine into a ball, push dowel into it and mould the plasticine up around the dowel so that it stays there.

Try spinning some greasy sheep's wool, teasing it out by hand or carding it with carding brushes.

A simple spindle and whorl.

The distaff

Later a distaff was added to the spinner's tool bag. It consisted of a stick onto which the carded fibre was loosely wound. The spinner would hold this in the hand or tucked under the arm so that the hand was free to feed the raw material into the spinning process.

As the spindle developed the spun yarn the added weight would make it spin for longer and more steadily. So that this would happen earlier and before much fibre had been spun a wooden or stone disc with a hole in the middle was attached to the bottom of the spindle. This is called the spindle whorl.

This would seem a labour intensive and slow method resulting in uneven thread. However, when practised by an expert it is the opposite. Of course, as the demand for spun yarn grew it was necessary to find mechanical means of spinning thread but the spindle is still used in parts of the world today and has even come back into vogue as a hobby. It can be therapeutic to pull, spin and wind thread.

Peruvian women spinning using a distaff, photo courtesy of Homer Alvarez.

Evidence of plying

Depicted on a wall of the tomb of Khnumhotep, in Memphis, is a painting made about four and half thousand years ago. It shows a stream of people involved in making flax into cloth. Firstly the flax is retted, then it is spun and finally it is woven. There is one particularly odd picture amongst the spinners. A figure, standing on a box and with one leg in the air, appears to be spinning with two spindles at once. It is possible this is a process for plying. Egyptian linen was finished by bleaching in the sun for up to eight weeks at a time after being woven.

The Great Wheel

Spinning wheels have been around for hundreds of years. The first wheel appeared in China and was used to reel the unbroken filaments of silk fibre from the cocoon. To call the article a wheel is a bit of a misnomer because it was not round but square.

In India the spinning wheel has been in use for much longer than in European countries. It was a small hand turned wheel that was primarily used for spinning cotton. It was called the charka and still exists in many homes in a virtually unchanged form.

The Saxony wheel with its foot treadle.

It wasn't until the Middle Ages that spinning wheels were introduced to Europe. The earliest picture known of a spinning wheel is in a Flemish illuminated manuscript from 1338. These early wheels, known as high, great or muckle wheels, were not operated by a foot pedal as they are today but had various other methods of turning the wheel. One type required the spinner to walk away from the wheel with a bundle of carded wool teased out into a length and held taut while the rotation of the wheel twisted the fibre into thread. The method produced a fine, even thread but the process still required a lot of stopping and starting. The spindle was made from a long, thin spike of iron.

The Saxony Wheel
In the Fifteenth Century the Saxony wheel, named after its birthplace but also called the low wheel, entered the spinning industry. This East German invention saw the addition of a foot treadle to power the wheel which meant both of the spinner's hands were free to work the wool. It also had the distaff attached to the machine and it is this type of spinning wheel that we are probably most familiar with today when we think of hand spinning.

The Saxony wheel was a major innovation as it spun thread and wound it onto a bobbin at the same time, therefore doubling the output in half the time.

Origin of the word spinster
The verb, to spin, is first documented in written form about 725 AD. It comes from the Old English word, *spinnan*, and the Middle English, *spinnen*. The root for this word is *spen*, meaning to draw out, which is the action of teasing out carded fleece to feed the spindle.

It wasn't until the latter half of the Fourteenth Century that the noun '*spinster*' is found in common use. The word is derived from the verb, spin, and the ending -ster, which means the verb is undertaken by a female. A '*kempster*', therefore was

Man spinning on the Great Wheel, photo courtesy of Annamaria Magnus.

a female who combed out wool. A *'webster'* was a female weaver. In the case of weaving, a male weaver was called a *'webbe'* but as men took over the activity professionally the female term was sometimes applied without the intention of its original meaning.

During early times of official record making the term spinster was often put after a woman's name in a register to denote her main occupation. It wasn't until the Seventeenth Century that it took the meaning of an unmarried woman. A century later it was used to talk about older unmarried women and by the Nineteenth Century in was well entrenched in our vocabulary.

Origin of the word draper

A male weaver, in medieval times, would have been called a *'webbe'*. Sometimes he was even called a *webster* although this was properly the term used for a female weaver. By the Fourteenth Century a weaver of wool, typically a man, was known as a *draper*. The etymology of the word goes back to the Anglo-Saxon *draper* and the Old French *drapier*, both of which came from *drappus*, the Latin word for cloth.

The term draper to denote a male weaver of woollen cloth did not stay long. The terms *webbe* and *webster* superseded it. It came to mean the person who sold or supplied the finished product though.

Industrial spinning

John Kay invented his flying shuttle in England in 1733. With the shuttle being pushed through the weft threads by means of a fly cord wider fabrics could be woven and much more quickly. There was a problem with this in that it meant that the weaver could produce a lot more fabric than the spinner could produce the yarn to weave it with. To remedy this, inventions were needed to improve the spinner's output.

It wasn't until 1764 that James Hargreaves devised the spinning jenny that could accommodate eight vertical spindles. The story goes that his wife's spinning wheel got knocked over and Hargreaves noticed that it kept functioning even though it was on its side.

Instead of the new inventions being welcomed as ways of speeding up spinning and weaving they were met with violence by workers who were afraid the new machines would put them out of work. John Kay's home was attacked, as was Hargreaves' in 1768.

Richard Arkwright worked on the model of a water-driven spinning device that had been invented by John Wyatt and Lewis Paul. He installed it in his cotton factory in 1771.

Between 1775 and 1790, Samuel Crompton took aspects of both Hargreaves' machine and Arkwright's and came up with the spinning mule. This was one of the major developments in the production of spun thread as it meant the output was vastly superior to the hand spun method.

John Kay – the flying shuttle

It wasn't until the Eighteenth Century that the next great leap of mechanisation was made in the spinning industry. In 1733 John Kay had invented the flying shuttle to facilitate weaving. It was an ingenious invention without doubt but unintentionally

Hargreave's Spinning Jenny.

caused a dilemma. Weaving could be done at a rate much faster than the thread could be spun to supply the looms.

In a need to rectify this problem the Royal Society set up a competition to invent a spinning machine that would match the output of the weaver.

James Hargreaves – the spinning jenny

James Hargreaves rose to the occasion and invented the spinning jenny. There is a pretty story concerning the germ of the idea for the machine. Supposedly Hargreaves startled his wife while she was spinning on her wheel and it toppled over but kept working in its prone state. Hargreaves took the spinning wheel as the basis for his new machine, adding eight spindles to it, all operated by a single wheel. It was revolutionary. One spinning jenny, some say named for his wife, others for his mother, could do the work of eight.

It may have sped up production but the spinning jenny was not the perfect answer. It still tended to produce uneven thread with the odd bump or two in it. It also spun a thread that was too soft to be used for warp threads on a loom.

Hargreaves may have been a fine inventor but his business skills were not up to the same standard. Firstly, he did not claim the Royal Society's prize and secondly he did not immediately patent the jenny. After Richard Arkwright's success with his patented water frame, Hargreaves tried to patent his invention. Unfortunately he had left it too late and his claim for patent was denied because it was discovered that he had already sold some of his machines prior to seeking a patent on them. Lancashire cotton mills had stolen his idea but Hargreaves could do nothing but sit back and watch other men reap the financial rewards of his hard work.

Richard Arkwright – the water frame

Richard Arkwright, on the other hand, was not so backwards in asserting the ownership rights over his own inventions. Arkwright worked on the basis of previous experiments made by Wyatt in Northampton many years before. Wyatt's idea was that the carded wool would move through a system of rollers which gradually drew out increasingly finer filaments of wool so that it could form a finer spun thread.

Arkwright patented his first machine in 1769 but did not leave the matter there. He continued to work on the idea of spinning machines for many years afterwards and brought a series of them.

Arkwright's water frame had just about made Hargreave's spinning jenny redundant by about 1777. One of the water frame's superior aspects was that it made a much stronger and more even yarn than the jenny.

Arkwright's inventions were sold all over the country but it turned out that he did not own the sole rights to his invention and the patent was made void. This did not stop him from amassing a large fortune through his work or from accepting a knighthood in 1786 for his services to industry.

Samuel Crompton – the spinning mule

Samuel Crompton was the next important innovator in the spinning world. In 1779 he took the best aspects of both Hargreave's and Arkwright's inventions, the jennys of one and the rollers of the other and combined them in a new machine – a hybrid fittingly called a spinning mule. Crompton did not attempt to patent his device and maybe in the light of it being the product of two previous inventions by two different people, it would not have been accepted.

As happened to spinning when the flying shuttle was invented, so the mule had an impact on the other aspects of the textile industry. Carding and combing, two vital steps in the processing of fibre for making yarn, needed to be mechanised as well.

It is interesting that a carding cylinder had actually been invented as early as 1748, not long after the flying shuttle. It did not come into common use until after Crompton's mule was well established. This was accompanied by more than one type of mechanised wool-combing invention around 1792 and 1793.

Crompton's Spinning Mule.

Edward Cartwright – the power loom

Technology had finally caught up with and overtaken the flying shuttle of the first third of the century and now the conundrum was that there needed to be new work done on the weaving side of things.

Dr Edward Cartwright, a clergyman of all things, had been tinkering with the idea of a power loom from 1784 or so. He did very well from his hobby and Parliament awarded him £10,000 in 1809 for his invention with the loom.

What was happening in America?

One of the most important inventions, that revolutionised the cotton industry, was made by an American, Eli Whitney, in 1792. He had not long left college when he devised his machine for removing unwanted seeds and twigs and other debris from the harvested cotton bolls. This had always been performed by hand and was seriously laborious work. The cotton-gin as it became known has changed little in its fundamental working principles since it was invented.

The cotton-gin consisted of a box with a roller, lid and a wire mesh. The bolls were placed on the wire and brushes with metal teeth dragged the cotton filaments through the holes in the wire. The detritus was too large to go through the seive.

From cotton to guns

Whitney patented his gin but to little effect. The design was too simple and so easily copied that Whitney didn't make any money out of it. The State of Carolina gave him $50,000 in royalties but it was spent on legal fees tyring to enforce his patent. In 1797 he received another commission from the government but it had nothing to do with the textile industry. He was paid a handsome sum to machine manufacture 10,000 muskets.

Wool in America

The processing of wool into yarn and fabric did not become industrialised to the extent it had in Birtain and did not become mehcanised for a long time. It relied on a hard working domestic system, using the 'worthy poor' to spin and weave fabric in enough quantities to make America more or else self-suffienct in woollen goods. Although during the War of Independence American soldiers were supplied with blankets made in England of English wool, even though the two countries were at war with each other.

The first wool spinning machine was established at Peace Dale, Rhode Isalnd in 1804. It was followed by a power loom in Massachussets in 1823.

Ring-spinning frame

In 1828, a new type of spinning machine was invented: the ring-spinning frame. It drew on the previous technology of the water-frame with its progressively faster spinning rollers to draw out the fleece. It is then fed onto a rotating bobbin via a clip called a traveller. This winds the thread around the bobbin as it moves around it.

The ring-spinning frame is still in use though of course it is highly mechanised and can work 500 spindles at a time with 12,000 revolutions per minute on average.

Watt's steam engine.

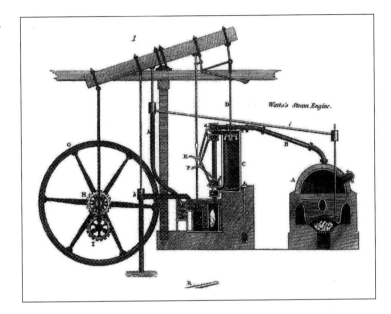

James Watt and the steam engine
Water had been the driving force behind the new inventions for spinning and weaving. Fulling had relied on water to drive the mill to pound the fabric for centuries. The next step was to make a faster and more effiecnt kind of power.

The Scottish engineer, James Watt, put together a new model steam engine after he was asked to repair an early, 1700 engine that had been invented by Thomas Newcombe. Watt's improvements and additions proved the start of a highly industrialised factory system of working. The steam engine replaced most water driven mechanisms, including those used for textile making.

- The ancient Egyptians were reknowed for their extrememly fine linen cloth. There could be 100 threads per centimetre
- Linen was a traditional material for wrapping mummies in as it was insect resistant
- Alfred the Great referred to the women he named as recipients in his will as the 'spindle side' of the family
- It is estimated that when women used the great wheel they could walk up to 20 miles a day
- Women in England during the Middle Ages, were given permission to own lands if they kept the local church well stocked with hanging, soft furnishings and embroideries
- The word spider originated from the Old English word spīthra, which changed to Middle English, spither. Both of these mean a spinner. The word web comes from an ancient German source which meant something woven. So spider is literally a spinner and its web is a woven thing

- It was considered vital that before a young woman could be considered marriagable she had to make herself all the necesary household trappings such as bed linen
- The word drab, meaning colourless and unattractive comes from the word drape, orignially meaning one who wove wool cloth. The connectoin supposedly being that woven wool cloth was not as bright and colourful as silk or cotton
- The shortage of woollen clothing and bedding was the main reason so many men left the army
- The surname Tucker comes from the families original occupation of fulling cloth

CHAPTER SIX

Weaving

In the days when the spinning-wheels hummed busily in the farmhouses – and even great ladies, clothed in silk and thread lace, had their toy spinning wheels of polished oak – there might be seen in districts far away among the lanes, or deep in the bosom of the hills, certain pallid undersized men, who by the side of the brawny country-folk, looked like the members of a disinherited race.

The shepherd himself, though he had good reason to believe that the bag held nothing but flaxen thread, or else the long rolls of strong linen spun from that thread, was not quite sure that this trade of weaving, indispensable though it was, could be carried on entirely without the help of the evil one.[1]

George Eliot sets her story about the weaver of the small village of Raveloe, around the last 20 years of the Eighteeenth Century. The domestic system of manufacture was still thriving, mechanisation had not made its presence felt in many rural communities. The craftsman, such as the weaver, was held in regard and would have been referred to, and addressed as Master, just as Eliot does for Silas.

Weaving is a craft as old as spinning. It is unknown which came first. The early looms were often warp threads tied to a branch and weighted at the bottom with pebbles or something similar. This kind of loom was still in use in the early Middle Ages in England although the tree branch would have been a piece of smoothed and straightened wood and the pebbles were specially made baked clay rings.

Woven rug, photo courtesy of A. M. Magnus.

The weft would have been woven in and out of the vertical warp threads. As the piece of weaving grew it would be rolled up over the supporting rod at the top. The weft threads would be further beaten upwards with a piece of wood and fine details adjusted with a bone tool.

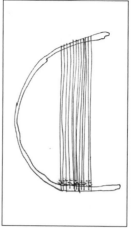

Some primitive looms.

In medieval times woven cloth went through a number of processes to finish it. It was washed and beaten and fulled, amongst others. At some point it was stretched out on a wooden frame. This was called a *tenter*, from the Latin verb *tendere*, meaning to stretch. This was to stop the damp piece of cloth from shrinking and warping out of shape as it dried. It was secured to the frame by a series of metal spikes that became known as *tenterhooks*. The term 'to be on tenterhooks' evolved in the Sixteenth Century to mean a stretching of one's conscience. It then came to mean a general state of anxiety.

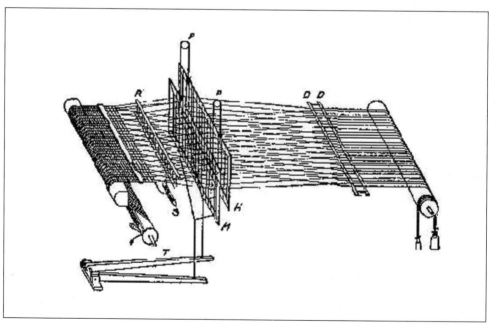

A modern loom, photo courtesy of A.M. Magnus.

The Lady and the Unicorn.

Tapestry

Tapestry is a woven picture. Unlike fabric that is woven to be made into clothing, the method for weaving tapestries is different. To make up the blocks of colour and the fine detail small parts of the weft are worked on at a time.

True tapestry is woven but it is sometimes the name given to elaborate embroideries. The Bayeaux Tapestry is actually embroidery, coloured yarn stitched onto a backcloth. In modern times tapestry is often confused with needlepoint an embroidery technique on open canvas.

Tapestry was once the typical furnishings of a castle or manor house, large pictures in woven wool used to drape over cold stone or to keep out the drafts in corridors. It was not only a European textile. All weaving cultures have used the medium to make pictures, be they ever so abstract; fabrics that are made not for covering bodies or any other use than for decoration and or ceremony or ritual.

Note

1. Eliot, George, *Silas Marner*, Penguin books, 1967 (first published 1861) p. 51.

CHAPTER SEVEN

Felting

When hair is un-brushed or fur unkempt it tends to tangle, flatten out and become a solid mat. This is felting in its most primitive form and is not derived through deliberate manipulation but is the natural result of neglect and is far from attractive or useful.

Felting is a process for making fabric out of fibre. It involves applying heat, pressure, moisture, movement, and combinations of these to a sheet of combed fibres.

Ancient fragments of wool felt that date back to 6500 BC have been found in Çatal Hüyük (in the area of modern Turkey). There has been an ongoing debate over whether the felt is a deliberate man-made construct or the result of unprocessed fleece, perhaps being used to insulate the shelter in which it was found, felting under a thousand years of compression.

As discussed, one expert[1] argues that the piece is man-made because the level at which it was excavated, level VIII, also contained detailed painted murals of motifs that are almost identical to those used in later and contemporary felting by people in that area. The juxtaposition of the motifs, known to be popular in felt products of later date, alongside actual felted fragments suggests that even if those fragments are not intentionally man-made then at least the technology behind the process was known at that time.

Myths abound about the invention or discovery of the felting process. It doesn't matter which culture the myth comes from the story is basically the same: someone puts shorn fleece into their shoes to keep the cold out. After a long and arduous journey (an essential element of the myth) the traveller finds that the friction and sweat from his feet in the wool lined shoe has matted it into a solid textile.

A nice variation of this story is one involving Noah's ark. The sheep on the ark shed wool, urinated on it and trampled it under foot. When Noah let the animals out onto dry land he found a felted rug left behind. It must have ponged a bit!

How Felt is Made

The felting process isn't peculiar to wool fibre. Felting cultures all over the world have, at some stage, made beaten bark-cloth by applying a felting technique.

Making cloth from the inner bark (the *bast* fibre found under the outer bark) of particular plants is an activity that can be found across a wide geographical expanse

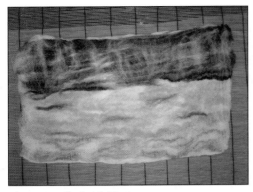

Fleece ready for felting.

Agitating the fleece.

of tropical and subtropical climates. Bark-cloth is made in Africa, Asia, the Pacific and the Americas.

Though a wide variety of plants can be used to make bark-cloth, certain types are more common than others. Wild fig, paper mulberry and the breadfruit tree are three of the most popular, with the paper mulberry producing the whitest and finest of this type of textile.

There is a structural difference between the fibres of inner bark and that of wool or hair. Inner bark fibres have a natural interlacing fibrous structure, which is

Paper pulp being turned into paper, photo courtesy of David Dunning for Anokhi Hand Printing Museum, Jaipur, India.

Pressing the felted paper and hanging it out to dry, photo courtesy of David Dunning for Anokhi Hand Printing Museum, Jaipur, India.

processed in strips or sheets, not as separated filaments (such as make up a wool fleece). The inner bark fibre interlocks with sheets of itself because, during the beating and soaking process, cellulose and non-cellulose elements are broken down to form a fibrous mesh. Wool, on the other hand, comprises multitudes of single fibres that need to interweave with each other in a random manner.

The sheet of inner bark is soaked or boiled in water until soft and pliable. It is then beaten to spread the interconnected fibres into a flat sheet. To make the sheet bigger another piece of softened inner bark is laid partially on top of the first and the process of beating repeated until it becomes interlaced with the fibres underneath. It is possible to create large pieces of textile in this manner.

To ensure extra strength or for decorative reasons the bark-cloth may have additives such as glue or gum to hold the layers together (though if the processing is done properly this is unnecessary) and/or stitching may be applied through the combined layers.

A paper-like textile is made from papyrus fibres in a similar manner. The pith from inside the *Cyperus papyrus* reed is soaked until malleable and then beaten to form a strip. Several strips are then placed side by side, edges together but not overlapping as in making bark-cloth. A second layer of beaten strips is laid crosswise over the first. The double layer of papyrus fibre is then subjected to the whole process again until the textile presents a smooth surface which is then finished by drying and polishing so that it may be used for writing on.

The fibres used to make felt from fleece have a completely different structure to bark-cloth and papyrus. Unlike the preformed sheets of the inner barks, fleece, fur and hair are single filaments that must be made to weave themselves together.

When a single fibre of wool is looked at under a microscope it can be noticed that the hair has a scaly appearance. This minute texture is enough to facilitate a multitude of similar fibres to cling together with the aid of water, heat, friction and pressure.

To make wool felt by hand a sheet of clean, combed (the combing process is called 'carding') fibres is taken, this is called a 'batt'. A sheet of carded batts is built up; the subsequent layers placed in alternating directions. Moisture is added, often hot water and/or an alkaline soap or a small amount of olive oil, rubbed into the piece by hand and gently massaged. It is important that the piece being felted is not made too wet but that it is kept damp and warm.

Eventually felting the fibres work their way out of their original combed order and being to interlock and shrink which is an important element to successful felt. More pressure can be applied and a more vigorous agitation of the fibres. In some cultures the piece being felted is rolled within another textile and manipulated that way, particularly for larger pieces such as rugs and blankets (or the sides of yurts).

Paper made from linen or cotton rag is formed in a related way. First; the woven fabric is broken down, by tearing it to shreds. It is soaked and then pulped. The separated fibres are then spread out in a bath of water (with or without additives), a frame with a wire mesh bottom is lowered into and under the mixture and pulp is collected onto it (as evenly as possible). The tray of pulp is laid flat and put under pressure, with or without heat, forcing the fibres to matt together as for wool felt.

Fulling is a felt related process and has been made with the aid of machines for centuries, particularly for making large sheets of felt. Fulling is what happens when a knitted woollen garment is put into a washing machine and washed in warm water. The water, heat and constant agitation of the machine causes the wool to shrink and *creep* (the ability of the fibre to move towards the root when pressure is applied)[1] so that the spaces between the original knitted stitches decrease. And the fabric becomes thicker, denser and more able to keep chilly winds at bay.

The earliest type of *fulling* machine consisted of a roll of fabric, wrapped in heavy canvas, being lowered into a trough of hot water. It was then beaten repeatedly as the roll of fabric was turned (like a spit roast). The roll had to be removed and rewrapped for the process to felt the entire piece of fabric.

Fulling was a popular process for making woollen textiles in England in the Middle Ages and guilds devoted to the craft arose, given legitimacy by royal charter. Broadcloth became one of the country's major exports and it was a woven wool fabric subjected to fulling to make a heavy fabric.

At the time of the Industrial Revolution steam was used to power the turning and beating mechanisms as it was for spinning and weaving machines.

Felt Hats

Felt is a common material for making hats. We have seen that felt hats have been around for thousands of years in various forms, some sewn, some moulded into shape. Felt hats are as popular as ever and include sewn felt, moulded wool felt, and also felt made from more exotic animal fur such as rabbit and beaver.

Felting animal fur is more difficult and involved than felting wool fibre. Only the fur from under the belly of the animal is used, which is soft and downy. It has to be treated with chemicals (traditionally a mercury nitrate mixture was used) first to lift the scales at the end of the hairs so that they will be able to cling to each other in the felting process. This is called 'carrotting' because it turns the ends a brownish red colour.

A wooden hat block.

The treated fur fibres are then mixed with wool fibres and felted in the same way as wool although not in a flat plane but a loose conical shape from which the hat shape can be refined with further steaming and stretching.

Wooden hat blocks are used to shape the felt to head shape. These are made in several basic sizes. Getting the basic shape of the hat is called blocking because it is performed in the wooden block. To finalise the head shape steam is used and a heated iron. Shaping the brim is called 'flanging' and is done off the block. The brim is cut to shape, ironed flat then rolled over a wooden flange (hence the name) then dried. The hat is often treated with a stiffening agent to help it keep its shape.

Try it yourself

It is relatively easy to try making a piece of felt by hand. Take a roll of carded fleece (it should also have been cleaned and had much of the lanolin removed). With one hand pull a thin wafer of fibres from the length and lay them on a piece of bamboo blind (or sushi mat). Build up a sheet (A4 size is a good place to start) of these wafers, placing them in rows with the fibres just touching each other.

Make another sheet on top of this but place the fibres at right angles to the first. Add another layer or two, each time alternating the direction of the fibres.

Sprinkle the fibres with warm water, perhaps with olive oil or an alkaline soap mixed in with it. With both hands, palms flat, gently massage over the surface, pressing down to apply pressure as you do so. Keep the sheet damp with warm water and repeat the massage process until the fibres begin to shrink and creep. As the felt develops rougher handling is needed and you can roll the felt up in the bamboo sheet and roll it vigorously. Once the piece is firmly felted (with no unwanted holes) it can be taken outside and thrown onto a hard surface (cement or asphalt). Rinse the piece several times and then leave to dry.

Needle Felting

Needle felting is a different process again for making felt without the use of heat, pressure or moisture. Industrial felting machines have been developed consisting of large flat metal plates covered in barbed needles. The plate is pressed down and lifted from the batting (carded fibres) multiple times. As it lifts the barbs catch on fibres and bring them up through the upper layers of batting. It is a successful method of felting a mixture of fibres that don't respond to the traditional methods; man-made fibres form a large part of this group.

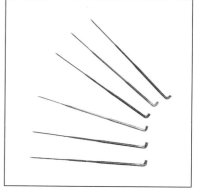

A set of needle felting needles.

By taking a single barbed felting needle and applying the principle to a ball of batting, that is, pushing down into and pulling up out of the fibres, small pieces can be felted and sculpted into 3D forms. It is a good method for adding small amounts of coloured batting as decorations to other felted items. It has become a very popular art form.

Felted textiles play a strong part in the culture, both ancient and modern, of Central Asia. It is still the preferred textile of Mongolian people who construct their large tents from it as well as saddle cloths, bags, hats, blankets and footwear.

While small, domestic items, such a clothing and accessories are made at home, the community comes together in autumn to work on large projects, like making yurts. The time is as socially important as it is practical. There is a lot of celebration and religious ritual that goes into making acres of felt.

The dry, cool atmospheric conditions of the Central Asian mountainous regions are ideal for preserving fragile archaeological pieces and it is here that ancient felted textiles have been found in numerous quantities in fair condition.

In the Tarim Basin, located in far western China, for instance, mummified bodies have been excavated that have been dated to between 3,000 and 4,000 years old. Many of the preserved bodies were found wearing shoes with woollen felt inserts. These were probably felted through the friction of walking on woollen batting placed inside the shoe for insulation. Interestingly mummies discovered in closely neighbouring areas, dating to a similar time, were found wearing felted caps. Apart from the Anatolian plateau finds (Çatal Hüyük) these are some of the earliest surviving evidence of felt textiles.

The Scythian people left tombs in the High Altai mountains in Siberia, dating back to 400–500 BC. The textiles found in these burial places include felt-made tents, saddlebags, carry-bags and socks amongst other items. The saddlebags were heavily decorated with leather appliqué and coloured felt appliqué and other embroidery techniques. The tents are very similar in style to the yurts that are still being used today. The intricacy of the decoration on the saddlebags shows the high level of craftsmanship developed such a long time ago. Felted hats were found that were not flat sheets of felt, cut and stitched together, but felt that had been moulded on a

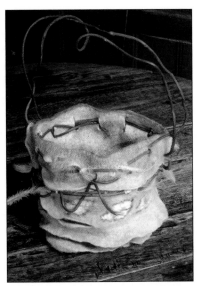

Felted vessel by Vanessa Taylor.

form to shape it into three dimensions without having to sew pieces together. This method, using steam to stretch the felted textile over a rounded shape is one that is still used for making basic felt hat shapes today.

The other significant Central Asian burial site producing felted textiles, dating to the First or Second Century BC, is in Mongolia where elaborately constructed carpets have been found. The carpets are made up of layers: a felted wool layer and a silk layer bound around the outside edges with silk, and the surface covered in embroidery, appliqué and cord work.

That silk is incorporated in the native-made felt carpets means that a trading relationship existed between the Mongolians and other people from more distant lands. The silk would probably have come from China but, as with other traded goods, this would probably have been obtained from a middle party, perhaps Arab traders, passing along the fabled Silk Road.

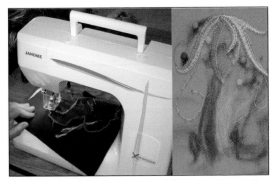

A domestic needle felting machine looks similar to a sewing machine.

Helen Evans telling a story with a felt story board she has made.

While silk was a specialty of the Chinese, it is not widely known that they were great producers of wool felt. They did use the product in mattresses and as part of armour. The famous terracotta warriors found guarding the tomb of Emperor Qin Shi Huang wear clay representations of heavy felt uniforms. It would seem that a possible payment for Chinese silk could have been felt.

Felt grew in popularity in England from the Middle Ages onwards so much so that from the Thirteenth Century felting guilds were formed to help regulate product quality and standardise prices. Hat making was England's largest felt product.

Felt as Art
Felting and fulling have seen a resurgence in popularity as a hand craft activity. Felting with fleece, incorporating a variety of objects has become a major art form. The boom in knitting has also seen the ancient art of fulling begin applied to all manner of items from children's toys to bags and clothing.

Needle felting with a single felting needle applied to fleece has grown to the status of sculpture in some cases though largely it is used for making soft toys and novelties.

Needle felting has become so popular that some major sewing machine manufacturers have brought out needle felting machines which will felt fleece and other items to a base fabric for decorative purposes.

- Felt is the material of choice for covering billiard tables although a cheaper woven covering is used for cheaper models
- Felt covered boards were a common child's story telling activity. Coloured shapes were placed on the board to make the pictures
- Ukulele plectrums are traditionally made of felt
- It is said that human hair from the victims of German concentration camps were felted into blankets and mattresses
- Constant exposure to the mercury nitrate mixture in the old days, used to 'carrot' the fur fibres, could lead to poisoning, the symptoms being memory loss and paralysis

---

Note
1. Burkett 1979, 1).

CHAPTER EIGHT

Knitting

… the innocent sleep,
Sleep that knits up the ravelled sleeve of care,
The death of each day's life, sore labour's bath,
Balm of hurt minds, great nature's second course,

Chief nourisher in life's feast (*Macbeth*, Act II Scene II)

The image of an old lady, sitting in front of the fire with a piece of knitting in her hands, is a popular one conjured up when the word knitting is mentioned. It has connotations of fluffy old women, plump and comfortable, who knit endless garments for their grandchildren. For many years in the Twentieth Century this image made hand knitting very unfashionable.

With the cost of finished items having dropped because they were made by machine in labour-cheap countries, and the rise in women going out into the workforce instead of staying at home and making clothes for the family, the activity of knitting became a thing of myth and legend. Almost.

Knitting has undergone a resurgence of interest and has attracted new recruits from all walks, ages and of life. Men, once proud and professional knitters, who left the hand knitting industry with the takeover by mechanisation and shunned it as a hobby, have returned in droves armed with their pins and balls of yarn. It is fashionable now to be seen knitting: in cafes, parks, restaurants, on buses and at the cinema.

An old lady knitting.

Thank goodness. The art of knitting was dying after such a long, long history. Knitting has been around as long as spinning and weaving, perhaps longer. In the early days its form was any kind of continuous looping, often only done with one needle.

Netting would probably have been the earliest form of knitting. Nets made from *bast* fibres are some of the earliest textiles that have been found on archaeological digs. In some instances the lengths of twine would have been looped and knotted and in others they were interlaced to make a loose mesh that had more give in it than the knotted type.

An early form of knitting is called 'naalebinding'. It is also called knotless knitting and knotless netting. It is a technique that is still practised in everyday life in some of the more isolated parts of the world. It too had two or more independent evolutions in different geographical locations. The term naalebinding, however, is a modern term for the ancient art.

It involves using one needle only. In some ways it resembles crochet in that the first step is to form a loop and pull the thread through that loop as one does in chain stitch crochet. It differs in that the thread is not pulled tight but left as a loose loop. The yarn is next passed through the newly formed loop and so on. When a row of these is made the thread may be passed through the length of it.

There have been pictures made by early mankind showing figures wearing all fitting garments that appear to have a knitted texture. To support the idea that they do indeed show knitted garments as the Bantu tribe in Zambia, still uses the same rituals and ceremonial gear that it has for centuries. Part of the ceremonial garb worn by the Bantu people is a close fitting all-in-one garment made from bark fibre and was worked in a looped style that strongly resembled knitting. The fabric of these items had the same give and stretch that knitting has. In light of the Bantu rituals it is tempting to think that those Neolithic depictions of figures were people wearing knitted body suits.

More early knitting

Knitting probably started where the earliest domestication of sheep started, though, as we've seen with the African tribes, knitting didn't necessarily begin with wool yarn. It possibly came to Europe via the Black Sea with the Celts. It is also possible that at least one group came after visiting the Mediterranean. Motifs common to Irish Aran knitting have been identified with similar, though less complex, designs in the Greek isles.

A piece of textile from 5 BC shows a definite pattern of knit and purl stitches suggesting that the two needle method was well established by then. Ribbed knitted fabric was used up until the Twelfth Century. The stitches were made: seven knit, three purl or seven knit, one purl. Apparently there was a religious and superstitious belief behind these combinations of numbers that regarded any item worked thus would offer a divine protection, or just plain good luck.

Two Needle Knitting

Within the two needle system there are two basic types of knitting: weft and warp, using terms we are more familiar with in weaving. The weft is the vertical, fixed threads in weaving and the weft are those that are threaded in and out of the other threads. Weft knitting is what we mean when we generally use the term knitting. One continuous thread is used and passed back and forth along the width of the item, looping into the stitches of the row beneath (at its most basic level).

Warp knitting on the other hand uses a separate length of yarn for each wale (column

288.—Casting On.

Casting on.

of loops running lengthwise like the warp of woven fabric). It is usually done by machine and includes: tricot, raschel, and milanese.

In the common two needle method, the weft method, the basic stitches used are knit (also called plain) and purl. These two stitches used in various combinations and by slipping, picking up and twisting, form a huge number of patterns with which to texture knitted products.

Two needles, more needles or one?

Modern knitting can be done on two needles, making and transferring the stitches on one to the other. Or to make a circular object, for example, a sock, then three or four double pointed needles can be used so that the knitting can bend around on itself and the end meet the beginning. The other method for doing circular knitting is to use, circular needles. These are not literally circular but resemble a double pointed needle cut in half and length of thick nylon inserted between them. The flexibility this offers gives means the work in progress can be pulled around so that the last stitches of a row can be joined to the first and the second row begun.

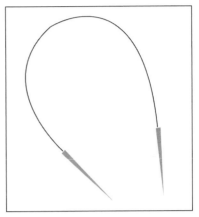

The circular needle.

Joseph's coat of many colours

A theory has been put forward that the fabled techni-coloured dream coat of Joseph, was in fact 'a knitted seamless coat traded from the Far East'. The style the same as the seamless coat we found on sculptures in Phoenician Cyprus at the Nicosia Museum. These sculptures wear the contemporary dress of Jesus, King of the Jews, who wore, as King David did, the 'Seamless Coat of Penitence' which was no doubt a knitted mesh.[1]

Sailors

Knitting garments for warmth was a common pastime amongst the sailing fraternity. There was no thought of it being a female only occupation. Men at sea needed warm clothing and they had long periods with little else to do. It seems that sailors of all ethnic groups and religious persuasions undertook knitting. It may well be how the art moved around the world.

While British sailors were content to fashion their own sweaters they tended to buy their knitted caps, called 'Phrygian' from a reputable craftsman. The sailors of the Sixteenth Century, who explored the world and discovered new lands, bought many of their caps in Monmouth, which is still known for its knitted caps.

Sailor Knitting.

Shepherds were another group of men who made their own warm clothing by knitting them. It is easy to see the link between shepherd and knitting as the raw material was always there before him in the field. It would have been from the sheep he tended that he took the fleece. His wife, or other female family member (a mother or aunt) may have combed or carded it and spun it in to thread for him to take out and work at while overseeing his flock's welfare. It would probably have been greasy wool, that is, only surface cleaned so much of the natural lanolin remained in the yarn. Greasy wool offers more protection from wind and rain than scoured wool.

Men knitting in the Twentieth Century
After the civil war in Russia in 1920, many Russians ended up in China where they were rounded up and detained. With China's own civil war imminent it put the Russian prisoners into camel caravans and shipped them to Eastern China. In this way the Russian men taught their Chinese guards how to knit using the available camel hair; having first spun a yarn using a very primitive spindle and whorl method. Captors and captives whiled away the long, arduous journey in this way, presumably amicably.

War
From civil wars to world wars, knitting was seen as a indispensible. Women left at home, working during the day and left worrying at night, could work away with busy fingers producing warm garments for their men folk on the front. They knitted: socks, balaclavas, vests, sweaters, blankets and scarves. It was seen as part of a woman's duty towards the war effort to produce these items and posters were put up to promote it.

Woollen blankets were desperately needed in the American War of Independence and, ironically, the woollen blankets provided to the army by the American government were made and sold by the English enemy.

Knitting for charity
Wars continue but hand knitted garments are no longer wanted or required for the people fighting them. However, knitting has become a standard media for raising money for charities. The knitted items can be supplied directly to the needy, blankets and rugs being common items. Or they can be sold to raise money for charity. Often these are novelty items or toys.

One seriously neglected area that is now being targeted by avid knitters is warm wear for undersized and disadvantaged babies. The infants are sometimes so tiny that clothes are made for them based on patterns for doll clothes.

Knitting samples
There are many different combinations of stitches that make many different kinds of textures in knitting. The most commonly used in western knitting are the stitches: plain and purl.

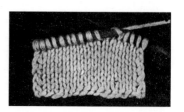

Plain knitting.

Purl knitting.

French knitting

French knitting is also known as spool knitting. It is a popular pastime with children. The spool is usually wooden with a hollow centre. Four pins are placed in the top and yarn is wound around this and looped over itself to form a long cylindrical textile. To make use of the textile it needs to be gathered, wound into a circle and stitched together to make a coiled flat fabric.

A common way of making a spool was to use and old cotton reel (in the days when they were made of wood) and hammer four nails into the top. Nowadays you buy super fancy ones.

For even younger children a very primitive but effective spool can be made out of a cardboard cylinder like a toilet roll. Four flat ice lolly sticks can be bound around the sides with masking tape so that they form the four pins protruding at one end. The size of this spool lets little fingers lift the wool over the yarn wound around the pins.

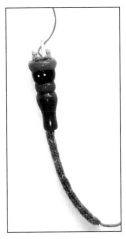

A fancy spool for French Knitting in the form of a doll.

Finger knitting

The earliest forms of knitting, including naalebinding, were performed with the fingers alone. A system of looping over a thumb and pulling the yarn through the loop is an easy task to perform. Finger knitting is a term given to the looping of yarn around the finger, following it with another loop and pulling the first over the second to form a chain.

This is a method used with young children in preschool. Thick, coloured yarn is an attractive option and children are content to sit and make yards and yards of it which can then be wound and stitched into objects such as hats or simple toys.

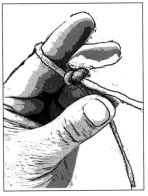

Finger knitting, the first knitting.

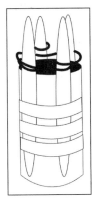

Toilet roll knitting!

A 1980s model knitting machine no longer in use.

William Lee and the knitting machine

According to legend, William Lee, a clergymen living in the latter half of the Sixteenth Century, got to work inventing a machine to knit so that his lady love could spend more time with him.

In 1589 he presented his new device to Queen Elizabeth and her court to consider for patenting. She did not grant it, requesting first that he knit her a pair of silk stockings, the woollen ones he had presented her with not being fine enough, and besides, since 1560 she had only worn stockings made of silk by her personal stocking maker, Mrs Montague.

Designer knitwear by Kaffe Fasset, photo courtesy of Kaffe Fasset's Studio.

When he brought the stockings forward, having fulfilled her request admirably, Queen Elizabeth still denied him the patent arguing such an invention would put the domestic makers of stockings out of business.

Consequently, the machine was offered across the channel to the French king and Lee set up business in foreign climes. Where William had failed, his brother succeeded and 30 years or so after William's first attempt at patenting, the stocking knitting industry was revolutionised by the first knitting machines. It did outrage hand knitters and it was not done without a fight.

Knitting machines were very popular in the 1970s and many homes had one. They fell out of favour and although still in use are nowhere near as popular as sewing machines.

Crochet

There are those people who are devoted knitters and then there are those who would rather crochet. Crocheting is done with a single crochet hook and the stitches are made with one on the hook at a time as opposed to a row of stitches on a knitting needle. The yarn is pulled through a loop with the hook end of the needle. Yarn is wound around the hook first to make different kinds of stitches.

Double Foundation chain.

Chain stitch.

Bobbin lace being made by Vicki Taylor.

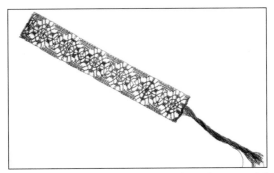

Bobbin lace made by Maureen based on an old Dutch pattern.

Lace

Lace should probably have a chapter on its own. It can be formed using several different processes: knitting, knotting, weaving and embroidery. True lace, defined as lace made by looping, twisting and braiding, was not in use until the Fifteenth Century.

In excavations of Roman towns bobbins resembling those used for lace making have been found. However, there is little evidence to show that this was what they were used for, certainly no textile fragments have survived and there is no documentary evidence of it being made at that time.

Lace making may well have started in Flanders in the Fourteenth Century, which was renowned for its fine weaving. Brussels became a big lace making centre later on.

Lace is categorised into the following types:

- Bobbin lace – is made on a pillow using fine thread and small wooden or bone bobbins around which the threads are wound. Pins hold the threads to each side as the work progresses. The lace is made by interweaving the threads
- Crochet lace – is made with a crochet hook and fine thread
- Cut work – an embroidery technique where threads are removed from the backing fabric and the spaces left are filled with needle made lace work
- Guipure – an embroidery made lace where the embroidery is done on a water soluble ground which is removed when the piece is finished so that only the embroidery thread remains
- Knitted lace – open work knitting such as Shetland lace made using ultra fine wool
- Knotted lace – includes macramé, the knotting of threads and tatting which uses a shuttle wound with thread that enables the thread to be looped and pulled through itself

A tatting shuttle.

Several types of machine made lace.

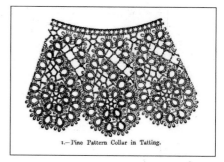

1.—Pine Pattern Collar in Tatting.

- Machine made lace – a variety of machines make different lace types, replicating those traditionally made by hand
- Needle lace – as the name suggests, this type of lace, for example, Kenmare lace, is made using a needle and thread. It is suggested by purists that this is the finest form of lace; it is not the quickest of procedures

---

- The first knitting trade guild was started in Paris in 1527
- Knit comes from *knot*, possibly from the Dutch verb *knutten*, to knot, though as it is similar to the Old English *cnyttan*, to knot, then it is likely there is an even older word that engendered both English and Dutch words
- The Craft Yarn Council of America has estimated that the number of women knitters aged between 25 and 30 rose by 150 per cent from 2002 to 2004. The trend is due to fashion not need
- Crochet and knitting are becoming trendy art statements. There is a movement around the world to bombard the streets with knitted graffiti. Nothing is safe: buses, poles, trees and even animals

---

Note

1. Kiewe, Heinz Edgar, Textile Design Anthropology ' History of Knitting', exhibition catalogue, Oxford, 1977, p. 6.

PART THREE

Surface Decoration

CHAPTER NINE

Dyeing

What should be the next natural step after having perfected the arts of spinning and weaving but colouring it? It must have been an early discovery because many of the textile artefacts unearthed by archaeologists are definitely coloured.

Perhaps we shouldn't really put dyeing in to a section on surface decoration as the nature of dye is to become integral with the fibre. However, it is a process that is added to the fibre, either before spinning, before weaving or afterwards.

The earliest dyes were found in natural objects that were available at the place of manufacture. Many of these dyes are still used today, particularly by hand crafters and environmentally concerned manufacturers.

There are three types of natural dye: substantive, vat and adjective. The first of these, the substantive dyes are those that can be used without the need of a fixative. The second lot of dyes are known as vat because they need to be fermented before they can be used. They will often not show their colour until taken out of the dye bath and exposed to the air. The third type of dye is called adjective and, in order to hold its colour in the fabric, it needs a mordant, a metallic compound of aluminium and iron or copper. A mordant is a bonding agent that acts on both the dye stuff and the stuff to be dyed.

One of the largest sources of natural dye is plants.

Hand dyeing in India, courtesy of David Dunning, Anokhi Hand Printing Museum, Jaipur, India.

Yellow

Yellow can be obtained from: dyer's broom, fustic from the mulberry tree, onion skin, osage orange (also from the mulberry tree), pomegranate, oak, rhubarb, weld, chamomile, goldenrod, blackberry, ragwort, tansy, turmeric powder and birch. Many of these dyes will need a mordant although, rhubarb, onion skin and pomegranate will hold quite well without.

Red

Red has been extracted from the madder root for thousands of years. It can tint a fabric a delicate pink or dye it a deep, rich red. Dye from this source may be used with or without a mordant although for the richer and brighter reds it will help the colour retain its brilliance.

It is not just the roots that can be used as a dye, the plant tops also produce a red colour though tending towards the tan and rust rather than true red. It too can be used effectively with and without mordants.

Madder root will also make deep and lovely purples if used with certain recipes.

Orange

Orange is a colour that can be achieved by using a red dye and certain mordants or modifiers, or yellow dyes and additives. One of the commonest ways of producing an orange is to firstly dye the yarn or fabric in one of the two colours, red or yellow, and then immerse the fabric in the other colour. In some cases it is possible to combine the two dye baths, rather like mixing paint.

Plants that produce an orange colour from red dyes are: brazil wood and madder root. Onion skin, traditionally a yellow dye has definite orange overtones and if used in a high proportion of skin to water the colour will intensify.

Blue

Indigo, like madder, is an ancient dye. It is also the only natural dye to obtain a real blue. It comes from a limited number of plants that happen to be found worldwide. Woad, the war paint of the early Britons and other tribes, is an indigo producing plant.

Being a vat dye, indigo plants need to be soaked for some time in a liquid mixture. Many recipes for indigo call for stale urine as a component of the dye bath which is considered offensive to our modern day sensibilities.

Indigo has had many rituals and superstitious beliefs attached to its properties and its processing. The island of Suva in South-east Asia has a mythology regarding the two different groups of people inhabiting it based on their matrilineal ancestry. It is believed that two sisters were about to be initiated by their mother into the secrets of true indigo making. One of the girls crept out the night before their induction into the dyeing process and stole the vat of indigo waiting for the next step. Through her ignorance she poured off the top layer of liquid thinking it would be sufficient for her to turn into a deep blue. Unfortunately for her she had taken the superficial layer which contained little colouring.

To make true blue indigo it is the bottom layer, that which has been fermenting that is the precious potion with which to make it. For the two sisters, one founded a family who could not produce the colour but only a thin ghost of it while the other, who waited for her mother's instruction, became the mother to the real dyers of the island.

Green and Purple
Just as orange can be made by mixing or over dyeing red with yellow, so purple can be made by dyeing red and blue. Purples can also be got from: bilberries, black currants, blackberries (look at how it stains the fingers when picking them), elder fruits, and sloe.

Green too, is another colour that is hard to find in one plant source and is therefore usually obtained by mixing a yellow and blue dye. It can be found in fairly dull hues in the following plant sources: bracken tops, goldenrod, ivy berries, privet, lily of the valley and nettle.

Plants are not the only natural source of dye pigment. Tyrian purple, or imperial purple is made from a shellfish. It was long considered a luxury dye and purple became synonymous with royalty.

Other dyes, like the lovely cochineal, are got from insects of the *Dactylopius* species; only the females are used. These insects are native to South and Central America and, while used by the indigenous people of the area since at least 3,000 years, it did not become known or available to people on the other side of the world until Europeans conquered South America.

Two other insect based dyes are a bright red or scarlet colour produced by the egg sac of the female *Kermes* insect that feeds on oak trees and the other is the *Lac* or *Sticklac* from Asia that produces a resin which is the source of the pigment.

Plants, insects and shellfish weren't the only sources of natural dye. Earth pigments like ochre are still used by people today. Earth pigment can range from white to yellow, brown and red. It was used straight from the ground, and apparently there is a tradition of burying the piece of fabric or thread to be coloured in the ochre in the ground and left there for a period of time until it has taken the hue of the surrounding earth. Mostly though, ochre was put into a pot of water which was then evaporated to leave a concentrated pigment that could be further dried for storage and later use or ground directly and further diluted or applied to the fabric.

Natural Mordants
Mordants were found in nature alongside the dye sources they needed to modify. Some of these come from plants too: tannin from oak galls, blackberry leaves and twigs and alder bark; oxalic acid from the poisonous rhubarb leaf and, less socially acceptable, urine.

An iron based mordant can be made if you soak rusty iron in a mixture of water and vinegar. The same can be done with copper.

Chemical dyes
Chemical dyes weren't really invented until the mid Nineteenth Century. In 1856 a chemistry student, William Henry Perkin, was conducting an experiment to try to recreate quinine. He was unsuccessful in his aim but he was successful in making a purple matter that he discovered could dye silk purple.

Drying the cloth, courtesy of David Dunning, Anokhi Hand Printing Museum, Jaipur, India.

Perkin's discovery, mauveine, led the way to a whole range of synthetic dyes including a version of madder, in 1869, and indigo, 1878. In 1878 a group of synthetic dyes were created called organic azo-dyes. These formed the basis for many of the dyes used today.

With the invention of spinning and weaving machines driven by steam power it was inevitable that someone would come up with a way of producing strong, bright and colourfast dyes.

Ways of dyeing

As with everything else, mankind is never content with the simplest form of anything and dyeing yarn and fabric is no exception. It was not long after the discovery of making dye and immersing fibres in it to give them colour that humans began experimenting with ways of making the colour even more interesting.

One of the simplest ways to achieve interest in decoration is to dye the spun yarn in several different colours along its length. This is not over dyeing in order to achieve secondary colours but only dipping portions of a skein of yarn into each different colour dye bath. When it is then woven into cloth it will be multi-hued.

This simple method has itself been taken to a high art with a form called ikat (meaning to bind). Bunches of yarn are tied at intervals along their length with a dye resistant cord (traditionally silk) and then dyed. Sometimes the process is repeated up to three times, covering the already dyed area with cord before re-immersing. The yarns then form the warp or the weft of the fabric to be woven. It is rare to have both warp and weft dyed in this way. The resulting geometric patterns are amazing and show how much planning is needed to achieve this effect.

Tie-dyeing

A less complex form of resist dyeing (the term used for a process where another substance prevents the cloth from dyeing in that spot) is tie-dyeing, the popular handcraft of the Seventies.

The cloth is tied tightly with pieces of string or bunched and held with rubber bands. Pegs have also been used to make a pattern by preventing dye from reaching the cloth.

The patterns this method can produce are simple but fun and certainly distinctive. It is a good activity to do with children using white tee shirts and a cold water dye.

To go a step further with this type of dyeing why not stitch and pull the surface of the cloth? This is called trikit. The stitching is only to make folds and creases in the fabric, the firmer the better and it is the pressure of these that provide the resistance to the dye, not the thread that makes the stitches.

Batik

Then we get to batik (meaning wax writing). The method of using wax as a resistance to dye is ancient and its origins are obscure. Linen used to wrap mummies in ancient Egypt (Fourth Century BC) was soaked in wax and a design scratched into the surface and then dyed. It has been used in several Asian countries but it is the Indonesian island of Java that has become famous for its batik fabric.

Batik cloth from Indonesia.

The dye for batik must be a cold water dye as any heat would melt the wax. The best wax mix is 30 per cent beeswax and 70 per cent paraffin. One of the desired effects of batik is to get a subtle crackling effect where the wax has cracked and let tiny amounts of dye into the fabric. This needs to be controlled and that is where it is necessary to have the right proportions of the two waxes. Beeswax is the most adherent of the two and does not tend to crack. Paraffin on the other hand is far too brittle to be used by itself.

A design is drawn onto the cloth and hot wax applied to the area that is not to be dyed the colour of the first bath (the baths need to go from lightest to darkest). The wax can be applied by brush or dripped on but special tools can be bought, little copper reservoirs with a fine pouring spout, that hold an amount of hot wax like a pen holds ink. These are called tjantings.

The first dye bath is made and the piece dried. More wax will be added to preserve the colour just dyed. Subsequent dyeings are made. Wax can be removed between dye baths, if they are uncovered to receive a pure colour. When the piece is finished and dried all the wax can be removed by immersing in a solvent or ironing between sheets of paper.

To make the dyeing process quicker and to make repetitive patterns carved wood blocks are used. The hot wax is coated onto the woodblock, adhering to the raised surface of the carving. It is then planted face down onto the fabric and held in place until the hot wax infiltrates the fabric. The process is repeated.

Batik cloth from Indonesia.

CHAPTER TEN

Printing and Painting

Printing on fabric is another ancient art, developed in India and China well before it took off in Europe.

Printing probably began using found items dipped in dye or paint and pressed onto another surface in order to leave an imprint of it. From there decorations would have been carved or cut into the objects used for printing. These may have been stone and quite possible things like potatoes and other soft but perishable materials. Hands and fingers leave excellent marks too and these kinds of prints have been left on the walls of caves and rocks by our prehistoric ancestors.

The intricacy and sophistication of printed design would have been fairly contemporaneous with other develops in spinning and weaving techniques.

In India, China and Europe printing on cloth came before printing on paper. Paper wasn't even introduced into Europe before the Middle Ages. Silk was a popular surface for printing onto.

The printing blocks were often made of wood and these were the first printing blocks to be used in China according to archaeological evidence. These early prints, surviving only in fragments were of flowers on silk and used three colours. Egyptian printed cloth evidence comes from a slightly later date, about 400 BC. India perfected the art of block printing executing exquisite designs of flowers in bright colours that caught the fancy of Europeans in the Eighteenth Century.

Ink suitable for adhering to the fibres of fabric is thickened with a substance called a colourant. This is to prevent the ink from running or bleeding into other parts of the fabric other than within the design. There are four main types of printing onto textiles. The first method is called direct printing and uses inks fixed with colourants so that the ink stays within its design.

The second method is to print a mordant only onto the cloth where the pattern is to go. When the ink is applied it will fix onto the fabric where the mordant is and nowhere else. The third method is the resist dye method which has already been discussed. Examples of this technique are batik, tie-dyeing and the like. The fourth method uses bleach to remove colour in a set design from fabric that has already received dye.

The Eastern countries successfully printed on textiles for centuries before the Europeans did. The art of block printing entered Europe through Spain via the Moors in the Twelfth Century as did so much technology. The European dyes were not as permanent as the Eastern ones and often ran marring the fabric. The problem was exacerbated by the need to wash items intended for clothing. Those that were for decorative purposes only tended to last longer.

Printing on fabric in England began in 1676 when a Huguenot refugee from France began his business in London. While England was new to the process it had already become established in mainland Europe and printers were becoming famous for their designs.

Calico printing had been popular in Germany and its neighbours for nearly a hundred years before it took off in England. The major influence on designs was France who had developed a reputation for the finest work in Europe.

The different methods of applying print to fabric are: woodblock, perrotine, engraved copperplate printing, roller printing, cylinder printing, or machine printing, stencil printing and digital textile printing.

Woodblock

Woodblock is the oldest form of printing on textile and has remained popular up until today. India was and still is a leading exponent of the art.

A piece of flat wood has a design drawn onto it and those parts that are not to be covered in ink are cut away. The raised design is then coated with ink via a roller, carefully placed onto the fabric and pressed down by hand or a clean roller to push the ink onto the fabric. In some countries it is transferred by hitting the printing block on the back with a wooden mallet.

One of the drawbacks of using wood blocks for printing is the wear of constant printing on the block. The finer details wear away quite quickly and so the quality of the print deteriorates over time. To overcome this problem the carved wood is often covered in metal, beaten into shape over the carved surface. If the design requires more than one colour a second and third block are prepared with the pattern cut into it. The designs must be lined up carefully so they integrate properly.

Perrotine printing

This is woodblock printing mechanised. What is the point of being able to produce yards and yards of woven fabric if it can't be decorated in an easy and quick manner? All parts of textile production must try to match the others in time and quality.

Perrot lived in Rouen and it was his machine that revolutionised the printing of textile fabrics in 1834. Surprisingly the machinery never became accepted by the English although the rest of Europe embraced the new technology eagerly.

Engraved copperplate printing

Perhaps the Perrotine printing machine was never popular in England because they already had the engraved copperplate system. It was first used by Thomas Bell in 1770. The plates were fixed to a letterpress at first but then the cylinder press came into use. The cloth went around the cylinder which transferred the ink to the cloth. This method was difficult to line up the various colour plates.

Roller printing, cylinder printing, or machine printing

This was another of Thomas Bell's inventions and he produced it in 1785. His first patent was for a machine that would print six colours at once but his design was not quite right and it was difficult to keep the six different plates in alignment. The problem was solved by Adam Parkinson in Manchester in the year of the machine's patent, 1785. This time the machine proved successful.

Bell and Parkinson's design could print 10,000 to 12,000 yards of fabric in a 10-hour day if only one colour was used. It was also excellent for reproducing any

Woodblock cutters workshop, courtesy of David Dunning, Anokhi Hand Printing Museum, Jaipur, India.

Digital print of artist's doll by Fiona McDonald, fabric printed by Spoonflower.

Preparing blocks for carving, courtesy of David Dunning, Anokhi Hand Printing Museum, Jaipur, India.

Carving woodblocks, photo courtesy of David Dunning, Anokhi Hand Printing Museum, Jaipur, India.

Preparing sheets of fabric for screen printing, photo courtesy of David Dunning, Anokhi Hand Printing Museum, Jaipur, India.

manner of designs. The main advantage was the precision in the matching up the different colours and its ability to print seamless repetitive motifs.

Stencil printing

Stencil printing is nearly as old an art as woodblock printing. They probably emerged in a very similar time frame and both were particularly close to the heart of the Japanese aesthetic.

Basically stencil printing involves a design cut out of a thin board, usually paper of metal. The cut away parts represent the coloured areas. The board is placed over the fabric and ink is brushed or rolled over the cut away design leaving a clear, hard edged design printed onto the fabric. The process can involve more than one colour plate. The subsequent plates being printed once the previous layer is dry.

A stencilling machine was built in 1894 by S.H. Sharp. The plate was made of thin steel and passed continuously over a cast iron cylinder as it turned. The fabric passed between the stencil and the roller and the ink was pressed onto it.

Screen printing

Screen printing was a development of stencil printing. Hand screen printing enjoyed a revival in the 1970s with people making their own silk screens. A design was cut in paper or card, laid over the fabric which lay flat on a table. Ink was applied with the aid of a squeegee; a length of tapered rubber held with a wooden block. The squeegee pulled the ink across the design in a smooth movement and left a clean print behind.

Screen printing has now become a highly technical business and companies print everything from road signs to tee shirts.

Screen printing, photo courtesy of David Dunning, Anokhi Hand Printing Museum, Jaipur, India.

Digital textile printing

Like everything else printing had to be digitalised. It is done through inkjet technology in the way computer printers print to paper. It is the most time efficient and accurate method of printing.

It is possible to upload images of an artist's work onto a website called Spoonflower in the US and have that design printed onto fabric from the computer image.

Preparation of cloth for printing

Just as with dyeing, fabric must be prepared before it is ready to be printed. All finishes need to be removed and the fabric bleached to give it an all over quality of whiteness otherwise the pattern will appear altered. As with dyes certain mordents or fixatives need to be added or applied beforehand so the fabric will hold the colour fast and it won't fade or run in the wash or in sunlight.

Painting

Hand painting fabric is a time consuming process. It is reserved for the most special fabrics and those who can afford such luxuries. The history of hand painting is another of those 'lost in time' stories but around 1000 BC a form of fabric painting emerged called 'kalamkari', which means pen work. The design was applied with a bamboo or date palm stick. A bundle of hair would be pushed into one end of the hollow stick to form a brush. At first the process was applied to cotton fabrics but it was later used on silk and other textiles. The technique was mainly used to depict Hindu religious and mythological scenes and deities.

From India the technique became accepted in China, Japan, Egypt and Greece. Europe came to it later.

- In the Americas the Incas and Aztecs had printing technology before they were invaded by the Spaniards
- In the Sixteenth and Seventeenth Centuries European ladies would send finished dresses of silk and cotton to India or China to be hand painted. The idea behind sending a completed garment was that the design could be painted all over without any loss in the seams
- When the owners died they often bequeathed their costly dresses to the church to be made into articles such as kneelers and cushions

CHAPTER ELEVEN

Embroidery

Decorating a piece of cloth with yarn stitched onto its surface is as old as sewing itself. The stitches used to hold pieces of garment together, be they skin or cloth, could form a decoration in themselves as well as performing a fundamental function. Embroidery has been used for pure decoration as well as serving religious and symbolic meanings.

Richly embroidered cloth has served the purposes of celebrating marriages, births, christenings and death. Death perhaps has had the longest history of embellished fabric being used for ceremony. The cross-over from the living state to one that is a universal mystery requires special care and preparation.

The household trappings that make life warmer and more comfortable, carpets, bedding, curtains and the like have always attracted by the need for decoration. Weaving and dyeing and printing onto fabric is one way to achieve these results but embroidery offers a chance to sit still and contemplate or relax while the hands move in a repetitive motion bringing colours and motifs to life.

Women have dominated the domestic embroidery scene but it is wrong to think that embroidery is only a female pursuit. Men tended to undertake professional embroidery just as they often performed professional weaving and knitting.

Embroidery exists in all parts of the world in many different forms and it arose in the American continent independently of its rise in Asia and Europe in the same way asspinning and weaving of wool and cotton did.

There are regional designs, motifs and colours but many embroidery stitches are common to all. There are some that can be traced along the ancient trade routes often originating in China or India and spreading slowly west, usually via the Arab countries into Spain and then the rest of Europe.

The basic stitches used in embroidery have not changed dramatically over the centuries; the biggest innovation to the craft being machines that will do the embroidery automatically for commercial purposes and machine embroidery being made by individual artists. This latter group use domestic sewing machines, they remove or lower the feed teeth, the effects that can be achieved are wide ranging.

One of the historically significant embroideries is the Bayeaux Tapestry illustrating the Battle of Hastings. It was embroidered by Saxon women, probably using English wool. Inspired by the Bayeaux Tapestry, two hundred Quakers drawn from eight countries made their own enormous embroidery showing the history of the Quaker community, from its inception in the Seventeenth Century to modern day. It took almost nine years to complete even with the large workforce. The piece is currently on view at the Quaker Meeting House in Kendal, Cumbria.

A traditional occupation for girls who were to become good housewives was to embroider samplers. These were cloths to showcase the stitches they had

Wattle Flat, The Escarpment, by Judy
Wilford.

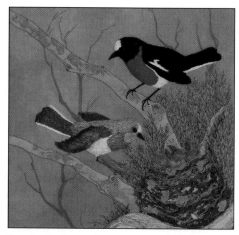

Scarlet Robins, the Nesting, by Judy
Wilford.

mastered. The children often began this task as early as four or five years old. They
would be required to make several samplers during their childhood as their skills
developed.

Texts from scripture were popular embroidery projects with flowers and other
decorative motifs.

Quilting

Quilting is not an embroidery technique though it will often employ embroidery
as its own surface decoration. Quilting is the piecing together of small shapes of
different fabrics to make a new, whole fabric. The idea was born out of necessity.
When clothing or furnishings wore out there was always good fabric left that
seemed to good to throw to the rag-and-bone-man.

Old Indian made quilt.

Quilt by Kaffe Fassett.

Needlepoint in blue and white by Kaffe Fassett, photo courtesy of Kaffe Fassett's Studio.

Needlepoint cushion by Kaffe Fassett, photo courtesy of Kaffe Fassett's Studio.

The old garments were cut into shapes and stitches together. The fabric made in this way was nearly always used for bed coverings. Overtime distinctive patterns and motifs cropped up and quilting was not just about using up leftovers but creating objects with their own intrinsic value.

After the patchwork was complete the quilt was backed with a solid piece of plain fabric such as calico and a layer of wool batting sandwiched between the two. To keep it all in one piece a design was stitch in a plain thread through the layers to form a pattern that resembled embossing.

Canvas Work

Canvas work, also called needlepoint, is embroidery worked on an open weave canvas with a thickish yarn so the holes are filled with the yarn. Wool is the usual medium for this embroidery technique. It was used for years to make beautiful upholstery for chairs and lounges, fire screens and bed hangings.

Kaffe Fassett, a leading UK textile designer has been instrumental in bringing the art back into fashion.

Eastern Scrub Wrens, Judy Wilford.

Embroidery Stitch Glossary
Back stitch: a simple outline stitch. Make a stitch and then take the needle back half a stitch and push through fabric to form next stitch.

Backstitch.

Blanket Stitch: and buttonhole stitch. Bring the needle out on the base line (say the edge of the blanket) take the needle and insert at upper line and bring back out at base line making sure the thread is held under the needle. The stitch forms a back-to-front L shape. It is a good stitch to finish a raw edge with as the base thread forms a protective line. This is the way buttonhole stitch is made but the stitches are very close together to prevent fraying.

Blanket Stitch.

Bokhara couching: is a filling stitch. A satin stitch is laid down and then small diagonal stitches are made regularly along the thread to hold it in place.

Bokhara couching.

Bullion stitch: is a knot stitch. The needle is inserted into fabric and brought out a distance from the first stitch. Thread is wrapped around the needle several times and the needle pulled through them to form a knot.

Bullion Stitch.

Chain stitch: is a looped stitch and can be used for outline work or filling. A stitch is made and the thread held under the needle and secured by the making of another stitch.

Chain stitch.

Cross stitch: a row of stitches is made with a diagonal slant. A second row is made crossing the ones previously made. Alternatively the crosses can be completed individually.

Cross stitch.

Daisy stitch: is a form of chain stitch in which the stitches sit individually to form a daisy flower.

Daisy stitch.

Eyelet holes: firstly a line of running stitches just in from the hole to be embroidered. Make small satin stitches from the running stitches to the edge of fabric. The stitches are next to each other.

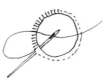

Eyelet holes.

Feather stitch: is a form of open chain stitch.

Feather stitch.

French knots: are small raised knots that add texture to embroidery and are very effective when used in clusters.

French knots.

Running stitch: is the most basic of embroidery stitches involving a simple in and out technique. It is probably the oldest stitch ever used.

Running stitch.

Satin stitch: is a filling stitch. Stitches of a certain length are placed immediately next to each other to create a flat plate of colour.

Satin stitch.

Stem stitch: is the next stitch up from running. A solid line is created by the running stitches being filled by a back stitch.

Stem stitch.

PART FOUR

The Industrial Revolution

CHAPTER TWELVE

The Industrial Revolution

Before the revolution

The raising of sheep for wool and the export of it had been one of early England's major economic staples. By the time of Henry VIII the sale of raw wool overseas had been well and truly overtaken by the manufacture of woollen cloth.

The rise of the newer industry meant that people all over England and particularly in rural areas participated in the various processes that turned raw wool into cloth. This was known as the domestic system and it suited the people of England very well. One did not have to be highly trained in order to do some of the jobs required. One could keep a sheep and sell its wool, and spin thread in the evenings after all the other day's chores were done. Weaving too could be done in the largest room of a cottage.

While this system worked well for centuries it began to fail with the advent of labour saving machinery.

For several centuries the industry of making cloth had been carried out under what was known as the 'domestic system', where people undertook work such as spinning yarn or weaving cloth in their own homes, often to supplement other income. While there had been town-based craftsmen for a long time, and once the guild members had dominated the work force, the domestic system meant that the output of work was no longer tied to urban areas. What then happened was particular crafts tended to proliferate in a particular rural area. Subsequently new centres emerged just as they had done in the time of the guilds.

Cotton factory, Manchester.

Birmingham, Halifax, Leeds and Manchester were leading lights of the domestic system of textile production, opening the way for the introduction of the factory-based manufacturing system. The centres often appeared as specialists in one or two areas of manufacture (e.g. fulling, spinning or weaving) because geographical attributes of that area were fundamental to the processes used in those processes. Fulling required running water to power the mills (already in operation in medieval times). Easily accessible water was also good for washing cloth and dyeing it.

Before the introduction of cotton as a raw material, wool and woollen cloth were the staple products of the textile industry in England. Spinning was done on spinning wheels powered by a foot treadle and looms were all hand operated as were knitting frames.

The Beginning of Mechanisation
The fulling mill was the first real non-human powered machine and it had been around for centuries. The mills were similar in construct to mills that gound wheat or corn into flour only they turned giant hammers to batter rolls of felt rather than large stones to grind grain.

The first real water powered textile factory was that built by Thomas Lombe in 1719 on the River Derwent in Derby. The secret behind this water driven mill for spinning organzine silk thread was stolen by Thomas's brother John from an Italian mill. John infiltrated the mill in disguise and took detailed notes of the structure and how it worked to take back to his brother in England. Unfortunately John did not live long enough to enjoy the stolen fruit of his labour because, legend has it, an Italian woman tracked him down and poisoned him.

Cotton, introduced to England by the East India Company, had given fashionable beings a taste for the light and elegant material. So much so that England began producing its own calico and lawn, and in the early part of the Eighteenth Century it was forbidden by law to print imported cotton cloth in the interests of the home product. Imported linen was exempt from this edict.

The manufacture of cotton and silk were relative newcomers to England's textile industry in the Eighteenth Century and they were successful. They did not oust the old woollen cloth merchandise and the demand for these continued to grow, slowly but steadily.

The increased demand for English goods from foreign countries meant that the organisation needed to meet the demand was no longer adequate, just as it had happened when England began making and exporting woven wool fabric instead of staying with the tried and true raw wool. Making cloth by hand was no longer a viable indsutry, people could not physically work hard and long enough to produce the volume wanted. Machinery, however, could. Techonology was advancing in great leaps and bounds in the Eighteenth Century and it is these inventions that played a major role in the Industrial Revolution.

Spinning was one of the most labour intensive steps. It was being done in a manner that had changed little for thousands of years. The drop spindle, while no longer a common tool, was still around and it was inevitably the implement used by the very poor to eke out a meagre existence. The spinning wheel in its various forms, in particular the great wheel, was the normal method of spinning. It was quicker than the ancient drop spindle but even so, one weaver could use the yarn made by five or six spinners in the same time frame.

Unfortunately it was an invention to facilitate weaving that came before one for spinning and so the weaver was soon able to far outstrip the production of the spinner. In 1738 John Kay invented the flying shuttle. Instead of thrusting the shuttle by hand through the lifted warp threads it could be manipulated by a system of pulleys and two cords. This was even more beneficial to weavers of broadcloth who required two men to operate the hand loom; one to thrust the shuttle through the uplifted warp threads and another to retrieve it at the other end and send it back again. Kay's flying shuttle meant that broadcloth could be woven by a single man.

Now the problem of needing more spun yarn was exacerbated. Weaving could be done in a fraction of the time it had been traditionally but the yarn was not available to enable it to be done. The Royal Society decided to launch a competition with a monetary prize for anyone who could complement the flying shuttle invention with one that would increase the speed of spinning yarn. Whist nobody claimed the prize it set in motion the steps necessary to make a more time efficient industry. One of the first successful attempts to make a spinning machine was James Hargreaves.

The Major Inventors

James Hargreaves
James Hargreaves, born in Lancashire, and was a carpenter and weaver until he turned to inventing in 1740. He began his new career as an inventor with a commission to make a more efficient carding machine. His innovative spinning jenny did not arrive on the scene until 1764. The story behind the invention was that he startled his wife who had been working at the great wheel; she jumped up in surprise and knocked it over. James observed that the wheel and the spindle were still going. He thought that if one could put several vertically placed spindles next to each other then it could be possible to spin more than one thread at a time from the one wheel.

His idea was that the one great wheel would make the spindle revolve via the means of a leather band made into a continuous circle. A pair of bars would replace the human hands that drew the carded wool from the distaff and guided it to the spindle with a pair of bars which could be consecutively separated and closed, moved closer or further away from the spindles on wheels, and so manage to spin several threads at the one time. It was named in honour of his wife.

The local community saw the machine as suspicious and were afraid that it would put them out of work. In 1768 Hargreaves' house was set on fire and everything within it was burned including the spinning jenny. Hargreaves left the district and set up a cotton mill in Nottingham with Thomas James. Hargreaves' invention spawned many similar ones and there were machines that could spin 20 or 30 threads at a time.

Richard Arkwright
Richard Arkwright was not aiming to copy Hargreaves's jenny but was engaged in trying to invent a more efficient one altogether. He had looked at the experiments of Wyatt from Northampton for inspiration. Arkwright worked on a succession of

rollers through which the carded fleece was fed. Each pair of rollers spun more quickly to the effect that the fleece was teased out to a fine amount, just as an expert human hand might. The patent for this spinning machine was taken out in 1769 and made a strong rival for Hargreaves' jenny.

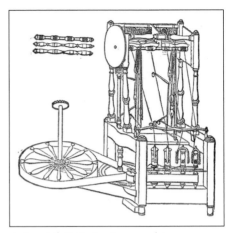

Arkwright didn't stop with the patented design but worked on it for years afterwards. He made and sold the machines himself and with various business partners in different districts. The patent was eventually revoked, the argument being that it contained not enough original material but relied too much on that of predecessors like Wyatt.

Arkwright's Spinning machine.

The outcome was that with the patent lifted the invention was open to manufacture by anyone who had the means or the money. Spinning machines invaded industry. Despite the loss of his patent, Arkwright managed to amass a healthy fortune for his spinning machine and was publicly acknowledged for his services to the industry and received a knighthood in 1786.

Samuel Crompton

Hargreaves had sparked an inventing frenzy and after Arkwright came Samuel Crompton, another weaver by trade. He took the best aspects of Hargreaves's jenny and Arkwright's spinner and in 1779 he formed a hybrid that became known as the spinning 'mule'. Crompton did not patent his improved invention and it became a popular device for spinning thread.

Just as the flying shuttle spurred on the invention of a faster and better spinning device, so the spinning jenny and mule sparked the search for a carding and a combing machine so that the fleece, ready for spinning, could be at hand. A carding cylinder was already in existence, having been invented by Paul in 1748. It now came into its own and was soon joined by wool-combing machines in 1792 and 1793.

Edward Cartwright

The process began to turn full circle. Now that spinning and fleece processing had been made faster by machinery, the looms were falling behind. As wonderful as the flying shuttle had been decades earlier it had, by the end of the Eighteenth Century become old technology and the need for power looms was pressing. Edward Cartwright, a clergyman, not a weaver this time, worked consistently on improving a design for one such piece of equipment. By the beginning of the Nineteenth Century Cartwright's power loom was the norm in the weaving industry.

Cartwright's power loom.

While Arkwright and Crompton had been unlucky in the patenting attempts of their inventions, Cartwright's device was seen as being not only original but an indispensable piece of industrial equipment and Parliament awarded him £10,000 in 1809.

As Britain developed its cloth manufacturing industry, so long based on wool, new fibres made their way from foreign climes. Cotton was one of these. By the time of the Cartwright's invention cotton was no stranger to the English mills.

Eli Whitney

Perhaps the most important invention for the processing of cotton was Eli Whitney's cotton gin. This was an American design and was so successful in removing seeds and foreign matter from the cotton bolls that it remained largely unchanged from the original of 1792.

All this machinery made production very much quicker. While the early spinning jennys could be installed in a domestic situation their later cousins were far too big and required too much manpower for a normal sized house, let alone a cottage. The need for something stronger to drive them led to the use; firstly of horse power, but eventually water power was much better. Where running water was available, mostly where mills were already set, water power was not a difficulty. The answer lay in the steam engine.

James Watt

James Watt patented his steam engine in 1769 and its first application to the textile industry was in 1785 when it powered a cotton mill. By the end of the century steam was far more prevalent for powering textile mills than water was.

The result of all this activity was that the new innovations required large amounts of capital, as well as adequate space, to run. Such machines were not even dreamed of by the cottagers who had formed the basis of the old domestic system.

Machines would spell the end of the long established domestic system. What took its place was the factory.

The Factory System

Men with money invested it in textile mills. The mills needed money to set up with machinery and then they needed a labour force to make them earn their keep. Even though machinery had revolutionised the industry, making cloth faster than humanly possible by hand, it still required many people to run them efficiently. Machinery plus men under the one roof equalled the first factories.

It was making cotton textiles that first became mechanised and organised into a factory. It was not long before the woollen cloth industry followed suit and eventually other industries all started using the new 'factory system' as opposed to the long standing 'domestic system' of production.

From 1760 until approximately 1800 the introduction of machinery and steam power altered the whole manufacturing process and, in this short time, it managed to produce a whole range of social problems too. Workers who had long been able to make extra money working from their own homes at their own times were now expected to go to the work site at specific times to work set hours. This automatically disqualified workers who lived any great distance from an industrial centre.

Cotton mill.

The Industrial Revolution

The Industrial Revolution means exactly that. Industry was revolutionised in a way that hadn't been done for centuries, probably with the adoption of the domestic system in late medieval times. It has set a paradigm for industry ever since with a need to utilise new and more efficient machinery and technology, to gather its workers under a centralised building and to have a large well of capital to draw upon.

The effect on the domestic manufacturer was devastating. They could not compete with machine-made yarn or cloth in either speed or quality. Many people who had subsisted on a bit of domestic manufacture and a bit of agriculture could not exist on either. Many people sold up their small farms and went to seek work in the towns and cities. Others stayed on the land as farm labourers after selling their small holdings to bigger farms. The era of the small farm was over, just as the small manufacturer was too.

The population underwent a dramatic shift. Rural areas were often abandoned and some villages disappeared altogether as people sought work or opportunities abroad. Still, in 1801, according to records from the time, only one fifth of England's population lived in urban areas and four-fifths stayed in the countryside. However, the Industrial Revolution had stimulated a major change and 50 years later the population had rearranged itself so that the percentage of town to rural dwellers was approximately half and half. By 1901 the numbers of 1801 had totally reversed and the towns held the bulk of the people and the rural areas had dwindled to a fifth of the overall population. For example:

- Manchester in 1800 had a population of 85,000; in 1850 it had expanded to 400,000
- Leeds in 1800 had a population of 53,000; in 1850 it had grown to 172,000
- Bradford in 1800 had 13,000 people; by 1850 it had become 104,000

Pollution

One of the negative outcomes for the increase of mechanised manufacture in the towns was air pollution. Charles Dickens paints a dark and dirty picture in *Hard Times*. Dickens, apparently, visited a Lancashire manufacturing town, Preston, at the time of industrial action by the workers.

It was a town of red brick, or of brick that would have been red if the smoke and ashes had allowed it; but as matters stood it was a town of unnatural red and black like the painted face of a savage. It was a town of machinery and tall chimneys, out of which interminable serpents of smoke trailed themselves for ever and ever, and never got uncoiled. It had a black canal in it, and a river that ran purple with ill-smelling dye, and vast piles of building full of windows where there was a rattling and a trembling all say long, and where the piston of the steam-engine worked monotonously up and down like the head of an elephant in a state of melancholy madness.[1]

As Dingle Foot says in his introduction to this volume, Dickens was bored by the town, out of his usual setting and did not give himself the chance to get to know the people. He describes Coketown in unflattering terms and equates its population with the town's physical attributes too.

Elizabeth Gaskell supports the idea that these textile factory towns were polluted. In *North and South*, her heroine, Margaret gets her first view of a northern industrial town, Milton, based on the author's own experience of Manchester, from the train which is carrying her to it and she notices the difference between it and the south of England. The country carts 'had more iron, and less wood and leather' and there was less colour. Everything, Margaret thinks, has a sense of busy purpose about it.

For several miles before they reached Milton, they saw a deep lead-coloured cloud hanging over the horizon in the direction in which it lay…Nearer to the town, the air had a faint taste and smell of smoke; perhaps, after all, more a loss of the fragrance of grass and herbage than any positive taste or smell. Quick they were whirled over long, straight hopeless streets of regularly-built houses, all small and of brick. Here and there a great oblong many- windowed factory stood up, like a hen among her chickens, puffing out black, 'unparliamentary' smoke, and accounting for the cloud which Margaret had taken to foretell rain.[2]

By 'unparliamentary' smoke Gaskell refers to the 'Act of Good government of Manchester' of 1844. The act commanded that every factory furnace had a chimney that would 'consume the smoke arising from such a furnace'. Obviously the act was not efficient in diminishing air pollution.

A city under a cloud.

Land Enclosure

With the disappearance of the small farms due to the decline of manufacture, the domestic system, the advances made in agriculture, plus large amounts of capital being pumped into the bigger farms, enclosure of common land was to be expected.

One of the profoundest effects on England through these changes was probably the social structure of the rural populations. Previously the boundaries had been somewhat blurred between the rural classes. With the emergence of the new factory system, the abandonment of small farming and the desperate need for work by the poorer people displaced from farm work and cloth making, the only option besides moving to the city, was to become labourers to the bigger and more impersonal farms.

At the top of the pecking order were the landlords who rapidly acquired more land. Secondly were the tenant farmers who leased the farms belonging to the landlords for large sums of money. They were professional farmers and could make the farms run at a profit big enough to pay their rent and themselves a decent wage. The labourers were at the bottom of the pile. They were paid pitiful wages for farm work, lived in rundown cottages, and had no land of their own. It is odd then that England was no longer self-sufficient in food production.

During the Eighteenth Century there was a big increase in population, from five million in the early 1700s to six and a half million in the middle of the century and approximately nine million by 1800. Within another 50 years the population of England had doubled to eighteen million. With a big part of the people involved in manufacturing non food stuff there was not enough emphasis put on domestic food production.

Urbanisation was responsible for a decrease in domestic food production but it also directed a change in the general eating habits of the English people. Before the Industrial Revolution people ate brown bread and unprocessed foods; but when people became urbanised they turned to white bread and began the tradition of tea drinking. There was a major decline in the home baking of bread. Bakery businesses grew as a consequence.

Overall living standards fell dramatically and between 1800 and 1834 they were the lowest they had ever been. Previously, farm labourers had usually lived within the confines of the farm with food plentifully provided by the farmer. As the Revolution steamrolled across England, this tradition was also lost. Farmers could sell excess food and for a good profit because of the demands of town dwellers. Farm workers moved out of the farm itself and had to find rented accommodation.

Women and children in the work force

> But how were these two little girls to find time to do all this work for me? The whole day they were engaged, from six o'clock in the morning till bed time... the poor little girls had to work so hard for more than thirteen hours every day that neither of them could awake in time.[3]

Women and children made up much of the work force in the young factory system. They were employed more than they had ever been in previous labour systems and were employed in the factories to a greater extent than men. For instance, a flax spinning mill near Leeds, in 1832 employed 1,200 workers of which about two thirds were under the age of eighteen. This was a fairly typical ratio of the early factories.

The attraction of having such a young work force was that they could be paid a lower wage and they were more easily brought into line through physical restraint and intimidation. Men were slower to take on factory work preferring to stay with the tried and true method of working by hand.

Children working in a textile mill in the Nineteenth Century.

The textile mills of the early factory system were not congenial places to work. They were noisy, hot and nasty and often dangerous. The hours were piteously long and the work repetitive to the point of insanity. There was no distinction made in the hours and conditions or types of jobs given to adults and children; all were required to work up to fourteen hours a day.

Pay could be irregular depending on the amount of production done at the time. It tended to be somewhat erratic and intense production could be followed by a lengthy and unpaid for lull. Not being able to pop out of the house and tend the garden or milk the cow, now that workers were congregating in the towns, meant that there was nothing to fill the gaps of inactivity and no wage. It also meant that the farm labourer and the factory worker alike were segregated even further from the rest of society and their potential for changing this was further diminished. Slums rapidly arose, not helped by the fact that the towns were just not equipped to manage the influx of population. The cramped conditions were highly unsanitary, depressing and degrading.

Children were the worst affected by the conditions often succumbing to infectious fevers that could not be fought because the small body was so weak and malnourished. Below is a report made on the appalling conditions that children were subjected to.

Report on the Condition of Children in Lancashire Cotton Factories [Report of Committee on Sate of Children in Manufactories, 1816 (III), pp. 139–140, 1796][4]

It has already been stated that the objects of the present institution are to prevent the generation of diseases; to obviate the spreading of them by contagion; and to shorten the duration of those which exist, by affording the necessary aids and comforts to the sick. In the prosecution of this interesting undertaking, the Board have had their attention particularly directed to the large cotton factories established in the town and neighbourhood of Manchester; and they feel it a duty incumbent on them to lay before the public the result of their inquiries:

1. It appears that the children and others who work in the large factories, are peculiarly disposed to be affected by the contagion of fever, and that when such infection is received, it is rapidly propagated, not only amongst those who are crowded together in the same apartments, but in the families and the neighbourhoods to which they belong.

2. The large factories are generally injurious to the constitution of those employed in them, even where no particular diseases prevail, from the close confinement which is enjoined, from the debilitating effects of hot or impure air, and from the want of active exercises which nature points out as essential in childhood and youth, to invigorate the system, and to fit our species for the employments and for the duties of manhood.

3. The untimely labour of the night, and the protracted labour of the day, with respect to children, not only tends to diminish future expectations as to the general sum of life and industry, by impairing the strength and destroying the vital stamina of the rising generation, but it too often gives encouragement to idleness, extravagance and profligacy in the parents who, contrary to the order of nature, subsist by the oppression of their offspring.

4. It appears that the children employed in factories are generally debarred from all opportunities of education, and from moral or religious instruction.

5. From the excellent regulations which subsist in several cotton factories, it appears that many of these evils may, in a considerable degree, be obviated; we are therefore warranted by experience, and are assured we shall have the support of the liberal proprietors of these factories, in proposing an application for the Parliamentary aid (if other methods appear not likely to effect the purpose), to establish a general system of laws for the wise, humane, and equal government of all such workers.

Finally action was taken to rectify this shocking state of child abuse. Sir Robert Peel, in 1802, put the facts before Parliament. Let it be noted that Peel himself was an employer of a thousand or so children. Outrage at the wretched conditions enforced on children led to a bill being passed for the health and moral welfare of the children in cotton factories. Children under nine were no longer allowed to be employed and the hours of labour were set at a maximum of twelve and none could be undertaken at night.

The factory buildings also had to be updated to comply with the new health regulations. Such requirements were: walls had to be whitewashed, ventilation had to be installed, and apprentices were to receive a new outfit once a year or more and were to attend church weekly so their souls could become as healthy as their bodies.

Children living in slums.

The Factory Act (1802)[5]

An act for the preservation of the health and morals of apprentices and others employed in cotton and other mills...Be it enacted that...all such mills and factories within Great Britain and Ireland, wherein three or more apprentices or twenty of more other persons shall at any time be employed, shall be subject to the several rules and regulations contained in this act...

...That all and every the rooms and apartments in or belonging to any such mill or factory shall, twice at least in every year, be well and sufficiently washed with quick lime and water over every part of the walls and ceiling thereof; and that due care and attention be paid by the master and mistress of such mills or factories to provide sufficient number of windows and openings in such rooms or apartments, to insure a proper supply of fresh air...

That every such master or mistress shall constantly supply every apprentice... with two whole suits of clothing..., one new complete suit being delivered to such apprentice once at least every year...

That no apprentice...bound to any such master or mistress shall be employed or compelled to work for more than twelve hours in any one day.... exclusive of the time that may be occupied by such apprentice in eating the necessary meals. Provided always that, from and after the first day of June, 1803, no apprentice shall be employed or compelled to work upon any occasion whatever between the hours of nine of the clock at night and six of the clock in the morning...

They must also receive some tuition in their trade and attend a church service on Sunday. Two independent inspectors were to have been appointed to visit the mills at regular intervals to ensure that the reforms were being carried out.

Real Reform?
The first 'factory act' paved the way for more reforms of working conditions, not limiting them to children nor to just the cotton industry. However, when evidence is examined from later sources it is rather difficult to see if the reforms really did much for the welfare of some of the workers or that many factories implemented them.

Evidence of Factory Workers of the Condition of Children [Report of Committee on Factory Children's Labour, 1831–2 (XV) p.192, etc.] 1832
Evidence of Samuel Coulson

5047. At what time in the morning, in the brisk time, did those girls go to the mills?

In the brisk time, for about six weeks, they have gone at 3 o'clock in the morning and ended at 10, or nearly half past at night

5049. What intervals were allowed for rest or refreshment during those nineteen hours of labour?

Breakfast a quarter of an hour, and dinner half an hour, and drinking a quarter of an hour.

5051. Was any of that time taken up in cleaning the machinery?

They generally had to do what they call dry down; sometimes this took the whole of the time at breakfast or drinking, and they were to get their dinner or breakfast as they could; if not it was brought home.

5054. Had you not great difficulty in awakening your children to this excessive labour?

Yes, in the early time we had them to take up asleep and shake them, when we got them on the floor to dress them, before we could get them off to their work; but not so in the common hours.

5056. Supposing they had been a little too late, what would have been the consequence during the long hours?

They were quartered in the longest hours, the same as in the shortest time.

5057. What do you mean by quartering?

A quarter was taken off.

5058. If they had been how much too late?

Five minutes...

5061. So that they had not above four hours' sleep at this time?

No, they had not...

5065. Were the children excessively fatigued by this labour?

Many times; we have cried often when we have given them the little victualling we had to give them; we had to shake them, and they have fallen asleep with the victuals in their mouths many a time...

And so it goes on listing accidents as a consequence of fatigue and the docking of pay while the child was off work due to the loss of a finger, regular beatings of children and instances of children, healthy before they began working in a textile mill but almost crippled after three years of labouring in one. This was a report made thirty years after Peel's reforms.

Such damning reports lead to another factory act being made in 1833 with particular detail being directed towards child labourers.

Factory Act (1833)[6]

An act to regulate the labour of children and young persons in the mills and factories of the united kingdom...Be it...enacted...that...no person under eighteen years of age shall be allowed to work in the night-that is to say, between the hours half-past eight o'clock in the evening and half-past five o'clock in the morning...in or about any cotton, woollen, worsted, hemp, flax, tow, linen, or silk mill or factory, wherein steam or water or any other mechanical power is or shall be used to propel or work machinery...

And be it further enacted that no person under the age of eighteen years shall be employed in any such mill or factory...more than twelve hours in any one day, nor more than sixty-nine hours in any one week...And be it further enacted that there shall be allowed in the course of every day not less than one and a half hours for meals to every such person...

And be it enacted that... it shall not be lawful for any person whatsoever to employ in any factory or mill aforesaid, except in mills for the manufacture of silk, any child who shall not have completed his or her ninth year of age...

The 1833 factory act also mentions that the previous act of 1802 had specified that two inspectors be allocated to make sure that the reforms were being carried out. It appears that the inspections were not made as stipulated so the 1833 act made it law that the King should appoint four people with authority to inspect the mills and factories to ensure the amendments to the factory act, in regard to the welfare of children were implemented.

Fluff

Another problem facing textile workers, particularly cotton mill workers, was cotton residue being inhaled and causing respiratory problems. We have an excellent illustration of this, again from Elizabeth Gaskell's *North and South*. A young girl, Bessy, lying tossing and turning on her sick bed, tells Margaret about her illness.

Working in a cotton mill.

'I think I was well when mother died, but I never been rightly strong sin' somewhere about that time. I began to work in the carding-room soon after, and the fluff got into my lungs and poisoned me.'

'Fluff?' asked Margaret enquiringly.

'Fluff,' repeated Bessy. 'Little bits, as fly off fro' the cotton when they're carding it, and fill the air till it looks all fine white dust. They say it winds round the lungs, and tightens them up. Anyhow, there's many a one as works in a carding-room, that falls into waste, coughing and spitting blood, because they're just poisoned by fluff.[7]

When Gaskell wrote her book the disease known as *byssinosis* had not been identified. Its common name was card-room asthma.

Industrial Revolution in London

While technology saw the rise of the factory system in many textile centres of England, London did not respond to the Industrial Revolution in the same way. There were no enormous textile mills or other steam powered manufacturing plants in London; it was very expensive to buy suitable land for factories in the city. This did not mean that the city did not play an important role in the textile industry.

What had been known as the domestic system before the Industrial Revolution became 'sweated' labour in London after 1800. The increased demand for cheaper goods, the influx of cheaper materials and a steadily growing population meant that for London to compete in the textile and clothing markets it had to take drastic action. Work standards broke down and semi-skilled labour replaced the skilled workers produced through rigorous apprenticeship. Lower wages were paid accordingly to the lesser level of skill and this kind of work attracted women who could often do the work at home. Others worked in what became known as 'sweatshops', mostly in salubrious attics or cellars supervised by a 'sweater' or 'garret-master'.

The growth of these organisations meant that trained tailors, called 'honourable' for their work ethics and attention to high quality production, were overtaken by the 'dishonourable' sweat shops that exploited their workers. The employees of the sweat shops worked long, long hours, received meagre wages and were often required to pay much of this back to the employer in return for food and rent.

The Sewing Machine

The invention and implementation of machinary to do the basic production work of spinning and weaving meant that fabric could be produced much faster than previously and therefore the cost of it could come down within the reach of the general public. It had negative impacts on some parts of the textile industry but ultimatley it took over tedious hand work.

An early model domestic sewing machine.

There was an invention, made by an American in Cambridge, Massachusetts, that was to revolutionise domestic sewing as much as it did factory clothing production. Elias Howe was a mechanic working in a shop that repaired fine machinery. He became intrigued with the idea of a mechanical sewing process.

It took him several attempts to come up with a machine that would sew quickly and use a stitch, lockstitch, that wouldn't just come out. Previously machines had been made and even patented but they relied upon chainstitch which was notrious for the stitches to pull out. Thomas Saint had brought one out 50 years before in England and in France Thimmonier employed 80 of them to make soldiers' uniforms. Unfortunately his workshop was broken into by angry tailors who smashed the machines fearing they would put them out of work.

Elias Howe was not the first to invent the lockstitch although there is considerable doubt as to whether he ever knew of a previous lockstitch machine by a man called Walter Hunt who had devised a machine but never took the inventoin to patent.

Howe attempted several versions of a sewing machine. He tried manufacturing and selling the first, which had multiple problems attached to it, not the least being the sale price for it.

The second machine saw many of the glitches of the first sorted out but it still did not take on, partly because of the workers' opposition to it. He did patent the second machine in 1846.

The sewing machine finally found interest in England with a corset maker who paid for the rights to produce it and pay royalties on machiens sold. Howe went to England at the invitation of the investor in order to design a sewing machine specifically for making corsets. It looked as though the sewing machine was set to take off.

Elias brought his family over from America, thinking they would all settle in Britain. Prosperity did not eventuate and Howe sent the family home again when he destroyed his relationship with the English corset maker. He followed not long after when he had gathered enough money for the ship.

On returning to America, Howe's wife died. Hoping to make a living though his sewing machine, Elias tried to restart his business. However, during his time away his machine had been reproduced by other people, including Isaac Singer, founder of the Singer Sewing Machine Company.

Howe and Singer became embroiled in a court case over the patent rights to the machine. After five years, Howe won out and Singer and his company had to pay Howe for royalties gained through Singer's machine sales.

Ten years later Howe set up the Howe Machine Company of Bridgeport, Conneticut. The new venture proved profitable and when he died, only two years later in 1867, he was well and truly wealthy. The company continued until the mid 1880s, run by the inventor's borthers-in-law.

A modern domestic Janome sewing machine.

Isaac Singer
Actor, inventor and industrialist, Isaac Singer is best known as the name behind the sewing machine. In 1851 Singer and Edward Clark, a lawyer from New York, set up a manufactory of sewing machines called I.M. Singer & Co. In 1865, well after the court battle with Elias Howe, the company was renamed the Singer Manufacturing Company.

Despite having to pay Howe a fortune in royalties for sales of a machine based largely on Howe's design for lockstitch, Singer and his company did nothing but prosper. Isaac Singer died in 1875, nine years after his rival. The company continued without him, just as Howe's did and in 1885 it brought out an improved machine with a vibrating shuttle.

During World War II a halt was put to the production of sewing machines so that full attention could be given to the making of armaments, specialising in artillery and bomb sights, though five hundred pistols had been made. Sewing machines returned to schedule after the war.

- In 1786 spun yarn of a particular quality was worth 38 shillings. In 1796 the same amount was only worth 19 shillings. The price continued to decline with it being worth 7 shillings 2 pence in 1806 and only 3 shillings in 1832. This devaluation meant that is certainly was no longer viable to produce hand spun thread
- Handcrafting stayed much longer as a viable production method of textiles in London than many of the other textile towns. One of its stable industries was tailoring
- In the late 1700s a man called Lieven Bauwens smuggled cotton spinning machinery out of England. He took it to Gent in Belgium and managed to kick start the mechanisation of the textile industry in his own country
- The American author, Alvin Toffler, born in1928, wrote, 'To think that the new economy is over is like somebody in London in 1830 saying the entire industrial revolution is over because some textile manufacturers in Manchester went broke.' Which shows how famous Manchester was for its textile industry
- During the Industrial Revolution Nottingham, was a major centre of lace production, particularly machine knitted lace

---

Notes
1. Dickens, Charles, *Hard Times*, Distributed by Heron Books, p. 24.
2. Gaskell, Elizabeth, *North and South*, Penguin books, Middlesex, 1978 (first published in Household Words 1854–5)
3. From Memoirs of a London Doll, Richard Henry Horne, 1846.
4. From English Economic History, pp. 495–6.
5. Sources of English Constitutional History, pp. 675–6.
6. Sources of English constitutional History pp. 726–7.
7. North and South p. 146.

PART FIVE

Textiles in the Modern World

CHAPTER THIRTEEN

Man-made Fibres

Not content with making marvellous cloth from the materials available naturally, human beings had to invent more sources of making fabric themselves. The first category is called regenerated fibres because they do in fact come from natural raw material such as cotton and wood fibre. These raw fibres are changed so significantly from their original state that there is very little natural about them.

In the second half of the Nineteenth Century a French chemist by the name of Hilaire Chardonnet was experimenting with the possibility of imitating silk. He finally came up with a fibre that suited. It was made from a derivative of plant cellulose, nitrocellulose or cellulose nitrate.

A selection of man-made fibres.

Chardonnet immersed his cellulose into an acidic solution to turn it into a liquefied state. It was then forced through tiny holes simulating the silk gland of the silk moth larvae, known as spinnerets. After drying the remaining substance was strands of nitrocellulose that resembled long silk fibres.

The process was not completely Chardonnet's invention. In 1883 the English inventor Joseph Swan had been producing fibre in a similar way but to use as the filament for his electric light bulbs and did not take it beyond that. Chardonnet's input was to further the process by making it into cloth which could be woven. Chardonnet exhibited his artificial silk at the Paris exhibition.

1890 saw another version of rayon made by another Frenchman, Louis Despeissis. In 1892 a pair of English chemists, Charles Cross and Ernest Bevin came up with viscose which did not require the use of the highly flammable cellulose nitrate. It was this version that forms the basis of today's viscose rayon.

Nylon
It was an American, Wallace H Carothers, who invented nylon, patenting it in 1935. It was the result of one of many experiments using different chemicals in the process of dissolving and pushing through spinnerets. Nylon's liquid form was particularly suitable for pouring through the tiny holes of the spinneret and when you look closely at the fibres of a nylon stocking it can be seen how fine the holes really are.

Six years later polyester came on the scene, the product of British chemists. After the war acrylics were invented using acrylic acid as the solvent.

The appearance of these man-made fibres took over the textile industry and although it didn't make natural fibres redundant by any means it certainly affected many of the textile factories producing yarns and fabrics that had been relied upon for thousands of years.

Nylon yarn.

Man-made Fibre Glossary

Acetate: Although a man-made fibre acetate originates from cotton which is melted in acid to make a thick, sticky liquid. It is then spun into fibre and woven into cloth. It was invented in 1921.

Acrylic: Consists of acriylontrile which comes from oil that has been made with carbon, nitrogen and hydrogen. It is then liquefied and spun into filament. Acrylic yarn is often further processed by steaming it and cutting it up so it can be spun like fleece.

Aramid: This textile was made especially for space travel. It is supremely strong.

Bi-component: These are nanofibres consisting of a nylon centre and a polyester outer skin. They are very fine and the threads resemble silk.

Nylon: Is made from a combination of benzene, a coal product and hydrogen. It is subjected to the melting process and pushed through the spinneret. It has elastic properties.

Polyester: Unlike nylon, polyester does not stretch. It is crease resistant and dries quickly. It is made up of a mixture of petroleum, ethylene glycol and trephthalic acid.

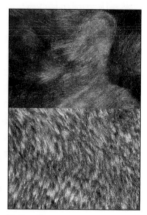

Rayon and Viscose: These fibres come from the woodchips of pine or spruce trees. Firstly they are steamed for about 15 hours and then caustic soda is added and the whole is transformed into a thick liquid, the consistency of molten toffee. The mixture is poured through spinnerets to make thread. It is generally used for anything requiring a shiny, satin finish.

Synthetic fibres, on the other hand, are completely man-made constructs. They are composed of long chains of chemical compounds called polymers.

Fake furs.

CHAPTER FOURTEEN

Fibre Art

In the Twenty-first Century in most parts of the world there is little need to hand spin and weave textiles in order to clothe ourselves. Mass-produced, western-style clothing like tee shirts and jeans will have found their way to even the remote spots, often at the cost of local traditional dress.

In the West no one produces their own cloth for their everyday clothes unless it is a passion or hobby. We may sew our own clothes, although the majority of the population now buys ready-made, but we don't have the time to spin enough thread to weave enough fabric to make a suit of clothes.

The tradition of doing things all by hand gave way when the factory system was fully implemented in the Nineteenth and early Twentieth Centuries, with the exception of sewing. The sewing machine became a common domestic feature and it was cheaper for a long time to sew your family's clothes rather than buy them ready-made. That is, of course, until the markets were flooded with the produce of cheap labour from third world countries in the last quarter of the Twentieth Century.

It looked as though hand spinning and weaving, dyeing and printing, embroidery and knitting would be skills that fell by the wayside and were forgotten. Luckily these arts intrigued enough people to relearn and keep the old skills alive and in time they became more than the retaining of historical crafts but art forms in their own right.

There are many, many artists who use textile mediums to express themselves and explore issues of the world around them.

Glenys Mann

Glenys Mann, renowned Australian textile artist says of her work:

> I am a contemporary quilt maker that works with 'found' cloth, namely old wool blankets and silk, all hand stitched. The cloth is natural dyed with leaves, bark, lichen and any found organic material. My work is inspired by emotions of the environment and emotions of everyday life. The 'horizon' series was an on going series that traced the emotions of always trying to achieve the 'horizons' that we set as goals, but never seeming to be able to attain. This series was finished with 64 art works.

It is easy to see in her work the emotions she, and many other Australians have for their 'sunburnt country, a land of sweeping plains'[1]

Glenys says that she began her Memory Cloth series in late 2008 thinking about the way cloth hangs in folds, free to 'retain' memories. While she was exploring the possibilities of this theme the infamous Black Saturday fires occurred in Victoria and her son and his family lost 11 of their friends as well as everything they owned.

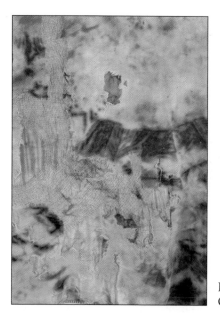

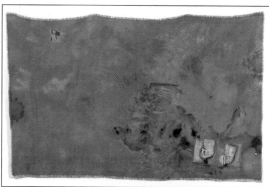

From the Memory Cloth series #6 Soft Footsteps.

From the Memory Cloth series #1 Environmental Chaos.

Josephine, inspired by the dancer Josephine Baker, a textile and mixed media sculpture, Courtesy of Lisa Lichtenfels and CFM Gallery, New York, NY, USA.

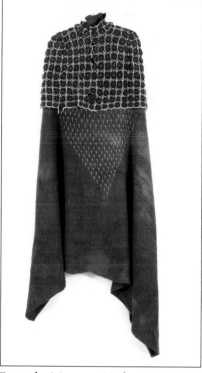

From the Memory Cloth series #13 Comfort Cope detail.

Clara by Lisa Lichtenfels, Courtesy of
Lisa Lichtenfels and CFM Gallery, New
York, NY, USA.

Kaffe Fassett sitting in front of one of his
textiles.

Kaffe Fassett: Fabric design.

Kaffe Fassett: Knitted quilt.

Kaffe Fassett: Tapestry.

This event caused Glenys to rethink her subject on an even deeper level. The yellow ochre of Environmental Chaos is evocative of the Australian bush, especially after the years of drought the countryside has endured. The overlaying black dye conjures up, in its smudgy application, the black smoke residue of fire. The bush fires that have ravaged, not only Australia but other parts of the world too are a major result of and a major contributor to environmental chaos.

Glenys Mann has been making quilts, as she calls her profound pieces, for more than 30 years. For quite a few of those years she struggled to conform to the rules expected of someone working in this genre. Her seams were never straight and her points never met perfectly and she wouldn't use only traditional cotton cloth. With the emergence of the contemporary quilt, now recognised as art rather than a hobby, Glenys found her niche.

In her artist's statement she states:

> To have the freedom to use cloth that held the knowledge of a previous owner.
> To use cloth that may be a bit worn!
> To hand stitch, but never with a perfect stitch or thread!
> To be able to play in the dirt and the leaves, to colour this precious cloth!
> To be able to set your own 'rules', if you really need them!
> And to have your work accepted by your peers, without any criticism!

Lisa Lichtenfels

Lisa Lichtenfels works in nylon – the nylon of pantyhose and stocking. Her work is figurative sculpture. It is very realistic in detail and individual in technique.

Lisa's work is highly refined; her technique immaculate. The viewer is first seduced by the beauty of the piece and then drawn further into it on recognising the medium she has used to construct it. Even without touching the skin of the figure it can be seen to be soft and warm with just the right amount of give in skin and muscle over bone; the illusion of realism is amazing.

Lisa has developed her technique over many years and describes the process below:

> The more realistic the superstructure is, the more realistic will be the figure, so, at each stage of construction, I try to use materials that are similar in density and character to the corresponding parts of the human body.
>
> The skeleton is anatomically drawn before it is fashioned out of sculptural aluminium armature wire, which is wrapped with yarn and then shaped to the proper thickness by sewing on compressed layers of white felt, which, as one of the densest fabrics, is useful in simulating bone.
>
> Where muscles need to be flexible, I will use elastic fabric, but for all other areas I use batting, which is a white non woven fabric, that when sewn onto bone has much the same feeling as muscle tissue.
>
> Fibrefill acts very much like fat, and can be slipped in between the batting and outer layers of nylon, which makes wonderful skin. Delicate surface features can be brought up by sewing the nylon layers with clear thread.
>
> Facial features of eyelids, brows, nose, lips and ears can be supported by copper wire scaffolding, covered with nylon and carefully needle modelled.

Kaffe Fassett

Kaffe Fassett is an undisputed master of colour. 'Glorious colour' was the name of a television series he created in the mid eighties. His first piece of textile art was a knitted garment incorporating 20 colours he had bought on a trip to a Scottish woollen mill. The colours he chose reflected those he had admired in the landscape. It was the beginning of a life long journey into textile colour and design.

From knitting needles to needlepoint tapestry, quilting and fabric design, Kaffe Fassett has explored them all, pushing their ability to portray colour to the limit. His designs are contemporary but always acknowledge the tradition they come from and quote the sources that have inspired him from around the world.

While some artists use textiles to give voice to social, political, environmental and political issues, designing works that provoke thought and cause discomfort, Kaffe Fassett, with his knitting, sewing, quilting and embroidery, on the other hand, unashamedly sings beautiful courtly love songs to soothe the ravaged soul.

It is easy to wax lyrical over Fassett's work but the truth is that behind the designs is hard work and research. He also has a passion to share his knowledge and has given slide shows, lectures, presented television programmes and published books on the how-to of the crafts he employs and he has instigated numerous projects involving people from all over the world. The first of these was the Pebble Mill at One Heritage Tapestry made up of over two and a half thousand pieces of needlework, each six-inches square, illustrating the favourite things of the people around Britain who made them. When they were all gathered together they were sewn together to form one large work.

Fassett's commissioned works include: tapestries for the Sea Princess cruise liner, an Elizabethan house in Yorkshire, the Edinburgh Tapestry Weaving Company and Marks and Spencer department stores; a mosaic mural for the entrance foyer of a theatre in California and many, many pieces for private clients.

Brandon Mably

Brandon Mably chose textile design in exchange for a career in cooking after a visit to the studio of Kaffe Fassett in the late 1980s. He was inspired by the range of colour and design, textile media and the wealth of inspiration that Fassett drew upon in his work.

Mably acted as Fassett's studio manager for several years and learnt all aspects of textile craft from knitting to needlepoint and fabric printing.

Mably also teaches and enjoys bringing out what he sees as a latent sense of colour in most people, encouraging them to open up and experiment with what they have felt too shy or nervous to display.

Jan Garside

Whites, blues and subtle greys imitate sand, pebbles and water in Jan Garside's delicately woven textiles. Translucent veils cascade downwards just like the waterfalls they represent. Shadows thrown behind the work form an integral part of the piece.

Jan uses traditional looms to weave her pieces, hand dyeing and incorporating vintage yarns with new and synthetic ones. She says her inspiration comes from a variety of sources but it is 'the ephemeral nature of light and the exploration of multiple imaging through translucent surfaces' that is a recurring theme.

Brandon giving a workshop.

Brandon Mably at work in his studio.

Brandon Mably: Fabric design.

Brandon Mably: Knitted bag.

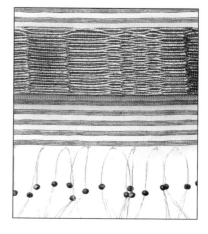

Jan Garside: Water.

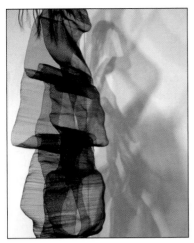

Jan Garside: Waterfall, Courtesy of Jan Garside.

Jan Garside: Pebbles.

Vicki Taylor: Bobbin-made lace sculpture.

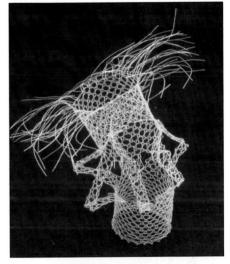

Vicki Taylor: Detained shows a stylised butterfly, made of bobbin lace, caught in a spiral of thick barbed wire. The juxtaposition of yarn and wire provides a tension that disturbs the viewer.

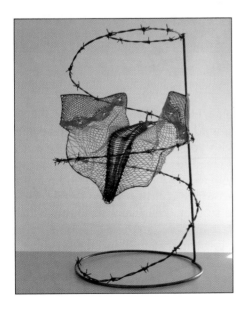

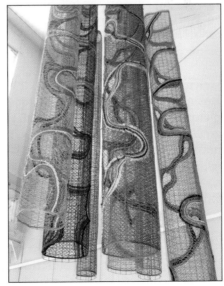

Vicki Taylor: Three Hanging cylinders.

The work shown here has a crisp and cool coherence that is imbued with light and shadow, redolent of the beach in the early morning or the late afternoon.

Jan moved from her career as a midwife to that of a textile artist, graduating from Loughborough University in 2002 with a BA Hons in Textile Design. From then on Jan has gone from strength to strength having been awarded Arts Council England grants, a Crafts Council award and she has been selected as a member of the Crafts Council Next Move Scheme and is a member of the Design Nation and Design Factory.

In her very contemporary art practice Jan looks to the past, particularly at the history of weaving to help her invent work for the present and future.

Vicki Taylor

The idea of bobbin lace conjures up images of dainty ladies in white caps sitting quietly at tables twiddling with small wooden things. On closer inspection the small wooden things turn out to be exquisitely turned wooden bobbins and the twiddling an intricate dance of threads so they interweave and form a structure. As for the dainty and demure ladies, Vicki Taylor will assure anyone that that aspect may well be a detail buried in the past. Vicki herself has recently returned from a trip through Europe in the sidecar of an ancient motorbike.

The cliché ridden images that still cling to our ideas of certain crafts and arts are ridiculous fictions born of ignorance. Vicki's lace work, produced by the same type of bobbin used hundreds of years ago, is not at all the type of thing that people think of when lace is mentioned. Her work is contemporary with a biting edge of social criticism.

Vicki also experiments with the abstract and finds that lace is the perfect vehicle to explore shape and subtlety of colour. She has participated in a project using long tubes of perspex that sat inside tubes of lace that hung from the ceiling.

Vanessa Taylor

Vanessa Taylor works in felt. She has been developing her technique over the last 15 years. Her passion for textile art has lead her to organise many textile workshops for schoolchildren and adults as well as instigating workshops for professional textile artists to come and share their special area of expertise.

Helen Evans

Helen Evans is a textile artist, writer and storyteller. Her small and intimate appliqué pictures depicting the local countryside and a wild and exotic interior landscape grew out of her storytelling skills. Working with young children, Helen began to make tactile picture books of her own stories to read to them while they interacted with the pictures. Colour features prominently in all her works and texture played an integral part of the books she made to encourage children to explore by feel. Often characters in the books were detachable so they could venture through the story in physical form at the same time they were involved in the words of it.

Producing books with lavish illustrations, sew, embroidered and often beaded, is a time consuming task and commissions for books took months to complete. Demand for Helen's work outstripped her capacity to make it and she began making one off pictures to satisfy the market.

While the techniques involved in the pictures are not significantly different to those used in the books, Helen's designs had broadened and her sense of colour and pattern have intensified in her work that doesn't have a written narrative.

Helen runs a gallery in Uralla, a small town just south of Armidale in New England, NSW Australia.

Judy Wilford

Embroidery made up of the minutest of stitches depicting birds, flowers and sweeping landscapes is the textile medium of choice for Judy Wilford who has won numerous awards and accolades for her work.

Fiona McDonald

Fiona McDonald never thinks of herself as a textile artist. Her training was in painting and drawing at Australia's oldest running private art school, Julian Ashton's in Sydney. Drawing and painting play a large part in her artistic output but she admits she can't get away from wanting to make things in cloth and yarn.

One of Fiona's favourite themes is toys, particularly dolls. These human-like imitations given to children to play with form the basis of many of her paintings, pastels and drawings.

After leaving art school Fiona began fashioning cloth dolls and painting them with the oil paints that she used on canvas. The first efforts were crude but as she experimented the figures emerged with wire armatures, striking facial features that often resembled bizarre performers and soon became life sized pieces. At this point she found she couldn't really refer to them as dolls. It caused a dilemma. What defined a doll? Was it purely a play thing for children? Was it the clothes or the painted features? Fiona responded to this by researching sculpture from the past.

She discovered that ancient Greek sculpture had been painted; it was not the pure white of the modern aesthetic perception of the classics at all. Later sculpture, mainly in the form of church statues of the Madonna showed figures that were sometimes articulated, painted and dressed in costly painted silks. These were not playthings but religious objects of reverence.

For a period Fiona left making dolls, figures or polychrome figurative sculptures as she called them and focussed on other things. When her interest returned to the doll it was in the form of a definite toy. Knitted dolls emerged from newly awoken knitting needles and decided they too would defy the generally accepted physical appearance of a knitted doll. Toys with sophisticated faces and wearing high fashion garments came out of the idea of the hand-made knitted doll of the past, made by a mother for her daughter.

Note
1. *I love a sunburnt Country* by Dorothy Mackeller.

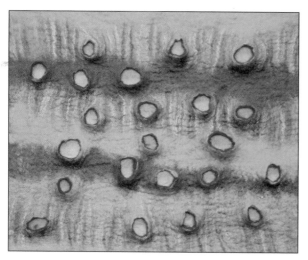

Vanessa Taylor: Hanging, felt.

Vanessa Taylor: Sculpture, felt.

Vanessa Taylor: Vessel, felt.

Vanessa Taylor: Vessel, felt and twigs.

Helen Evans: An illustration from Jacob's Tree.

Helen Evans: Landscape in New England.

Helen Evans: Fantasy Landscape.

Judy Wilford: Button Grass Flats Tasmania.

Judy Wilford: After Rain, Desert Flowers.

Knitted Dolls.

Johann, life size cloth and mixed media sculpture.

The Wife Of Bath.

CHAPTER FIFTEEN

Literary Textiles – Quotes, Metaphors etc.

Rumplestiltskin by Walter Crane.

Walter Benjamin (1892–1940), the German theologist, writer and essayist applies weaving as a metaphor for good writing:

> Work on good prose has three steps: a musical stage when it is composed, an architectonic one when it is built, and a textile one when it is woven.

An American writer, Ambrose Bierce, journalist and editor, 1842–1914 has an interesting idea about ghosts and how they always appear in shrouds or clothing:

> Accounting for the uncommon behavior of ghosts, Heine mentions somebody's ingenious theory to the effect that they are as much afraid of us as we of them. Not quite, if I may judge from such tables of comparative speed as I am able to compile from memories of my own experience. There is one insuperable obstacle to a belief in ghosts. A ghost never comes naked: he appears either in a winding-sheet or "in his habit as he lived." To believe in him, then, is to believe that not only have the dead the power to make themselves visible after there is nothing left of them, but that the same power inheres in textile fabrics. Supposing the products of the loom to have this ability, what object would they have in exercising it? And why does not the apparition of a suit of clothes sometimes walk abroad without a ghost in it? These be riddles of significance. They reach away down and get a convulsive grip on the very tap-root of this flourishing faith.

Perhaps the answer to ghosts wearing clothes lies in Grandma's prayer by Eugene Field:

> I pray, that, risen from, the dead,
> I may in glory stand
> A crown, perhaps upon my head,
> But a needle in my hand.
> I've never learned to sing or play,
> So let no harp be mine;
> From birth unto my dying day,
> Plain sewing's been my line.
> Therefore accustomed to the end
> To plying useful stitches,
> I'll be content if asked to mend
> The little angels' breeches.

William Butler Yeats, the great Irish poet (1865–1939) is attributed with having put these thoughts into a poem:

> I made my song a coat
> Covered with embroideries
> Out of old mythologies
> From heel to throat;
> But the fools caught it,
> Wore it in the worlds' eyes
> As though they'd wrought it.
> Song, let them take it,
> For there's more enterprise
> In walking naked.

Shakespeare often used textile imagery in his plays:

> O fello, come, the song we had last night.
> Mark it Cesario, it is old and plain.
> The spinsters, and the knitters in the sun,
> And the free maids that weave their thread with bones,
> Do use to chant it…
>
> *Twelfth Night*, Act 2, Scene 4

From the same play a Nineteenth Century author, Ella Rodman Church, in *The Home Needle*, 1882, has slightly altered a very famous line:

Children seldom achieve greatness, in the way of sewing, unless it is thrust upon them.

Robin Goodfellow, in *A Midsummer Night's Dream*, chances upon the rude mechanicals practising for their performance of Piramus and Thisbe. Robin, overhearing their

Twelfth Night.

plans recognises them as 'hempen homespuns' which does not reflect well on one of them, Bottom, a weaver and probably a guild member.

Alfred Lord Tennyson's lonely lady locked in a tower and cursed if she ever tries to leave it took solace in creating woven images from the things she saw in her mirror, the Lady of Shallott.

The enigmatic song, *Scarborough Fair*, which requires the singer's lover to make him a shirt without needlework, perhaps she considered felting it instead?

The Lady of Shallot at her loom.

There are a whole spate of wool related sayings:

- No wool is so white that the dyer cannot blacken it. Which is to say that no one is so perfect that nothing can be found that mars their character or reputation
- Wool gathering. Maybe this is related to that sleep that knits up the ravelled sleeve of care? To be distracted from the task in hand. Perhaps it goes back to the time when children were sent out to pick up wool left on fences and in bushes by the sheep and who would get sidetracked by some other interest
- To go for wool and come home shorn is to have the tables turned against you
- Dyed in the wool is a saying that means you are not able to be budged from your beliefs or opinions. It comes from the tradition of dyeing the fleece before it is spun so that the colour will mix evenly and through the wool
- Pull the wool over the eyes means to deceive another. It came about through the fashion of men wearing powdered wigs in the Eighteenth Century. If the wig didn't fit perfectly or was knocked awry through an accident then the wearer was rendered blind until the wig readjusted. It was not hard to tip a wig as they were heavy and clumsy. Added to this the fact that judges still wear wigs the meaning can take on an added connotation meaning that it is possible to fool a judge

CHAPTER SIXTEEN

Care of Textiles

Most garments that are made these days carry a label with detailed instruction on how to wash and care for them. In the urge to be universally understandable symbols have been developed to illustrate the procedures necessary. Unfortunately many of these are just too cryptic. How you care for a fabric depends on the purpose it was bought for, its age and whether you want to preserve it or just wear it out.

There are other fabrics that do not have labels and their care needs a bit more attention. Older fabrics, such as handmade quilts, wall hangings, baby's christening gown and Grandma's wedding handkerchief all need a bit of thought to their display and storage so that they will last for at least another generation.

A few commonsense steps should help you preserve them.

An old Bear.

- If the textile is very old, precious (even if only for sentimental reasons), or you are unsure of its worth or provenance and you suspect it may be worth quite a bit then the best thing is to contact an expert in the textile field at a museum. If the local museum does not have an expert on hand then they will know where to direct you to one
- Do not under any circumstances throw your textile into the washing machine! Domestic machines are rough enough for everyday items and they will make and older piece of fabric disintegrate entirely
- Equally disastrous is to put them in the dryer. Don't even joke about it
- Gentle dusting can be undertaken without too much worry unless the textile is disintegrating. Some fabric is so old or has been through so much stress that it should not be touched but taken straight to an expert
- Depending on the nature of the textile and its worth it may or may not take a gentle wipe

A lace handkerchief from a 1949 wedding.

with a damp cloth. This kind of cleaning I would only recommend for something like a beloved toy that cannot be left out of the owner's sight for a second. If it is truly and antique or collectable this must not be done

- I have heard of antique bears being bought at auction and then found to be playing host to minute creatures. I'm not sure I would take this step myself but they can be put into plastic bags, sealed and placed in the freezer for a week or so to kill the inhabitants
- Minor repairs can be done at home on items that are precious to the owner but not necessarily to anyone else. These can involve a surface wipe with a slightly moistened cloth, a good dusting, darning, stitching that kind of thing

While repairs are often needed leave it to the experts unless is a minor fix on an object known to be of insignificant value. The best way to preserve textiles is by prevention rather than cure.

Storage and Display
It is understandable that people want to show off their treasures. This is not always a good idea for the health of the object. Again, it all depends on the item, its age, provenance and value. However, here is a list of dos and don'ts if you are going to have them on display and how to store them afterwards.

- Never, ever put a textile of value in direct sunlight
- Keep away from any damp places
- Do not leave them where animals or children can reach them
- Keep them away from food preparation areas and where food can spill, splatter or fall on them
- Dust the objects regularly and check for insect activity, do not spray chemicals near the item
- If possible put the item in a glass cabinet with a door, this will help minimise dust damage and some insect damage too
- Do not display in a room with an open fire or too close to a covered one. Smoke will cause discolouration and bad odour

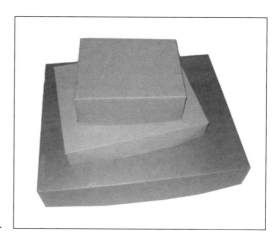

Archival storage boxes.

- Try to give the item a rest after a few weeks on display (depending on what it is)
- Storage can be in an archival-quality, air-tight box (not just any cardboard one). Plastic tubs with lids can be an option thought I wouldn't place anything really precious in one
- Try not to fold the item to be stored. If it is a garment search for a large archival-quality box and place the garment in it between layers of acid free tissue paper
- Hanging in cupboards can put stress on shoulders and straps of garments, it is usually preferable to store flat
- Moth balls do repel moths who will seek out textiles for their young to feed on. They smell horrible. Air tight containers are a far better option. Look out for new products that are environmentally friendly as well as anti insect
- To avoid moth balls at least in direct contact with your textile, which is a no-no, try using vacuum seal bags. These are available at department stores and through mail order catalogues. Put the items in the bag and follow the directions to suck out the air with your vacuum cleaner. Do not use this on valuable items and be careful in the procedure as it may be too rough for some fabrics

It will always be a fine balance of showing and caring for your textiles. Resting pieces in dark, dry and cool conditions is the best place for them and then bringing them out for your enjoyment.

I do want to stress that if you are in any doubt call in the experts!

Glossary

A

Abaca: A *bast* fibre, rather like hemp, grown in the Philippines, used mainly for cordage.

Absorbency: The amount of moisture the fibre or fabric can absorb.

Acetate: A man-made fibre from the cellulose found in cotton and/or wood pulp. It is fast drying and not easily creased. It is often a sumptuous looking fabric imitating silk. Acetone or alcohol will melt the fabric.

Acid Dye: A colouring solution for protein fibres, acrylic, polypropylene and nylon fabrics made with an acidic base. It is resistant to fading in sunlight and will not run in the wash.

Acrylic: A man-made fibre that consists of synthetic polymers, acrylonitrile. It has a soft, woolly texture. It is not very absorbent, doesn't crease easily is quick drying, soft yet tough. It can withstand direct sunlight and chemicals.

Adjective Dye: A dye which requires the use of mordents.

Alizarin: A rich red dye, once made from the root of the madder plant but mostly now made from chemicals.

Alpaca: Part of the llama family native to South American. It is has a fleece that is softer, finer but stronger than ordinary sheep's wool. It is technically a hair not a wool fleece. It was once a specialty fibre but is becoming quite common with the popularity of the animal spreading across the globe. Farmers in Australia often keep an alpaca or two to chase away wild dogs and other predators from their sheep flocks.

Alum: A commonly used mordant made from hydrated double-sulfate of alumina potassium

Amercian Pima Cotton: A cotton grown in Arizona, USA. It is a cross between Sea Island (considered the finest cotton) and Egyptian cotton.

Ammonia: An alkaline liquid used in natural dyeing.

Ammonium Sulfate: A chemical which makes an acid-forming salt. It is used with acid based dyes.

Alpaca scarf.

Aniline Dyes: Also called coal tar dyes. It is an early synthetic dye that was once extracted from aniline (coal tars). The term is now used to refer to all classes of synthetic organic dyes as opposed to dyes with an animal or vegetable base and synthetic inorganic pigments. Aniline dyes are graded according to their brightness and their resistance to light.

Animal Fibres: Hair from animals used to make textiles: wool, fur, cocoons and hair.

Angora goat: The fleece from this animal is called mohair. It is a luxury fibre that has a lustrous appearance.

Angora rabbit: A rabbit that is native to Asia Minor and Turkey. The fur is long and fine, light weight and fluffy. It has a tendency to matt and to shed hair. It has to be blended with another, longer haired fibre, such as wool, in order to be spun or felted. It is sometimes used to make felt hats.

Anthrax: or 'wool sorter's disease' is a highly infectious and often fatal disease caused by *Bacillus anthracis*. It got its popular name through the fact that people who regularly handled fleeces were often at risk of contracting it through any cuts in their skin coming into contact with infected animals.

Apparel Wool: Wool that is specifically used for making garments.

Applique: Stitching one piece of fabric on top of another to form a design. Reverse applique requires two or more pieces of fabric placed together and the top layers cut away to reveal the lower ones to form a design.

Aramid: Is a man-made fibre that is flame proof and cannot melt.

Assisi work: Is a counted thread embroidery where the central motif is outlined and the background filled in with embroidery stitches so that the motif is a negative shape. Originated in the town of Assissi in Italy.

Astrakhan: True Astrakhan is the skin of a caracul lamb from the Astrakhan area of Russia. The black curly texture has been imitated by using wool sometimes woven using a mohair warp. A pile is woven and then cut to simulate the soft curly wool.

Attenuation: The act of drawing carded fibres from the distaff into a strand of a particular thickness.

Axle: The central shaft of a spinning wheel.

Axminster: A town in England which was the original home of the Axminster carpet made from wool.

B

Baby Combing Wool: or French Combing Wool as it is also called is a worsted wool yarn, characteristically short and fine.

Backlining: The application of a louse-killing chemical along the backbone of a sheep.

Backstrap loom: A loom that uses the weaver's body to supply the necessary tension for the warp threads. It is held in place by a belt.

Bactrian Camel: The type of camel which produces hair that can be made into textiles.

Balanced: A plied yarn that doesn't twist back on itself. If you over twist a yarn you will find that it will want to double back and twist up its own length.

Bale: The measurement and packaging in which Australian and New Zealand Wool have their fleeces made into. Each bale weighs 150 kg (330 lb). In the US they are called 'bags'. This is to facilitate transporting. Cotton is also made into bales for shipping, they weigh approx 226 kgs (500lbs).

Banana fibre: A popular Asian fibre taken from the stem of the tree, not the fruit, and made into textiles and paper.

Basic Dyes: These are usually synthetic dyes that form bases for other dyes. They are aniline dyes. If the base is converted into a salt then it may become water soluble.

Basket Weave: a type of weave that has a characteristic basket-like appearance.

Bast: A fibrous plant whose stem consists of a hard outer coating and bundles of fibres inside. Hemp and flax are both common *bast* fibres.

Baste: A temporary form of stitching to hold fabric in place while a more permanent process is used to fix the pieces together. For instance in tailoring, collar faces are often *basted* in place before the sewing machine stitches them together. It is also referred to as 'tacking'.

Batik: A decorative process involving wax and dye. Melted wax is applied to a cloth to cover areas of the pattern not to be coloured. The piece is then immersed in the dye bath. When this has dried more wax may be applied to areas that need to retain that dye colour. At the end of the process the wax is removed through heat.

Baptiste: Named after the French linen weaver, Jean Baptiste this light weight, semi-sheer fabric is made from cotton, rayon or wool. It is woven from tightly twisted yarns with a mercerised finish.

Batt or Batting: Padding or stuffing made out of wool, cotton, manmade fibre or a combination of these which is made into sheets. It is often used in quilts between the decorated outer layer and the practical under layer. Its primary use is to add warmth.

Beading: A surface decoration where beads are sewn onto the fabric.

Beaver cloth: An English textile made to imitate beaver fur. It is made from wool or cotton and is napped on both sides. It has a twill weave that is heavily napped and then fulled. It is a heavy luxurious fabric that is used mainly for coats.

Belly Wool: The fleece that grows on the underside of a sheep, hence its name. It is a different grade of fleece from that which grows on the back of the animal and is characteristically uneven in quality and has shorter, weaker fibres.

Applique.

Woven Wool Astrakhan coat from the 1960s.

Machine-made braid.

A heavily beaded bag.

Upholstery Brocade.

Beetle and beetling: A large wooden mallet, the beetle, is used to soften and flatten cellulose fibres in woven fabric such as ramie and linen. It helps produce a lustrous finish to the textile. The process of pounding the fabric is called 'beetling'.

Bias: When fabric is cut across the bias it means the warp and weft threads are on a diagonal, not straight up and down. This gives a stretch to the piece of fabric and good for using on necklines and other curved seams.

Binders: The individual hairs in a sheep's fleece that run from one staple to another.

Binding Threads: Threads used to unite two or more ply into one composition.

Black Wool: Wool that contains coloured fibres. A fleece containing some coloured fibres, though predominantly white, will be put into the black wool pile. This will later be dyed a uniform colour.

Black-top Wool: Fleece that contains high quantities of natural grease that gathers at the ends of the wool staples and attracts dirt. It is often very good quality wool.

Blanket cloth: Made from a variety of fibres including wool, worsted, cotton and synthetics and blends of these. It is heavily napped by putting fabric over rollers covered in tiny wire spikes called teasels (after the plant it resembles). The textile is then fulled. It takes its name from the Flemish weaver Thomas Blanket (Blanquette) who lived and worked in Bristol, England in the Fourteenth Century. Blanket cloth is used for bedding and overcoats.

Blanket Stitch: An embroidery stitch that finishes the raw edge of the blanket fabric, acts a bit like an overlocker stitch in that it helps prevent the edges from fraying.

Bleaching: The removal of all impurities in fibre or a textile so that its whiteness is as bright as possible. It also refers to the total removal of colour from a textile but is not always the case.

Bleeding: When dye from fabric runs, often discolouring other fabrics.

Blend: A mixture of different fibres or grades of fibre in a piece of fabric or a yarn.

Blocker and Blocking: A frame used for drying skeins of wool. The damp yarn is wound firmly around the frame and left to dry. The skein can then be removed as a whole skein. The purpose is to dry it under tension. A similar effect can be achieved by winding the damp yarn around the legs of an upside down coffee table or chair.

Bobbin: The storage facility which yarn or thread is wound on to; traditionally a wooden spool. Domestic sewing machines use bobbins for the under thread. Bobbins are also used to make bobbin lace with.

Bodkin: A long, needle with a large eye, usually thick in diameter and bluntish or a small slim tool with a sharp point used for making holes in cloth or leather.

Body: Refers to the fullness and bounciness of fabric or wool staple.

Boiled Wool: The process for 'fulling' a piece of knitted wool fabric. The fibre mats together to form a solid, felt-like piece of textile.

Boiling Off: The process used for removing seracin from silk threads before they can be reeled.

Bombazine: The name comes from the Latin word *bombycinum* which means silky. Of course it is connected to the name of the moth from which silk is harvested, *bombyx mori* in China. Bombazine is an English textile, originally made of silk. It was popular in the Nineteenth Century as a mourning garment when dyed black.

Botany Wools: Derives its name from the fleece sent from Botany Bay in Australia. It now refers to high quality wool.

Bouclé: The name comes from the French word meaning buckled. It is a base yarn that has another, fancier twisted yarn wrapped around it to form loops and bobbles. It is also a fabric made with the yarn so that has a distinctive texture. It can be a heavy or light weight fabric depending on the weight of the yarn.

Braid: Is a form of interweaving threads, similar to plaiting. Is also the name given to a narrow, often continuous band of material with a decorative motif or design woven into it used to trim garments for decorative purposes.

Braid Wool: A coarse but lustrous wool, the coarsest grade of wool in the US.

Brandenburg: Decorative braid formed into a roll to make a fastening.

Breaking: The point in the process of removing flax fibres from its outer coating after it has a rollers or beaten with wooden paddles to break the fibre into a pliable substance. It is essential that the fibres are not damaged in the process. This is also called 'scrutching'.

Breaking Load: The point at which a fibre, yarn or fabric will break under tension.

Breech or Britch Wool: Fleece of very poor quality that comes from the back end of the sheep. It is often very dirty. It can be cleaned and used for hand spinning.

Breed Characteristics or **Breed Type:** The particular characteristics of a particular breed of sheep, for instance Merino which is a fine, crimped fibre or the Lincoln, which has a much coarser fibre with less crimp.

Bright: Term used for ultra clean and white wool. Cormo is a breed that produces this kind of fleece.

Brittle: Refers to harsh, dry, 'wire-like' fibre; much like the split ends in hair.

Broadcloth: Originally made from the spun yarn of short stapled wool, it was woven on a broad loom and then fulled to make it thicker and more durable. It is napped and then closely sheared to give a velvety texture. Broadcloth was one of England's major cloth exports. It is now sometimes made of cotton, silk or polyester.

Broadloom: An especially wide loom capable of weaving wider fabrics.

Brocade: Brocade is a jacquard weave with an embossed effect and contrasting surfaces. Can also be woven with synthetic or man-made fibres. Brocade is recognisable by its elaborate design in low relief and is often reversible so that the same figure appears on the reverse side but in the opposite colours (somewhat like a photographic negative).

Broderie Anglaise: A type of embroidery in which the fabric and thread are the same colour. Parts of the fabric are cut out to give a decorative, lacy type effect.

Brushed Wool: Fabric or yarn that is brushed to raise loose fibres to give a distinctive finish.

Buck Fleece: A fleece from a ram. The wool often has a heavy shrinkage rate because of the excessive oil in the fleece. This wool is not of the same quality as that of wool from ewes or wethers. It can also have a strong odour.

Buckram: A loosely woven fabric made in cotton or linen that is heavily sized to make it stiff. It is used for stiffening in clothes, such as in the collar or cuffs. It is also used to stiffen the brim of hats.

Bulk Grade: The largest percentage of grade in a lot of original-bagged wool.

Bump: Is a commercial measurement and delivery system for fibre. It consists of a cylinder of coiled fibre already for spinning.

Burlap: The American name for hessian.

Burry Wool: A fleece or wool fibre that is full of extraneous matter such as: burs, leaves, seeds, and twigs. It requires a lot of cleaning of these things in order for it to be used.

Bursting Strength: A mechanically applied strength test done commercially on fibres.

C

Calendering 1: Method of adding sheen to a fabric. For instance, if the fabric is dyed with indigo then one traditional method of calendering is to coat it with a mixture of egg white or blood and then beat it into the fabric until the sheen appears.

Calendering 2: The process of passing fabric through a machine consisting of heavy rollers, which rotate under pressure to smooth and flatten fabric, to close the intersection between the yarns, or to confer surface glaze. Often used with cellulose fabrics like linen and cotton.

Calico: Is one of the most common cotton fabrics available and one of the cheapest to buy. It is a coarse weave and is sized before selling to make it crisp. When the starch is removed calico can look rather drab. Calico originally came from Calcutta in India.

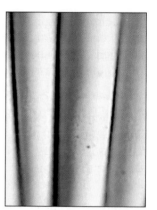
Calico.

Cambric: A cotton or linen fabric that is closely woven. It is calendered on the right side to give it sheen. It originates from Cambria in France.

Camel Hair: Hair, mainly from the belly, of the Bactrian camel, which has two humps and is native to China and Mongolia. It is a soft, light and fragile fibre that makes a light but warm fabric that is water resistant and wrinkle free.

Camelid: Any animal that comes from the camel family. Obviously camels, but also alpaca and llama.

Canary-stained Wool: A discolouration occurring in wool which may be caused by bacteria or urine It is difficult to remove this kind of stain by ordinary scouring and washing.

Candle: Is the fat on an unwashed fleece that stiffens as it sits.

Candlewick fabric: The base fabric is plain weave cotton or wool. Onto this candlewick (heavy plied yarn) loops is placed to form a design which is then cut to form a pile. It is often found made into bedspreads.

Canvas: A family of fabrics, usually made from cotton that have a heavier, more open weave made from plyed yarns. It is used to make things for heavy duty use and often is waterproofed to add protection. Artists also use canvas as a base for oil painting in which case it is covered with a layer or two of white sealant called gesso.

Carbonising: A chemical process for removing vegetable contamination from animal fibres.

Carded Fibres: Fibre, usually, wool, cotton or flax, that have been processed ready for spinning.

Carders: The brushes which are used in the carding process. For hand spinning, hand carders are used. For commercial spinning carding is done with large mechanised drum carders.

Carders.

Carding: A process involving the brushing fibres between two metal plates covered in bristles. The process rids the fibre of any contaminants such as burs or twigs, straightens the fibres and makes them parallel to each other. Once fibre is carded it can be spun.

Carpet: A heavy duty textile, often made of wool though also man-made fibres and in some cases silk. Carpets can be made by weaving or knotting short lengths of yarn onto a heavy open weave canvas.

Carpet Beetle: The larvae of the beetle that eats wool and other protein fibres.

Carpet Wool: A wool with coarse, heavy duty characteristics that will withstand the wear and tear of being walked on.

Cashgora: A fleece from the animal resulting from the cross breeding of cashmere and angora goats.

Cashmere: Is the fleece, or hair, from the Kashmir goat that is found in Kashmir, India, Tibet, Iran, Iraq China, Persia, Turkestan and Outer Mongolia. It is soft, silky and fine. It is a very good insulating fabric and doesn't crease. Of all hair fibres this one is most like wool and tends to be rather delicate. It is a luxury fleece.

Castle Wheel: The flyer is usually mounted above the wheel to keep the wheel compact. It is similar in design to other portable spinning wheels.

Cellulose Fibre: Is made from the cell walls of plants such as: cotton, hemp and ramie.

Chambray: Is a plain weave cotton using a dyed warp thread and a white filling. It has a faded look. It was originally made in Cobrai in France and is used for dresses, children's wear and aprons.

Chaffy Wool: Wool containing a considerable amount of chaff, that is, finely chopped straw.

Chain Stitch: An embroidery stitch involving looping the thread around the needle to form a chain like stitch. It is often used as a fill stitch in Indian embroidery.

Challis: This is a soft, lightweight fabric made from wool, cotton or man-made fibres. It was invented in Norwich, England in1832. The name comes from an Indian word, *Shallee*, meaning soft. It often has a delicate floral pattern printed on to it. It was generally used for making women's and children's clothes.

Chambray: A plain weave fabric that usually consists of a coloured warp but a white weft.

Character: The quality of wool in respect to its uniformity and amount of crimp.

Charka: Means 'wheel' and was used in India for spinning thread. It was made famous by Gandhi when he advocated that all Indian people spun their own thread and wove their own cloth in order to assert their independence.

Charmeuse: Is a satin weave silk with a crepe back sometimes called crepe-backed satin.

Cheesecloth: Is traditionally a loose plain weave cotton originally used for pressing cheeses. It is gauzy in appearance. It became popular for clothing in the seventies and a variety of fancy weaves were applied to it.

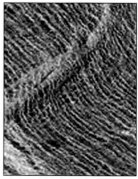

Cheesecloth.

Chenille: What gives chenille fabric its character is the chenille yarn filling of the weave: it has a pile, like velvet, all around the core fibre. Chenille is the French word for caterpillar which the yarn resembles ever so slightly.

China Grass: Is another name for the *bast* fibre, ramie

Chinchilla: Despite its name this fabric does not try to imitate the fur of the chinchilla (a small and now rare rodent from the Andes). The name is actually associated with the town of Chinchilla in Spain where the cloth originated. It is a woollen and sometimes cotton fabric with a twill or sateen weave and has a nubbed surface. It is used for making overcoats as it is a heavy fabric.

Chintz: A lightweight cotton from India. It was famous for its beautiful flowery printed designs. It became very popular in Europe in the Eighteenth Century. It is often finished with a wax or starch glaze which is only temporary. Permanent resin glazes can be applied and these will stand regular washing. Chintz that isn't glazed is called cretonne. Chintz gets its name from the Indian word, *chint*, meaning broad, gaudily printed fabric.

Classer: The person in the shearing shed who trims the fleeces and grades them into categories before baling.

Class-one Wool: The best quality fleece, usually produced by Merino sheep. The fleece has a fine, short, strong fibre with high elasticity and a strong crimp. It is a warm wool.

Class-two Wool: Not as good as Merino but still a superior fleece.

Class-three Wool: A coarse wool with fewer scales and not as much crimp as the other two classes of wool. Because they are smoother they have a more lustrous quality although they lack elasticity and strength. This wool is still able to be used for making clothes.

Class-four Wool: The least desirable of the classes of wool. The fleece is hair-like and coarse.

Classification by Fleece: Shows whether it is from lambs or older sheep, live or dead beasts.

Clean Content: The measurement of wool after it has been scoured and cleaned of all extraneous material.

Clean Wool: Wool after it has been scoured but sometimes refers to greasy wool that has had vegetable matter removed.

Clear Finishing: Is a process applied to worsted fabrics. The finished fabric is sheared, not brushed, to give it a smooth finish and crisp feel.

Clip: Amount of hair taken from a single angora goat.

Clock Reel: A device for winding hanks of yarn: some have counters to measure the number of winds.

Cloth: Another name for fabric.

Clothes Moth: In fact refers to the larvae of the moth that eats wool and other protein fibres. Moth balls made from naphthalene were a popular deterrent but tended to leave a strong odour. Sandalwood is also supposed to deter the moth.

Cloud Yarn: A term given to yarns of irregular twist obtained by alternately holding one of the component threads while the other, being delivered quickly, is twisted around it, and then reversing the position of the two threads; thus producing alternate clouds of the two colours.

Cloudy Wool: Discoloured wool often because it has been stored in damp conditions.

Coated Fleeces: Have you ever seen a sheep wearing a coat? Some farmers put coats on their sheep to keep the fleece from getting dirty and picking up plant matter.

Cockle: When a fabric has been shrunk the cockle is the wrinkle left where the shrinkage was inconsistent.

Colour and weave effect: Is the characteristic pattern made when different coloured warp and weft threads are used together in one piece of fabric.

Colour Matching: When a sample of dyed material is given from which to make a larger batch of dye and the proportions of pigments has to be managed to get the same hue.

Colour Fastness: The amount of colour retained by yarn or fabric after subjected to washing or exposure to sunlight.

Colour: The natural colour of the fleece. White and cream are preferable to coloured wools or those with canary stains or other discolouration.

Colour Defect: Anything that taints the white or cream fleeces such as canary stains, coloured wool mixed in with the white or any other form of discolouration.

Colour Fastness: That property of a dye to hold its colour even when put under certain stressful conditions, e.g., exposure sunlight, heat, immersion in water.

Combed fibres: Fibres that have been combed to remove the short fibres and straightening the longer ones so they lie parallel to each other.

Combing: The process of straightening carded fibres and to further remove impurities. As its name suggests combs are used. Combing can be done dry, that is without oil being added, or with oil so the fibres are easier to control.

Combing Wool: Wool that is long enough to comb.

Common: A US grade of wool, one up from the coarsest grade. It is supposed to have got its name from the common sheep from which it is shorn.

Complements: These are complementary colours that as found on a colour wheel. The primary colours are red, yellow and blue. When these are added to each other they make the secondary colours of: green (yellow and blue), purple (red and blue) and orange (red and yellow). When these have been added to the colour wheel their opposites are: yellow and purple, red and green and orange and blue. These are known as complementary colours.

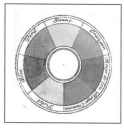

Colour wheel.

Composition: The components and their amounts that make up a particular fabric.

Condition: The moisture present in a textile fibre in its raw form. Also with regards to wool it is the amount of impurities it contains. A fleece said to have a heavy condition means it will shrink a lot.

Cone: Conical base onto which yarn is wound producing a cone.

Copp: Is the cone of fibres that build up on the spindle.

Corduroy: A fabric, traditionally made from wool which has a distinctive ribbed effect produced by weaving a cotton foundation in plain or twill weave with vertical cut-pile stripes, called wales.

Core-testing: The coring of bales or bags of wool to determine the clean content

Core Yarn: A yarn made by winding one yarn around another to give the appearance of a yarn made solely of the outer yarn.

Cortical Cells: The spindle shaped cells forming the inside structure of a fibre.

Cotted: A fleece that contains matted or felted fibres.

Cotton: A cellulose fibre from the boll of the cotton plant.

Cotton Damask: Fabric woven on a Jacquard loom using mercerised yarn.

Cotty Wool: Wool that has matted or felted on the sheep's back. The problem is caused by an insufficient amount of oil being produced by the sheep.

Count: The number given to a yarn of any material, usually indicating the number of hanks per pound of that yarn. May also refer to the fineness to which a fleece may be spun.

Crabbing: Is a process of rotating the worsted fabric over cylinders through a hot-water bath, or series of baths, each hotter than the one before, followed by a cold-water bath.

Crease-Resistant: This refers to the ability of a fabric to resist and recover from creasing during use. Wool is considered to be very crease resistant, while cotton is not. And don't even get me started on linen!

Creel: Is a storage rack for rolls of textiles

Crepe: A fabric with a distinctive, puckered surface due to different tensions used in the weaving process. Similar effects can be produced by using different types of yarn or applying chemicals.

Cretonne: Heavy ribbed fabric made from cotton.

Crewel Embroidery: Is an embroidery technique worked in wool and consists of an intricate design outlined and filled with a number of different stitches. The effect is rich. The origin of the word crewel possibly comes from an old word describing the curl in the fibre of the wool.

Crimp: Is the amount of waviness in wool fibre.

Crimp Recovery: A measurement for assessing how well a fibre returns to its natural crimped state after being pulled straight.

Crocking: The act of dye rubbing off fibres or fabric by friction.

Crinkle: The amount of waviness retained by a single fibre after it has been taken from a lock.

Crochet: A manner of making fabric using a stick with a hooked end. It is related to knitting but only uses the one implement and the loops are made by pulling the thread through itself and other stitches.

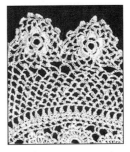

Crochet.

Crop: To remove loose fibres from the cloth's surface after it has been woven.

Croop: The name of the sound made by silk when rubbed or compressed.

Cropping: The trimming of the pile of a fabric to make it even or the trimming of loose threads and fibres from a piece of finished weaving.

Crossbred or **Cross Breed:** Wool produced by interbreeding different species of sheep.

Cross colour: The use of different coloured warp and weft threads.

Cross-stitch: An embroidery stitch in which one stitch is laid down diagonally and another of the same length is laid across it, also diagonally to form a small cross. If has become a popular form of embroidery in which to make complex pictures, as subtle shading effects can be obtained.

Crutching: The shearing of a sheep's rear end before the annual shearing of the whole fleece. This is to help prevent blowfly strike.

Crutched Wool: Wool that has been clipped from rear end and udder area of ewes in the early spring to prevent collection of manure and fly strike.

Cuticle: The outer layer of cells of a woollen fibre. They are hard and flat and overlap rather than fit snuggle together.

D

Dags: The fleece of a sheep's rear end when matted with urine and faeces.

Damask: Has a reversible pattern woven into it. On one side the pattern is satiny and on the other side the ground has the lustre.

Damp Wool: Wool that has become damp or wet before or after storage.

Darn: The term used for making woven repairs in woollen products, typically socks. Traditionally a round wooden block is inserted into the sock to spread it while working on it. Small warp stitches are inserted across the hole and these are then woven across until the hole has disappeared.

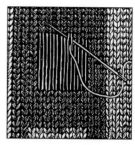

A darned hand-knitted sock.

Dead Wool: Wool taken from the carcass of a sheep that has died in the field or been killed. It is sometimes called 'merrin'. It is an inferior grade of wool.

Decatising: A mechanical process using steam for smoothing out fabrics, particularly wool. Fabric is placed around a roller with perforations in it from which steam issues through and around the fabric.

Defective Wool: Wool that contains excessive vegetable matter, such as burs, seeds, and straw, or which is kempy, cotty, tender, or otherwise faulty.

Degreasing: Any method that removes yolk, suint, and dirt from wool.

Degumming: The boiling-off of silk in silk and hot water, in order to dissolve and wash away the natural gum (seracin) which surrounds the fibre.

Delaine Wool: Fine combing fleece, originally from Ohio and Pennsylvania. The Delaine-Merino breed of sheep is a particular breed that produces this class of wool.

Demi-lustre Wool: A semi lustrous wool but not enough to be classed as lustre wool. Romney sheep grow this class of wool.

Denier: A unit of weight indicating the fineness of fibre filaments and yarns.

Denim: A basic cotton or blended fabric woven in twill with a strong, hard wearing surface. It is characteristically blue. It gets its name from the French term *serge de Nimes*.

Density: The number of wool fibres per unit of a sheep's body. The finer classes of wool have denser measurements of fibre.

Devore: A technique for decorating fabric in which the pile of the fabric is burnt away with acid.

Differential Dyeing: Term for the same kind of fibres which may have different dyeing properties from the standard for that type.

Dimity: Is a plain weave cotton with a crosswise of lengthwise rib or crossbar effect. It is sheer with the ribbing effect slightly less so. It is crisp in texture and resembles lawn in its feel and look.

Dingy: Wool that is dark and tends to shrink heavily. May be caused by excessive yolk, poor farming conditions, or parasites.

Dipping: A chemical bath for sheep to reduce louse infestation

Direct Dyes: Aniline dyes which are good for dyeing cellulose fibres like cotton or flax. They do not need a mordant to fix them. They are characteristically duller than acid or basic dyes. They are very colourfast.

Direction of Twist: The twist is the natural direction the yarn wants to twist in. S typifies one way, Z the other. You can find out which ways a yarn will twist by holding it in a vertical position and looking closely at the angle of the spiral. The angle of the S twist will match up with to the centre part of the S. The angle of the Z twist will match up with the centre of the Z. When spinning, the wheel should rotate counter clockwise for an S twist and rotate clockwise for a Z twist.

Dirty Tips: The weathering that occurs on the ends of some locks. These may not completely wash out or take dye evenly.

Discolour: Fleece, yarn or fabric which has become stained through contact with something else, such as another dyed product, fading in the sun, water stain or anything else which has altered the intended colour.

Distaff: Wooden rod to which carded wool, flax or cotton is loosely wound. It is held under the arm or tucked into the belt and fibres drawn from it which are then fed into a spindle. The distaff was originally this hand-held one but as spinning wheels became generally used the distaff became attached to the machine leaving two hands free for guiding the thread.

Diz: This is a tool to help form an even top when combing wool. Diz were originally made of carved horn.

Dobby: A fabric woven on a dobby loom. Small, geometric figures are characteristic of dobby fabric.

Dobby: A mechanism that controls the heald shaft movement of a loom.

Doggy: Inferior fleece that lacks quality of distinctive breeds. These wools are usually short fibred and coarse.

Domestic Wools: All wools grown in your own country as opposed to those imported.

Doubling: The process of combing by twisting together two single yarns to form a double yarn.

Double Coated: Some breeds of sheep have two coats. Sometimes it refers to different colours; for instance a darker, longer coat over a shorter lighter coloured coat.

Double Cloth: A textile product made from two pieces of cloth woven together.

Double Drive: Both the flyer and bobbin are driven by belts from the drive wheel. The bobbin pulley (or whorl) is smaller, which determines the spinning ratio.

Double Fleece: A fleece consisting of two year's growth.

Doupion or Doupioni: Term used for the phenomenon of double silk worm cocoons. It is also used to refer to the rougher quality of silk made from these cocoons. Because the filaments are tangled and sometimes broken they cannot be reeled off

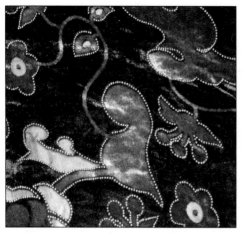

Sevore scarf.

Fabric.

in the same manner as top quality silk and it has to be spun instead. Commonly found in shantung or pongee silk.

Down Wool: Also known as 'Hill Wool'. The fleece of medium fine quality from breeds such as the Southdown and the Shropshire. They tend to have a fine and curly short staple particularly suitable for felting.

Drafting (or Drawing): A term used for the process of pulling fibres out of the carded bundle, usually attached to a distaff in order to feed them to the spinning device itself, such as a drop spindle or spinning wheel.

Paper patterns.

Drafting Triangle: Refers to the triangle made by the fibre being drawn from one hand and fed to the other, spinning hand. The height of the triangle should never be more than a length of the fibre being used.

Drape: This is the term to describe how a fabric hangs. Many factors affect the drape of a piece of cloth: the fibre it is made from, the weave, the dye and other finishes. Some fabrics have a naturally good drape others are too stiff,

Drenching: Squirting liquid worm medicine into a sheep's mouth.

Drive Band: The cord that runs between the wheel and the flyer of a spinning machine.

Dress: Means a woman's garment, the act of getting into one's clothes, clothing in general, men's or women's. It can also refer to the finish on a piece of cloth.

Dressmaking: The art of turning fabric into clothing for women and children. Paper patterns became very popular so that anyone could make a fashionable outfit.

Drill: A cotton twill with closer, flatter wales than gabardine. It can be left a natural grey or dyed and bleached. When it is dyed khaki the fabric itself is then called by that name.

Drip-dry: The term for hanging a garment on the line or on a coat hanger to dry without other artificial means. Many newer man-made fabrics are drip dry so that they don't require ironing or drying in an electric dryer.

Drive Ratio: Ratio of wheel diameter to flyer whorl diameter (or bobbin whorl on a bobbin lead wheel). Governs how much twist you get in the yarn for each treadle.

Drop Spindle: A spindle that hangs freely from the fibre.

Drum Carder: A rotating drum, covered with carding cloth, used to card fibres mechanically.

Dry clean: A purely chemical method of cleaning fabric. Used for clothing made from fabric not liking immersion in liquid because it is delicate or it is handmade, has much embroidery, bead or is tailored and might shrink in a bath.

Dry-Spun Flax: Flax spun without added water; results in a coarser, hairier yarn.

Duck: A fabric originally made of linen but now mainly in cotton. It has a plain weave and sometimes a crosswise rib. Its other name is canvas. It became known by the name 'duck' in the Eighteenth Century when British sails were given the trademark of a duck. It has a very firm weave and is used for all sorts of things from clothing to painting portraits on.

Duffle: Is a thick, heavy material made from wool. It takes its name from its place of origin, Duffel, in Belgium. We know it for the coats and bags named after the fabric they are made from.

Dull: A yarn or fibre with no lustre.

Dusting: The second step in commercial wool processing (after sorting). The purpose is to remove as much dirt and sand as is possible before scouring.

Dye: The source of colour to change the colour of yarn or fibre or cloth. Dye can be chemically made or got from natural sources such as plants.

Dye Activator: A pure alkali powder for use with all reactive dyes on cotton and cellulose fibres.

Dyeability: The capacity of fibres to accept dyes.

Dye bath: The solution (usually water) containing the dyes, dyeing assistants and any other ingredients necessary for dyeing.

Dyed in the Wool: Fleece or spun yarn dyed before it is processed.

Dyeing: The process of applying a dye colouring to fibre, yarn or fabric.

E

Earmark: Marking a sheep's ear for identity purposes.

Eastern Pulled Wool: Wool is pulled from the skins after it has been loosened, usually by a depilatory. Pulled wool should not be confused with dead wool.

Ecru: The natural colour state of a fabric before it is exposed to the colouring processes.

Elasticity: The ability to return to its original length after being stretched or compressed. Wool has more elasticity than cotton.

Elastomer: Is a man-made rubber-like textile that can stretch three times its own length. After stretching it will return to its original shape.

End: A warp yarn.

English Combs: Hand combs used in preparing top.

Evenness: This term refers to the uniformity of the fibre throughout the fleece.

Ewe: Female sheep

Exhaustion: The amount of dye absorbed by the fibre, yarn or fabric from the dye bath.

F

Fabric: Any cloth woven, knitted or made using other processes from fibres.

Face: The finished, visible side of a piece of fabric.

Fall Wool: American term for fleece shorn in the autumn.

Fast Colour: A dye that is very good at retaining its hue in conditions like harsh sunlight.

Fellmongering: The process of gathering wool from the fleeces of dead sheep.

Felt or **Felting:** Non-woven fabric made by layering thin sheets of carded wool fibres, then applying heat, moisture and pressure to shrink and compress the fibres into a thick matted cloth. Not the same as fulling which is the shrinking of a pre woven or knitted fabric subjected to a similar process to felting. The finished pieces look very much the same.

Feltability or Felting Property: The ability for certain fibres to interlock in the felting process.

Fibre: The basic raw materials in textiles which can be natural or man-made, such as wool, silk, cotton, flax or nylon.

Fibre Fineness: The diameter of a fibre usually measured in microns.

Fibre Length: The staple length of the fibre. On combing wools, this is often 3–8 inches, on the down wools 1.5–3 inches. With cotton, it may be ¼–1 inch long. *Bast* fibres, likes flax, may have a staple length of 36 inches.

Fibre Thickness: The average diameter of the fibre usually measured in microns.

Filament: A fibre of indefinite or extreme length, some of them miles long. Cultivated silk is a natural filament, while nylon and polyester are synthetic filaments though they originated when imitation silk was begin invented. Filament fibres are generally made into yarn without the spinning operation required of shorter fibres, such as wool and cotton. Filament yarns are smoother and more lustrous than spun yarns.

Fine Wool: The finest grade of wool.

Finishing: Any further process applied to fabric after it has been woven and removed from the loom. It can even mean anything that is done to a fabric after it has been dyed or decorated in some way. Sometimes chemical or other applications are applied to the fabric to make it stiff or shiny. In some cases these need to be removed before the product can be used.

Flame Retardant: Is both the measure of a fabric's ability to withstand heat and flame or an additive that will increase that resistance.

Flammability: The ability of a textile to burn under specified test conditions.

Flannel: A woollen fabric of plain or twill weave, made of wool worsted, cotton or rayon, which originated in Wales. It has a dull finish with a soft napped surface. It must be pre shrunk or washed before making into garments as it will shrink.

Flannelette: A cotton fabric woven in plain or twill and finished with a nap, usually on one side only. It is often used for making sleepwear.

Flax: The plant whose long stalk provides the source of *bast* fibres for spinning linen thread.

Fleece: The wool from one sheep, either as it comes from the animal or after it is rolled into a bundle and tied. Is also the name given to a fabric made of wool, cotton and some specialty fibres. It has a deep soft nap and is a thick, bulky material. Used mainly for making coats.

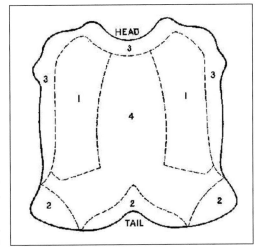

Fleece.

Fleece rot: An infection on the sheep's skin caused by a lot of wet weather.

Float: A length of yarn on the surface of a fabric between adjacent intersections of warp and weft threads.

Flock: Is the collective noun for a group of sheep. It is also the name given to unspun wool or cotton that is used for stuffing things like pillows.

Flock.

Footrot: a disease in sheep that affects their feet and ability to walk.

Flyer: A rotating device that adds twist to the slubbing or roving and winds the stock onto a spindle or bobbin in a uniform manner.

Flyer Bearings: Holds the flyer it is made from the same material as used in wheel bearings

Folded Yarns: Another term for plied yarns.

Flyer Lead: A single band drives the flyer. The bobbin has an adjustable friction band to slow it.

Follicle: The skin structure from which hair or wool fibre grows.

Footman: The vertical connection between the treadle and the crank.

Frame Spinning: The manufacture of yarn by easing a sliver of fibre by means of rollers and then inserting twist by means of a flyer, a ring and traveller, or a cap.

Frame Wheel: The flyer is usually mounted above the wheel so that it takes up less room. Also called a 'castle wheel'.

Free Wools: Usually means wool that is free from defects, such as vegetable matter.

French Combing Wool: Wools that are medium length between strictly combing and clothing. French combs can handle fine wools. French combing is done dry.

Fribby Wool: Wool containing an excessive amount of second cuts and/or sweat locks.

Frowzy Wool: A harsh wool, lacking in character.

Fugitive Colours: Dyes that fade especially in sunlight or through washing.

Fulling: The operation of shrinking and felting wool that has already been made into fabric.

Fulling Agent: A chemical, usually a surfactant, that acts as a lubricant during the process of fulling.

Fustian: Is an old fabric that was very popular in the Middle Ages and up to the Seventeenth Century. It is a mix of wool and linen or cotton and linen. It gets its name from Fustat near Cairo in Egypt.

G

Gabardine: Is a fabric made of worsted cotton, rayon or mixtures of these. It has a twill weave and is tightly woven. It is hard wearing. Used mainly for men and women's suits and coats.

Gingham: Plain weave lightweight cotton with a distinctive check pattern. It derives its name from the Italian expression *ging-gang* meaning striped.

Ginning: Is the mechanical process that removes the cotton fibres from the seed. The cotton gin was invented by Eli Whitney toward the end of the Eighteenth Century.

Glauber's Salt: Sodium sulfate. An acid used in dyeing to help protein fibres take colours evenly.

Grade: Is the term given to the size of knitting needles used for knitting a garment. The larger the number of the gauge the smaller in diameter the needle is and therefore this will make the knitting itself finer. And the reverse is true too. The smaller the gauge the larger the needle and the chunkier the knitting.

Grading: Is a term used for classifying fleeces according to their qualities in fineness, length of staple and whiteness.

Grey Wool: Is the term given to fleece that is not pure white but contains some fibres of a darker colour which happens more often with sheep that have black faces.

Greasy Wool: Unwashed, unprocessed sheep's wool complete with the natural lanolin produced by the sheep.

Great Wheel or Walking Wheel: An early form of hand turned spinning wheel. The spinner would turn the wheel with one hand while drawing out the carded wool with the other. The spinner would then walk away from the wheel while the yarn twisted into thread. It would then need to be wound onto the spindle and the process started again. It is estimated that a woman spinning eight hours a day could walk 20 miles just using the Great Wheel.

Grist: A measurement of yards per pound of weight. Grist is synonymous with 'count'.

Guanaco: A woollen fibre from the Guanaco, a relative of the llama.

Guar Gum: Is an industrial strength gum used to thicken the paste used for burning out the fabric design in devore.

Guard Hair: Is the wool which sticks out from the undercoat of an animal. It is typically coarse and hair like.

Gummy Wool: Wool that has been scoured but retains some of the yolk in it.

Gutta: Is the French word for 'resist' and it is a form of resist dyeing using a water or solvent soluble gum or resin to create the pattern on the fabric. Similar in function to wax in batik.

H

Hessian: Is the German name for a coarsely woven fabric, usually made from jute fibre. It is also known as burlap. It is mainly used to make sacks for storing things like potatoes. It is not often used as a clothing material. A hessian like textile was used to make a sackcloth or hair shirt.

Hessian.

Habick: A device used in Medieval times to hold fabric under tension during its final preparation and dressing. It is related to the frame used

Hackles: The comb for preparing flax or hemp fibre by removing any bits of outer stem.

Hackling: The process of removing any extraneous material from flax or fibre after it has been retted. The flax is pulled through a comb called a hackles, sometimes there is a series of hackles getting progressively finer.

Hair Fibres: Wool-like fibres from animals other than sheep, including the alpaca, llama, vicuna, cashmere goat, angora goat, angora rabbit and Bactrian camel.

Hand or **Handle:** Term used for how the wool feels to touch whether it is soft, coarse, fine, long is springy or straight.

Hand-washed Wool: Wool washed on the animal before it is shorn from the sheep. Really has to be done by hand.

Handspun: Yarns which are spun by hand using a spindle or spinning wheel.

Human hair.

Hank: A measurement of yarn which, for some fibres is a specific amount.

Hard Twist: A yarn with increased twist.

Harsh: A coarse, rough wool.

Harris Tweed: Is a tweed fabric hand woven in the islands off the North coast of Scotland. Harris Tweed comes in two types: that made from hand-spun yarn and that made form machine-spun yarn. Because it is handmade it is very time consuming to make and is very expensive.

Heald: A small device made from steel, wire or even cord with an eye through which a warp thread can be inserted.

Heald Shaft: A weaving frame that has healds in place

Heavy Wool: Wool that still has a lot of grease or dirt in it and therefore will shrink a lot during scouring.

Hemp: The fibre from the plant *Cannabis sativa*.

Herringbone: A combination of twill weaves in which the direction of twill is reversed to produce stripes resembling herring bones.

Herringbone Stitch: Is an embroidery stitch that imitates a herringbone pattern.

Herringbone Twill: A type of twill weave made up of vertical stripes alternately right hand and left hand in direction, giving it a herringbone look.

Hogget Wool: Hogget is a sheep that is 12 to 14 months old and has never been shorn. It is more mature than lamb's wool but is still fine and soft and strong.

Homespun: Named for the fact that this fabric was originally produced in the home for the use of its occupants. It was generally a coarser yarn making a coarser cloth that is tough.

Houndstooth: Describes the check pattern more than the fibre it is woven from. It is a distinctive check pattern where the checks are not square but more star shaped.

Hue: The colours that appear in the spectrum: red, orange, yellow, blue, green violet. It is also used to describe colours that tend towards one of those colours.

Hungry Fine: Is a fine wool fibre that has been caused by poor nourishment.

I

Ikat: Resistance dying method in which the warp and/or weft threads are dyed before they are woven in order to produce a decorative pattern.

Impurity: Any extraneous material present in a fleece or textile product such as seed heads or twigs.

Inchworm: A name given to spinners who are too slow and careful about drawing out and spinning their fibres due to lack of inexperience. Such methods halt the flow of spinning and the production of consistently smooth yarn.

Indigo: A blue dye obtained from plants of the *Indigofera* family. It is used as a vat dye and must ferment for a certain time to be of any depth of colour.

ISO: International Standards Organisation is an international body which looks out for the quality of goods.

J

Jacquard: An invention from the late Eighteenth Century to enable weavers to lift several warp threads at a time in order to produce complex patterns in the fabric. It was invented by Joseph Jacquard in France.

Jersey: Is a knitted fabric made of a number of different fibres. It has lengthwise ribs on the right side of the fabric and cross wise on the back. It is stretchy and crease resistant. Named after the island of Jersey where it was invented.

Jute: A vegetable *bast* fibre often used for basketry, rope and coarse fabric used to make sacks.

K

Kapok: A vegetable seed fibre from the kapok tree.

Kemp: A type of wool fibre that doesn't function as normal wool fibre does. It won't felt or take dye and is very coarse in texture. It is often found around the head and legs of the sheep.

Keratin: A protein substance which is the chief component of wool fibre.

Khadi: A type of Indian cotton that is spun and woven by hand. Gandhi advocated the weaving of it to make clothes for the Indian people so they could shun British made goods.

Knitting: A process for making fabric involving two needles that loop the yarn over previously made loops.

Knop: A group of fibres appearing along the length of yarn, giving a textured effect.

L

Lace: A textile that has an open, net like structure, used for decoration on garments. It can be made by knotting, knitting, crochet, needle and thread, tatting or with bobbins.

Lambwool: Wool from lambs before they are 7–8 months old. It is a soft fibre and is better for spinning than wool from older sheep.

Lanolin: The natural oil from a sheep's wool.

Latex: Is a natural material that has a milky colouring and texture. It is used to make a variety of textiles

Lawn: A plain weave cotton that takes its name from a city in France, Laon, where it was made. It is lightweight, soft and can be dyed, left plain or printed. Used for making dresses, shirts, curtains, children's wear and handkerchiefs.

Lazy Kate: A device for holding bobbins ready for plying. Traditionally made to look like a ladder.

Jar of liquid latex.

Lea: A measurement for linen yarn in length to weight.

Leader: This is yarn attached to the bobbin or shank of a spindle to help when starting spinning a length of yarn.

Lehariya: Indian tie dyeing method.

Level: A dye term referring to even colour. This will only happen in some cases with the use of an additive.

Light Fastness: Resistance to the fading effect of light or sunshine.

Line Fleece: A fleece which can be thrown into one grade or another because its quality lies between the two.

Line Flax: Line fax is the long fibre that will be spun differently to tow, the shorter fibre.

Linen: Fabric made from flax or hemp. It is one of the oldest fabrics produced by mankind.

Llama: An animal of the camelid family and is native to South America. It is a relative of the Alpaca. The fibre is lustrous and light weight.

Lock: A tuft or group of wool fibres that cling naturally together in the fleece.

Loden cloth: A fabric originally made from wool but now made from wool mixes such as mohair or camel. It is thick, warm and durable with a water resistance.

Lofty Wool: Wool that is open, springy, and bulky in comparison to its weight. This type of wool is desirable.

Loom: A machine for producing cloth by the interlacing of two sets of threads substantially at right angles to each other.

Loom State: What a piece of woven fabric is called just as it leaves the loom and before it undergoes any other process.

Long Wool: Fleece from breeds like the Lincoln, Leicester, and Cotswold. Each fibre is thick and very long.

Lowland Wool: A fleece that is often coarser than most and has either a shorter, curlier fibre or a longer straight one; often used in worsted fabrics.

Lurex: A modern textile consisting of a metallic thread given a plastic outer layer to make it shiny.

Lustre: The natural gloss or sheen of a fibre, usually of long-wool breeds.

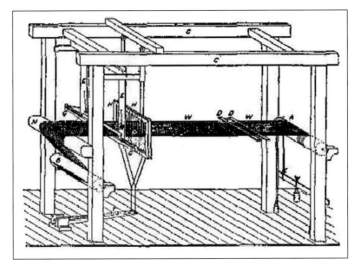

Loom.

Lye: Sodium hydroxide. Strong alkali used with vat dyes such as Indigo. Always add Lye to cold water not warm!

M

Mackinaw: Wool fabric composed of ordinary grade wool and recycled or low grade wool blended with it. It is often fulled or felted. It is also known as ski cloth and snow cloth because of its thick, heavy weight that makes it a natural choice for outdoor winter pursuits.

Madder: The root of the *Rubia tinctorum* plant and used as a natural dye for thousands of years. It can produce hues ranging from reddish brown, deep red to purple.

Madras: Cloth originally made in Madras, India, hence its name. It is usually made from cotton and is often a plain coloured background with stripes or checks.

Magnanery: Shed for housing silk worms.

Maiden: The name for the posts that support the flyer on a spinning wheel. Maiden, and the base that supports them, is called the mother-of-all.

Man-Made Fibre: A man-made fibre is one that has been manufactured using chemical processes and additives even if the base for the fibre is something natural like cellulose. The fibres, broken down into a liquid state by acids, are then pushed through a spinneret to simulate the thread of a silkworm or spider, after which more processing may take place.

Market Class: The class into which animals are put for their end product: meat or wool.

Marl Yarn: A yarn consisting of two or more single ends of different colours plyed together.

Martindale: An abrasion test used to measure the durability of fabric. The warp and weft threads are abraded simultaneously.

Mawata: Silk cocoons that have been heated in lightly boiled in water put out on wooden frame.

Mercerisation: A process of treating fabric with caustic alkali so they swell and stretch in order to increase the lustre.

Medulla: The core of a single wool fibre.

Mercerizing: The process of soaking fabric in a cold, concentrated solution of sodium so that the fabric will have a lustrous finish. It was invented by John Mercer.

Metamerism: The effect of light on the appearance of colour in fabric.

Micron: A measurement used in grading wool.

Milling: A fulling process by immersion in water and agitating it to make it shrink and thicken up. Called after the mills where it was made. Fulling mills were the first water-driven machines used in processing textiles. They were being used in medieval times and earlier.

Modacrylic: This is fire, chemical and abrasion resistant yet is a soft man-made textile.

Mohair: The hair of the Angora goat. The fibres are long, lustrous and silky it is also stronger and more resilient than wool. It accepts dye more easily than many other hair fibres.

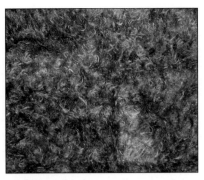

Mohair yarn.

Moity Wool: Wool that contains straw or other, non-seed-or-burr vegetable matter.

Mordant: A material used to fix a dye in or on a substance, by combining with a dye to form an insoluble compound. Commonly used mordants are chrome, iron, aluminium, and tin.

Mother-of-all: The whole stand that supports the maidens, bobbin, and flyer.

Mulesing: The removal of the wrinkled skin around a lamb's rear-end so that no wool will grow there.

Mungo: Wool fibres recovered from old and new hard worsteds and woollens of firm structure. The fibres are less than .5 in. in length, and owing to their reduced spinning and felting qualities, they are largely used in cheaper woollen blends. Mungo fibres are usually shorter than shoddy fibres.

Mushy Wool: Wool that is lacking in character and is often dry.

N

Nap: A pile raised on the fabric by brushing it. The appearance of the fabric is altered by the way the nap catches the light. It is important to take the nap into consideration when dressmaking.

Napping: The process of raising fibres from the base structure of a fabric or felt by brushing.

Natural Dye: Dye obtained from substances such as roots, bark, wood, berries, lichens, insects, shellfish and flowers.

Natural Fibre: Fibre obtained straight from the source whether that is: animal, vegetable or mineral sources. Regenerated and synthesised fibres are not natural fibres.

Navajo Ply: A hand-crocheted loop used to create a three-ply yarn.

Neps: Small knots of tangled fibre, usually consisting of short, dead or immature fibre, or caused by over-processing and not the result of deliberate planning.

Nettle Fibres: Fibre obtained from nettles such as Ramie in China. These are *bast* fibres.

Man-made fibres.

Novelty yarns.

Noils: These are the short fibres taken from the wool when it is being combed. Noils are used for spinning and felting.

Novelty Yarns: Yarns with a quirky appearance that may well have a short fashion run. Often they are made from artificial fibres.

Numerical Count System: A wool grading system. It divides all wools into 14 grades, and each grade is given a number.

Nylon: The generic term for man-made fibres composed of polyamides derived from coal and petroleum. Characteristics: high strength, elasticity, low water absorption and quick-drying, resistant to insect attack, abrasion and resistant to some dyes. It is used for making everything from pantyhose to fishing lines and rope.

O

Olefin Fibre: A man-made fibre that is very strong despite its light weight. It will resist mildew, staining, abrasion and chemicals. It is used to make clothing and many of the interior components of cars.

Organdy: A fine cotton fabric made with slightly twisted yarn. Typically sold with a crisp finish which is deceptive because it is the result of a starch that will wash out.

Organzine: Silk thread that has been thrown, doubled and twisted to make a four-ply yarn.

Off-sorts: The by-products of sorting wool. Off-sorts includes: short fibres, britch wool, kemp, grey wool and stained wool.

Open Wool: Wool tends to grow sparsely on a sheep and shows a distinct part down the ridge or middle of the back. Usually found in the coarser wool breeds.

Opening: The term given to the second step in commercial wool processing after sorting. The fleece is thrown flat so that scouring will be more efficient.

Overlocking: The joining of two pieces of fabric by double stitching over and around the edges. Overlocking machines are very popular and give a professional finish to seams.

Oxford: A cotton fabric with a basket weave look. It is popular for making men's shirts.

P

Patchwork: A new fabric made out of smaller pieces cut from other fabrics and stitched together to form a design. It was a way of using up scraps and material from clothing that had worn out or was too small.

Pick: A weft thread passing through a warp thread.

Piece Dyeing: Fabric that is dyed after it is woven.

Pelt: The skin from a slaughtered sheep before the wool on it has been pulled or processed into a sheepskin.

Pilling: Small balls of fibre that develop on the fabric due to general wear and tear. It is common in knitwear made from cheap yarn.

Pina: The vegetable leaf fibre from the pineapple plant.

Pieces: The skirtings and other less-desirable pieces of wool removed from the fleece (an Australian term).

Pilling.

Plain Wool: Wool lacking character and with few crimps.

Plant Fibre: A textile fibre taken from a plant, e.g., cotton, flax.

Plied Yarns: Yarns produced by two or more single ply yarns being twisted together.

Ply: A single thread of yarn. If two or more of these are twisted together then they will form a multiple ply.

Plying: The process of taking multiple singles and twisting them back against themselves.

Polishing: A process involving burnishing a plied yarn to give it a sheen.

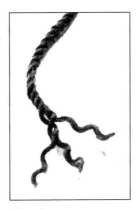

Plyed yarn.

Polyester: A manufactured fibre made from long-chain synthetic polymers. Characteristics: crease-resistance, quick-drying, great shape retention, high strength, abrasion resistance and easy care. Its original shape is determined by heat and will not be damaged with exposure to sunlight.

Poplin: A fabric similar to broadcloth but with a more pronounced filling. It is usually mercerized. If it is intended for outdoor use it is coated in a water repellent finish.

Pot Ash: Potassium Carbonate. A natural mordant for dye.

Presser: The person who puts the sorted wool of the shearing shed into a mechanical press to be made into bales.

Primitive: A fleece that contains long and short fibres.

Printing: A form of surface decoration applied to fabric by applying thickened dye to a plate carrying a carved or engraved motif that is to be transferred to the fabric.

Production Sequence: With regards to wool: Shearing, sorting, opening, cleaning, carding, drawing, possibly combing, possibly roving, twisting or spinning.

Protein Fibre: A fibre composed of protein, including such naturally occurring animal fibres as wool, silk, alpaca, llama and other hair and fur fibres.

Pulled Wool: Wool pulled from the carcass of a slaughtered sheep after the flesh side has been treated depilatory.

Purity: Refers to the absence of dark fibres, kemp or hair.

Q

Qiviut: Downy undercoat fibre from the musk ox.

Quality: Refers to the degree of fineness in wool fibre and fabric.

R

Rafia: A fibre taken from the rafia palm.

Ramie: A species of nettle that has *bast* fibres used for making cloth.

Range Wool: Wool produced under range conditions in the West or the Southwest. With the exception of Texas and California wools, it is usually classified as territory wool.

Raw Silk: Silk reeled straight off the cocoon and without degumming so it retains its stickiness.

Raw Wool: Another name for greasy wool.

Rayon: A generic term for man-made fibres composed of regenerated cellulose derived from trees, cotton and woody plants. It has good drape-ability, is highly absorbent, can have a bright lustre or a dull one and takes dye readily. It is also very strong and resistant to household bleaches and other chemicals.

Reclaimed Wool: Wool that is reclaimed from new or old fabrics.

Reed: Comb-like feature of a loom through which the warp-end pass.

Reeled Silk: A long strand of silk reeled from a number of cocoons and not twisted or spun. In order for this silk to be harvested the pupa in the cocoon has to be killed first with heat.

Regain: The weight of moisture present in a textile fabric expressed as a percentage of the oven dry weight.

Regenerated Fibres: These are man-made fibres that have natural fibre bases. Rayon and acetate are two common types. Rayon is made from wood chips and acetate from cotton. Both are modified by immersion in an acid type bath.

Rejects Fibres: Those not good enough for processing further with the quality fibres. For example: in fleeces, those with excessive coloured fibres and alien matter (twigs, dirt, burrs etc.).

Reprocessed Wool: Scraps and clips of woven and felted fabrics made of previously used wool. These remnants are garnetted; that is, shredded back into a fibrous state and used in the manufacture of woollens (spun like short fibre fleece).

Resilience: The power of recovery to original shape and size after removal of the strain which caused the deformation. A fibre may possess this quality to spring back to its original state after being crushed or wrinkled. Resilience is sometimes referred to as memory.

Retayne: A cationic dye fixing agent. Used on cotton fabrics to improve wet fastness of direct dyes and to colour paper pulp. Is helpful as an after treatment for reactive dyes where washing facilities are not adequate for complete washout, though tends to lower light fastness qualities.

Retting: This is the process in flax production that weakens the fibres in the flax plant. Several retting methods are used:

Dew or Grass Retting. Small bundles of the uprooted flax plants are left outdoors for 3–5 weeks.

Pond Retting. Small bundles are left submerged for 4–8 days. Many books refer to an unpleasant stench as a side effect of this process.

Stream Retting. Small bundles are anchored in a body of moving water. This is the quickest and the cleanest of the processes.

Reused Wool: Wool that has been made into fabric, used and worn out, the less desirable parts of a fleece and fleece that is not good quality can all go into the shredder for processing to be re-spun or felted. Wool can be recycled at home in many other ways too:

Cut up old jumpers and full the pieces for different projects – bags, toys, wall hangings

Unravel garments that are too small or out of date, wind the yarn into balls and knit into something else.

Cut up old garments of any fabric and use the fibres to make punch rugs or latch hook rugs in an age old tradition.

Rippler: The name of the coarse comb used for removing seeds from flax fibre.

Rippling: The process in flax production that removes the seeds. The seeds are removed before retting takes place, that is the breaking down through soaking in water of the outer casing of the plant stem.

Robust Wool: Strong wool with plenty of bulk.

Rolag: A roll of carded fibre that is rolled from the hand carders. It is light, soft and fluffy, looks a bit like candy flow. It is then ready for spinning.

Rooed: Shetland sheep are not shorn. Their fleece is plucked from them by hand. Rooing is the name of the process. The sheep's fleece will naturally start to loosen at a particular time of the year.

Rouseabout: The Australian term for the person in the shearing shed who gathers up the fleece from the floor and keeps the place tidy.

Roving: Fleece after is has been cleaned and carded ready for spinning.

Rug Making: Rugs have been made for centuries and many different methods have been used. Felt was an early type and weaving. Later there have been hooked rugs where the wool is cut into short lengths and hooked through holes in an open weave canvas and pulled through the loop it has made so that it remains knotted in place. Punch rugs became popular as a way of using old, worn out clothing and sacking as the back. A punch tool was used to push the strips of fabric through the loose hessian weave. The pile on the other side could be left looped or it could be cut. Plaiting strips of material and then stitching them in a coil has also been popular for thrifty homes.

S

S-Twist: Spinning clockwise. Traditionally, this is the direction single plies are spun.

Sackcloth: Originally a coarsely woven fabric made from goat's hair but then associated with hemp. It later came to mean an item of clothing worn by the Israelites during the mourning period. It was also symbolic of submission and was worn by prophets. Later again to wear sackcloth was a type of penitence and was known as a hair shirt and worn on Ash Wednesday.

Sailcloth: Takes its name from one of the popular products made from it. Sailcloth is a heavy weight canvas or duck.

Sateen: A cotton or rayon fabric with a sateen weave that is lustrous. It can be given a mercerized finish for extra sheen.

Satin: A very lustrous fabric that can be quite heavy, draping well. It can be made of silk. It is a luxury fabric and used for glamour wear.

Saxony Wheel: The spinning wheel featuring a treadle for the foot that came into favour in the Sixteenth Century and replaced the hand turned Great wheel.

Scotchguard: The brand name of a chemical compound that is used to finish fabrics that will come into contact with dirt, water etc. Upholstery is often treated to a layer of scotchguard.

Scouring: the process of washing a fleece to remove any excess oil and dirt. A fleece can lose 50 per cent of its original weight after scouring.

Scroop: The rustling sound produced when some silk is compressed.

Scrutching: After flax has been retted the softened outer stem is ready for scrutching which entails beating and breaking the outer fibres so that the inner *bast* fibres can be separated from the other.

Sea Island Cotton: A type of cotton. Its white silky texture gives it the title of the world's finest cotton. It was for a long time grown in the Carolinas and Georgia but is now grown in Mexico and Central America.

Seersucker: A cotton or rayon fabric with a crinkled texture produced by using slack and taut yarns in the warp. The name derives from a Persian word *shirushaker* which means milk and sugar. While the texture is traditionally woven in there are now seersuckers produced by other methods including chemicals and heat, these last two are not necessarily permanent.

Selvedge: The edge of a woven fabric where the weft turns back on itself to be woven across the warp again. Selvedge edges cannot fray.

Semi-bright Wool: Grease wool that lacks brightness due to the environment under which it is produced, though it is white after scouring.

Semi-worsted Yarn: Yarn spun from sliver carded (not combed) and pin-drafted on worsted spinning system machines.

Sequin: Small flat bead made of metal (or plastic) with a single hole in the middle to be sewn onto fabric for decoration; they are usually shiny.

Sericin: The glue like substance binding silk filaments together so they form a cocoon.

Sericulture: The art and craft of raising silk worms, harvesting the silk and preparing it for spinning and weaving.

Serge: A wool based fabric made in a distinctive twill weave. A diagonal appears in the weave running from the lower left corner of a piece of fabric to the upper right corner. It is hard wearing and has a hard, smooth finish which will go shiny with wear. Traditionally is made into suits and coats.

Serrations: The outer or epidermal scaly edges on the wool fibre which can be seen under a microscope: usually the finer the wool the greater the number of serrations. Serrations assist in felting by interlocking.

Sett: A term used to define the weft or warp density of a woven fabric, usually in terms of a number of threads per inch.

Setting the Twist: After you have plyed your wool, you need to set the twist. There are several approaches to this. One school of thought says that you wash your yarn and then dry it under tension. This approach is fairly popular with weavers. Another approach says that you wash your yarn and **don't** dry it under tension. This approach is more popular with knitters. Yet another approach, promoted by Judith MacKenzie, says, really shock your wool and let it do what it's going to do. This is done by washing in alternating hot and cold baths. A more detailed description is written up by Marie-Christine Mahe in *Yarn Abuse*.

Shafty Wool: Wool of extra good length, sound, and well grown.

Sharkskin: Not literally. It is instead made of wool and is worsted. The weave has distinctive diagonal lines running across it that gives a 'step' effect. It is very smooth to the touch and is used mainly for suits.

Shatush: This is an unusual fabric made from the hair of wild goats and is usually white, silver or grey. It is very fine in its texture and is one of the rarest fabrics in the world.

Shearing: The process of removing the fleece of wool from the sheep by means of hand shears or machine clippers.

Shed: The gap formed when warp threads are separated during the weaving action.

Sheepskin: The wool of the sheep still on the pelt or skin.

Shetland: Fleece from the sheep of the Shetland Islands in Scotland. The wool is not shorn from the sheep but plucked from it by hand. It gives three grades of wool: coarse from the outer coat, fine from the undercoat and superfine from the belly area. It is often left in its natural colourings of off whites, greys and browns. It is rarely dyed.

Shifu: Thread made from paper is an old Japanese tradition and has been used historically in clothing.

Shoddy: Wool fibres that are recovered from either new or used woven or felted cloth and which must be designated as reprocessed or reused. Wool fibres included in this classification usually run 0.5 inches or more in length, they are of longer fibre length than mungo fibres.

Shorts: Short pieces or locks of fibre that are dropped out while fibres are being sorted.

Shrinkage: The loss of weight in wool resulting from the removal of the yolk and other foreign matter in scouring or carbonisation.

Shuttle: The mechanism on a loom that carries the weft thread through the shed to interlace with the warp.

Silk: The product of the silkworm when it spins its cocoon in which it will pupate then turn into an adult moth. The most common cultivated moth is *bombyx mori* and was first domesticated in China. In order to harvest the long unbroken filament of the cocoon it must be thrown into hot water to kill the moth before it hatches. Once the cocoon is broken the thread will have to be spun like wool and the silk is felt to be less fine.

Singles: A single ply of yarn.

Sirospun: The term for spinning and twisting two strands together in a single operation to create a two ply yarn. The resulting yarn is more elastic, less hairy and is firmer than normal two-ply yarns.

Sisal: A vegetable fibre that is made into strong, coarse twine. It has been used for other textile products.

Size: Any of various gelatinous or glutinous preparations made form glue, starch, etc., used for coating the threads and yarn.

Sizing: Applying a size to fabric or yarn.

Skein: A length of yarn taken from the reel, wound into a long bundle, not a ball, and tied at one or more points to prevent tangling.

Skeining: The processing of winding a skein of yarn. This process can be done with a small frame-like structure.

Skew: What results in weaving when the warp and wefts are not at complete right angles to each other.

Skirting: Trimming all the dirty and less desirable parts of a fleece before shearing the whole.

Skirtings: The inferior quality wool that has been removed from the fleece.

Slippage: Unintentional shifting of warp or weft threads in weaving resulting in gaps in the fabric.

Sliver: A strand of loose fibres after carding.

Slub Yarns: A yarn which is deliberately made with slubs or bumps in it to create texture.

Snarls: Small, curly or knotted sections of yarn.

Soda Ash: Sodium Carbonate. Use as an alkali fixative for reactive dyes.

Sodium Acetate or **Sodium Acetate Crystals:** An acid-forming salt that acts as a levelling agent for Sabraset/Lanaset dyes.

Sodium Bicarbonate: Bicarbonate of soda or baking soda. An alkali used to set reactive dyes by steaming or ironing.

Sorting: The process of separating a fleece into its various qualities according to diameter, length, colour ,strength and cleanness.

Soutache: Decorative braid, woven or crocheted.

Space-Dyed: A yarn or fibre that has been dyed at irregular intervals.

Spandex: A textile that can stretch five times its own length and go back to its original shape. It is lightweight and is used mainly for sportswear and foundation garments (corsetry).

Spindle: An ancient device for making yarn. At its most basic level it can be just a stick. The spinning is more efficient if a weight is added to the bottom of the stick, this is called a spindle whorl.

Spindle Spun: A yarn produced on a hand spindle.

Spinner's Type: A fleece that is good for spinning without too much cleaning and preparation.

Spinning: The drawing out and twisting of fibres to produce a yarn.

Spinning Jenny: An early spinning machine having more than one spindle, enabling the spinning of several threads at once.

Spinning Wheel: A device used for spinning fibre into yarn or thread, consisting essentially of a single spindle driven by a large wheel or a flyer driven by a treadle.

Spinster: Originally meant a female who spun thread. It was not used in England with its unflattering modern connotations until the Eighteenth or Nineteenth Century.

Spun Silk: A yarn composed of fibres of silk which have not been reeled from the cocoon but have been gathered from wild cocoons or are cultivated cocoons that have been damaged. The silk fibres are short, not the long unbroken filaments of cultivated silk and need to be spun in a manner similar to wool.

Stained Wool: Discoloured fleece which will not scour clean.

Staple: A cluster or group of wool fibres naturally clinging together in the fleece.

Staple Length: The sample fibre length from a fleece.

Staple Length: The length of sheared locks measured as it comes straight off the animal and without stretching or disturbing the crimp.

Stenter/Tenter: A finishing machine used for drying and to set fabric width.

Stock Dyeing: Dyeing of the whole fleece. Most stock-dyed wool is made into woollen yarns unlike worsted wool which isn't dyed until it has been combed.

Storage Bobbins: Bobbins used to store yarn that will be plied later.

Strength: How much weight the fibres can bear.

Stretching: When the fibres are pulled taut while spinning.

Strick: The bundle of prepared (hackled) flax fibres.

Stubble Shearing: The practice of shearing different lengths of fleece from a sheep to be used as samples.

Suint: A component of the natural oil sheep secrete to keep their fleece in order, it is sometimes called perspiration. Suint is made of potash and fatty acids, free fatty acid and saline matter. It is soluble in water.

Superfine Wool: The ultimate class of wool and is produced by merinos.

Supplementary weft: An extra weft thread that is deliberately woven in to form a pattern.

Style: The combination of crimp and crinkle ranging from good crimp and good crinkle to no crimp and no crinkle.

Synthetic fibres: Man-made fibres produced using petrochemicals.

Synthetic Dye: A complex colourant derived from coal tar.

T

Tacking: A simple and temporary stitching on a garment to hold parts in place while the real stitching is performed.

Tags: The faecal laden britch wool of a sheep that is worthless for spinning. Also called 'dags'.

Tagging: The removal of faecal matter matted into the fleece of a sheep. In Australia is called 'dagging'.

Tag Locks: Large locks of britch wool clotted with dung and dirt. In Australia they are known as 'dags'.

Tahkli: A small, metal-whorl supported spindle.

Tailor: A man who makes clothes, mainly for men. He is a professional who will have undergone an apprenticeship.

Tapestry: A woven picture traditionally made with wool.

Tatting: A way of making lace using a small shuttle onto which the yarn is wound. The lace is formed by manoeuvring the shuttle and the yarn over and around itself to form a knotted material. Lace made in this way is very fine.

Tease: To disentangle and loosen fibres before carding.

Teasel: A plant with a large prickly head traditionally used for fulling fabric.

Tencel: A man-made fibre that appeared commercially in 1992. It is a fibre made from the wood pulp trees (chosen for their environmental sustainability) and processed in a non-chemical. It is the first new man-made fibre to appear in over 30 years. It is a good tough fabric that won't shrink or tear easily.

Tender: Wool that is weak at one or more places along its length.

Tentering: Fabric is stretched tight on a frame and held in place with pins, called tenterhooks and then steamed or left to dry in the sun. The object of the stretching is to help the fabric keep its shape.

Tensile Strength: The amount of pulling a fibre can withstand before it stretches and breaks.

Tensile Strength: The breaking strength of a fabric, usually measured in Newtons.

Terry Cloth: Known as terry towelling in Australia but is also called Turkish towelling. It is usually made of cotton, sometimes linen and is a jacquard and dobby with a pile weave. It is, as the Australian name suggests, often used to make towels out of.

Tex: A unit of weight indicating the fineness of yarns and equal to a yarn weighting one gram per each 1,000 meters.

Texture: The look and feel of the yarn or fabric. A texture can be smooth and silky or bumpy and rough.

Textured Yarns: All yarn has texture but this term is applied to man-made fibres that have had deliberate effects put into them to make them seem like the natural fibre they are imitating.

Thigh-spun: The most primitive form of spinning, pre-spindle. The thread is made by rolling the fibres down the thigh or between the fingers.

Thimble: A metal, porcelain or leather cap to be worn on the finger, traditionally the middle finger. It is used to help push the needle through the fabric. A bronze thimble was dug out of Pompeii. It is believed to have been made in the First Century AD.

Ticking: Known as a fabric for covering mattresses, its stripes are unmistakable. It is cotton woven in a firm twill weave and is very sturdy.

Tie-dye: A resist dyeing method using string or thread to tie up knots in the fabric. Where the ties are made the fabric will not be able to take the dye.

Tippy Wool: Wool staples which are caked with wool grease and dirt on the outer ends.

Tops: The soft long fibres removed from the lesser fibres through combing.

Total Fleece Weight: The weight of the entire raw fleece before any processing other than shearing has taken place.

Tow Linen: Made from the tow fibres, the shorter flax fibres that are combed out and put aside for spinning in a manner similar to wool.

TPI: Twists Per Inch (or Turns Per Inch).

Tow: The shorter flax fibres removed by hackling.

Thread: The result of spinning fibre.

Treadle: A plate attached to the spinning wheel or sewing machine which, when it is pedalled it will turn the wheel so the hands are left free.

Tritik: Similar to tie dyeing but the fabric is folded and stitched prior to dyeing.

True-to-Type Wool: A fleece showing strong breed-specific characteristics.

Turmeric: A plant spice used in cooking for both colour and flavouring. Also used as a dye, it comes from root of the plant.

Tussah Silk: The wild silk of India and China where the silk worms are fed oak leaves. This gives the silk a gold colour.

Tweed: This is the Scottish name for twill and taking its name from the river Tweed. Originally made from wool but now uses a variety of fibres and mixtures. Traditionally used for making suits and coats.

Twill: A diagonal weave effect created by the passing of weft threads over two or more warp ends.

Twist: Refers to the turns made to the yarn as it is being spun to hold the fibres together. The more twist the stronger the yarn, as in worsted yarns. Woollen yarn is less strong and has less twist. It is usually indicated as turns per inch or tpi

Twitt: Refers to unevenly spun yarn the cause of which is the carded wool is not drawn at an even rate probably because the spinner is not very experienced.

Tying: The term given to the tying up of a fleece after it has been shorn.

Type: A class of wool that has a particular set of characteristics. These are based on: breed, condition, length, spinning quality, soundness, style, and colour.

U

Unevenness: The quality of the fleece is never the same all over the sheep and this is the term used to refer to this.

Unfinished Worsteds: The term unfinished is misleading. The fabric is made of worsted yarn which is brushed to give it a soft nap finish.

Unwashed Wool: Wool that has not been washed or scoured to remove the natural oil.

Upright Wheel (also traveller or parlour): So called because it was designed to be portable. The flyer is mounted above the wheel to make it so.

Urea: A synthetic nitrogen compound used with dye to help its solubility.

V

Value: The relative lightness or darkness of a colour.

Vegetable Matter: Any kind of bur, seed, chaff, grass, or other vegetable matter found in your fibre source.

Velvet: A luxury textile with a short but thick pile. It is woven on a special kind of loom and two pieces of velvet are woven at the same time.

Velveteen: Usually made of cotton but is now made from some man-made fibres; it has a very short filling pile that gives it a soft, furry feel. Better quality velveteen has a twill backing. Cheap quality velveteen loses its pile quickly and ends up looking threadbare.

Velour: A plush pile fabric with a plain or knitted ground. It can be made of natural or man-made fibres. It was invented in France in 1844 in Lyons and its name means 'velvet' in French.

Venetian: A fabric, often wool based that has a good lustre that resembles satin. Used mostly for lining.

Vicuna: A member of the camelid family and is a close relative of the llama which it resembles except for its small size. The fibre produced by this animal is finer than merino wool and has a lovely natural colour range including caramel and chestnut. It is a luxury fibre and is very expensive. Vicunas can only produce a small amount of fleece and the Peruvian government is very strict about its availability.

Virgin Wool: Wool that has been shorn from a live sheep not undergone any of the processing that follows.

Voile: A light sheer fabric made from cotton or wool (when it is called Voile de laine). The tighter the twist in the yarn the better the quality of fabric; its hard, crisp finish is partly due to the method used of singeing away surface fuzz.

Vyella: A fabric blend of wool and cotton that has the appearance of fine flannel. It is good for pleating and is machine washable.

W

Warp: The yarns that run the length of the loom. The warp yarns are pulled through the loom as the weft or filling yarns are woven across the warp to make the fabric.

Warping: The term for putting the warp threads onto a loom.

Wax print: A resist dyes fabric printed with wax before dyeing to prevent the waxed area from absorbing dye.

Warping Board or Frame: A wooden frame with strong pegs inserted in the sides around which the warp can be wound.

Warping Reel: A mechanism, whose purpose is similar to that mentioned above for winding the warp and to keep the threads from moving about and getting tangled. It takes the form of a rotating frame that can be mounted horizontally or vertically. It's used to wind a warp and help keep the threads in order.

Washability: Refers to the reaction of wool to washing. It has a reputation for shrinking unless treated with the utmost care. One new technique being developed is to chlorinate the fleece before spinning and get rid of the tips of the scales (that in the fibre structure cause shrinkage and creep). It is then given a coating of fine resin.

Washed Wool: Wool washed in cold water while on the sheep's back before shearing (industrial term).

Wastage: A term used in both spinning and weaving. In spinning it refers to the fibre that is waiting to be spun. Some of it will be unusable because it is too dirty and is therefore called wastage. In weaving, it refers to the part of the warp that cannot be used because it is wound around the loom at both ends.

Wasty Wool: Wool that is short, weak, tangled or matted and usually quite dirty and not suitable for spinning.

Weave: The making of fabric by interlacing fibres at cross angles to each other. The upright threads that will determine the length of the fabric are called the warp fibres. The threads that are intertwined across the warp threads are known as the weft.

Webby Wool: A thin fleece with poor staple formation and a large number of cross fibres.

Weft: The thread that is woven across the warp (perhaps from weft to wight?).

Weft-Face Fabrics: Any fabric in which the warp is completely covered with weft.

Weighting: The term used for adding mineral salts or something similar to fabric to make it heavier. This is usually practised in material sold by weight rather than by the yard.

Wether: A male sheep or goat that has been castrated. Not only does this procedure prevent unwanted breeding taking place but it also means that energy that would have been taken up in hormonal needs can go directly into the quality of the fleece.

Wet-Spun Flax: As opposed to dry spun flax. As the name suggests a lubricant of some sort used during the spinning procedure. The fibre can be kept moist by licking the fingers or by dipping them in a bucket of water kept by for the purpose.

Wether Wool: The term applied to fleece taken after the first shearing, usually from a sheep older than 14 months. The fleece can be quite dirty.

Wheel: A mechanism for facilitating spinning. It originated in China with the silk reeling wheel and in India with the small hand turned wheel for spinning cotton.

Whipcord: Has a finish like gabardine and is made of worsted, woollen cotton and rayon and blends of these. It is very hard wearing and is often used for making work clothes such as overalls.

Whorl: Spindle whorls were the weighted bottoms of spindles to help them spin more quickly and efficiently. Later the same principle was applied to mechanical spinning.

Wickability: The ability to draw moisture through the fibre.

Width: The measurement made of fabric from selvedge to selvedge.

Wigging: Shearing around the sheep's eyes before annual shearing is due so the animal can see.

Winding: A spinning term that refers to twisting the spun yarn onto a bobbin and held in place so it won't come undone.

Windle: A reel or swift.

Wiry Wool: Wool that is not very elastic. It does not spin well. The fibres tend to be very straight and are likely to result from poor breeding or unhealthy sheep.

Woad: A blue dye produced from *Isatis tinctoria*, it is not as strong as indigo.

Woof: An old term for weft.

Wool: The hairy covering of sheep and related animals. Hair is harsher and has a different structure.

Wool Clip: The total yield of wool shorn during one season from the sheep of a particular region, or in other words, the total number of bales of wool produced by the sheep of one region or farm.

Wool Classer: The person who sorts the newly shorn fleeces into their grades.

Wool Combs: These are tools for preparing wool for worsted spinning. They come in different sizes.

Wool-Dyed: or dyed-in-the-wool are terms given to wool that is dyed before it is spun.

Wool in the Grease: Wool in its natural condition as it is shorn from the sheep.

Wool Roller: The person in a shearing shed who skirts the fleece, then rolls it. The fleece is then classed.

Woollen: Yarns spun from shorter fibres after being carded. The shorter fibres tend to stick out from the twisted yarn giving it a fuzzy texture. They are called woollens so as not to be confused with worsted which, while they may be made from the same fibre, e.g. wool, they are processed differently. Worsted is made from the longer fibres undergoes several preparatory phases and is then twisted tightly to form the yarn. Woollens, on the other hand, use short fibres and are just carded then spun with a looser twist.

Woollen Count: A measurement system for wool in which 1,600 yards of yarn equals one pound.

Woollen Spinning System: Another term for Woollen spun. It is the process used for turning shorter fibres into yarn and is also good for blending different fibres.

Woollen spun: The term used for wool that is spun in the ordinary way from short fibres. It is first carded and then spun, unlike worsteds that are made from longer fibres and undergo a more complex preparation.

Worsted: There are two different processes which are combined to make a smooth, clean yarn. The term comes from Worstead in Norfolk England, and was only applied to woollen yarn. Nowadays worsted yarn can be made from any number of fibres as long as they are long, combed and then spun tightly. The characteristic of fabric woven from worsted yarn is its smooth finish.

Worsted Count: The system used for measuring numbers of hanks of wool needed to make a pound of yarn.

Worsted Spinning System: A way of processing yarn to be spun that will end with a strong and compact product. Medium length and longer wool fibres are used and they are then: opened, blended, cleaned, carded, combed, drawn and finally spun.

Worsted spun: Yarn that has been spun from long wool fibres that have been combed and spun tightly. The end product is a strong, compact yarn.

Wuzzing: A term used for the process of removing excess moisture from yarn. To do this at home you hold the skein firmly at one end and whirl it around your head.

Y

Yardage: A measurement for fabric. In non-metric countries material is sold by the yard, in metric countries it is sold by the metre or part thereof.

Yarn: A generic term for cordage made from various fibres. It is spun or twisted into very long lengths and can be made in many different thicknesses, often according to the material they are made from.

Yarn-Dyed: Yarn that is dyed after spinning as opposed to dyed in the wool where the fleece is dyed before spinning.

Yellowing: Discolouring of the fleece often caused by urine, faeces, bacteria or fungus. Most stains cannot be removed by washing.

Yield: The amount of wool got from a fleece after is has been scoured. A 'high yield' is one that did not lose much wool in the cleaning process.

Yolk: The natural grease excreted from glands in the sheep's skin to help repel water from the fleece and to help prevent it tangling. The finer the grade of wool the more yolk will be present.

Z

Z-Twist: Spinning counter-clockwise which is the way plied yarns are spun.

Zibeline: Fabric named after a small animal of the sable family that is found in Siberia. The fabric is made from wool of cross-breed sheep. It has a sleek and lustrous finish. It is often dyed in strong bright colours. It is used mainly for making coats, cloaks and capes.

Textile Places of Interest

The American Museum in Britain, Claverton Manor, near Bath, England. Has a large collection of exhibits of pieces throughout American history, including 200 quilts

Armley Mills Leeds Industrial Museum in Armley, West Leeds, West Yorkshire, England. Has a large collection of textile machinery. The building housing the museum was previously one of the largest woollen mills in the world

Bankfield Museum in Boothtown, Halifax, England. Has a textile gallery

Blackburn Museum and Art Gallery is the local museum service for the borough of Blackburn with Darwen Borough Council. Houses the contents of the former of the former Lewis Textile Museum

Bradford Industrial Museum, in Moorside Mills, Eccleshill, Bradford, United Kingdom, has a large collection of textile machinery, kept in working condition for regular demonstrations to the public. www.bradfordmuseums.org

The **Colne Valley Museum** in the Colne Valley at Golcar, Huddersfield, West Yorkshire, England. The museum is housed in three converted Nineteenth Century weaver's cottages. The museum provides an insight into what life was like for a weaver in the early 1850s. The museum includes a handloom and a spinning room

Cromford Mill in Cromford, Derbyshire, England. Richard Arkwright's first water water-powered cotton spinning mill constructed in 1771

Derby Industrial Museum in Derby, England. Also known as the Silk Mill because it is situated in a former silk mill built 1717–1721 for the Lombe brothers for their machinery for doubling or twisting silk into thread

Derwent Valley Mills in Derbyshire, England, early cotton spinning machinery of Richard Arkwright was set up here in the Eighteenth Century

The **Fashion Museum** in Bath, Somerset, England. Shows off the collection of fashionable dress through the ages from the Sixteenth Century until modern day. The collection was started by Doris Langley Moore

The **Hat Works** in Stockport, Greater Manchester, shows hat making equipment

Mossley Industrial Heritage Centre, Mossley, Greater Manchester, England. Is housed in part of the old Longman's cotton waste mill. Contains artefacts and old photographs supplied by former mill workers

The **Museum of Domestic Design and Architecture (MoDA)** in North London, England. Comprehensive collections of Nineteenth and Twentieth Century decorative arts including wallpapers and home textiles

The **Museum of Science and Industry (MOSI)** in Manchester, England. Contains exhibits to do with Manchester's textile industry
www.mosi.org.uk

The National Woollen Museum in Drefach Felindre, Llandysul, Carmarthenshire is part of the National Museum Wales

New Lanark on the River Clyde, approximately 1.4 miles (2.2 kilometres) from Lanark, in South Lanarkshire, Scotland. Founded by David Dale in 1786 who built cotton mills and housing for their workers.

The **Quaker Meeting House** in Kendal, Cumbria, England is home of the famous Quaker tapestry depicting the history of Quakerism from the Seventeenth Century to modern times. It was made by 200 or so people from eight or more countries between the years 1981 and 1989. It is not a true tapestry but an embroidery in crewel work and inspired by the Bayeaux tapestry

Quarry Bank Mill in Cheshire, England. This mill is one of the textile mills that existed during the Industrial Revolution. It has been preserved and is now a museum featuring the cotton industry

The **Quilt Museum and Gallery** in York. It is dedicated to the history of British quilt making and textile arts. It is situated in St Anthony's Hall, Peasholme Green

Stott Park Bobbin Mill in Newby Bridge, Cumbria, England. It was a factory, a water powered mill, for the making of bobbins which were sold to the Lancashire weaving and spinning industries and up to a quarter of a million bobbins per week

Thwaite Mills in Leeds, West Yorkshire, England. It is a fully-restored working water-powered mill and industrial museum

Verdant Works in the Blackness area of Dundee. It was originally a jute mill but now houses a museum of the textile industry.

The **Victoria and Albert Museum** in The Royal Borough of Kensington & Chelsea, London, England. Huge collection decorative arts and design including textiles and cotumes

Wardown Park Museum in Luton. Houses a collection of the traditional crafts of Bedfordshire, such as lace and hat making

Whitchurch Silk Mill in Whitchurch, Hampshire. Was originally built as a fulling mill, then became a silk weaving mill

Textile places of interest USA:
The Textile Museum 2320 S Street, NW, Washington, DC www.textilemuseum.org

The Cotton Museum, at the Memphis Cotton Exchange, 65 Union Avenue Memphis, TN 38103 www.memphiscottonmuseum.org

The Fabric Workshop and Museum 1214 Arch Street Philadelphia, PA 19107 www.fabricworkshop.org

Hat and Fragrance Textile Gallery, Shelburne Museum 6000 Shelburne Road Shelburne, VT www.shelburnemuseum.org

Mission Mill Museum, 1313 Mill St SE Salem, Oregon 97301
www.missionmill.com/

Quilters Hall of Fame, 926 S. Washington St. Marion, IN 46953
www.quiltershalloffame.net

San Jose Museum of Quilts and Textiles, 520 S. First Street, San Jose CA 95113, 408.971.0323, www.sjquiltmuseum.org

The Metropolitan Museum of Art, 1000 Fifth Avenue, New York, New York 10028–0198
http://www.metmuseum.org/visit/general_information/

Textile Museum of Canada, 55 Centre Avenue Toronto, Ontario M5G 2H5
www.textilemuseum.ca

Textile places of interest Australia
Bendigo woollen mills, 4 Lansell St, Bendigo, Victoria, 3350
www.bendigowoollenmills.com.au

Nundle woollen mills, 1 Oakenville Sy, Nundle, NSW, 2340
www.nundle.info

Power house Museum, Woodbridge Hill Handweaving Studio, 269 Woodbridge, 7162
handweaving@learnetworks.com.au

Other Places of Interest:
Kurdish Textile Museum Kurdistan, Erbil citadel, Kurdistan
www.kurdishtextilemuseum.com

Textile Museum – Barcelona, Avinguda Diagonal, 686, Barcelona, Spain, 08034
www.dhub-bcn.cat/en/museus/museu-textil-i-dindumentaria

Lyon textile museum France (MUSEE DES TISSUS ET MUSEE DES ARTS DECORATIFS), 34 rue de la Charité F-69002 Lyon
www.musee-des-tissus.com/museum

Museum of Fashion and Textiles France (Musée des Arts Décoratifs – Musée de la Mode et du Textile), Palais du Louvre – 107, rue de Rivoli, 75001 Paris
Disabled access via a lift at 105, rue de Rivoli.

Anokhi Hand Printing Museum, Anokhi Haveli, Kheri Gate, Amber, Jaipur
www.anokhi.com

Calico Museum in Ahmedabad India, Sarabhai Foundation, Opp. Underbridge, Shahibag, Ahmedabad-380 004, Gujarat, India
www.calicomuseum.com

Museum Tekstil Indonesia, Jl Aipda KS Tubun 4 Menteng Jakarta, Java 11421 Indonesia

Textile Museum Sna Jolobil Mexico, Calzada Lázaro Cárdenas 42, San Cristobal de las Casas, Chiapas 29200, Plaza Santo Domingo, between Navarro and Nicaragua

National Textile Museum Bhutan, Norzin Lam, City Centre

Bibliography

Albinia, Alice, *Empires of the Indus*, John Murray, Great Britain, 2008

Amos, Alden, *The Alden Amos Big Book of Handspinning*, Interweave Press, USA, 2001

Asher, Catherine B. and Talbi, Cynthia, *India Before Europe*, Cambridge university Press, Cambridge, 2006

Ashley, Maurice, *England in the Seventeenth Century (1603–1714)*, Penguin books, Middlesex, 1952

Bindoff, S.T., *Tudor England*, Penguin Books, Middlesex, 1950

Bland, A.E., Brown, P.A., Tawney, R.H. (eds), *English Economic History: Select Documents*, G. Bell and Sons, Ltd, London, 1914

Brabbs, Derry, *England's Heritage*, Cassell and Co, UK, 2001

Cannon, John (ed.), *The Oxford Companion to British History*, Oxford University Press, Oxford, 2007

Cheyney, Edward P., *A Short History of England*, Ginn and Company, USA, 1927

Cheyney, Edward Potts, *An Introduction to the Industrial and Social History of England*, Macmillan & Co., LTD New York, London, 1916

Clyne, Densey, *Silkworms*, Angus and Robertson, Australia, 1984

Cohen, J.M. (ed. & trans.), *The Four Voyages of Christopher Columbus*, The Cresset Library, London,

De Moor, Antoine, *3,500 Years of Textile Art*, Lanou, Holland, 2008

Dean, Jean, *Colours from Nature – A Dyer's Handbook*, Search Press, UK, 2009

Emery, Irene, *The Primary Structures of Fabrics*, Thames and Hudson, London, (1966, 1980, 1994, 2009)

Evans, Ivor H. (revised edition), *Brewer's Dictionary of Phrase and Fable*, Guild Publishing, London, 1985 (1959 – Cassell Publishing)

Filbee, Marjorie, *A Woman's Place*, Book Club Associates, London, 1980

Flavell, Linda and Roger, *Dictionary of English down the ages*, Kyle Cathie Ltd, Great Britain, 1999

Flavell, Linda and Roger, *Dictionary of idioms*, Kyle Cathie Ltd, Great Britain, 1992

Flavell, Linda and Roger, *Dictionary of proverbs*, Kyle Cathie Ltd, Great Britain, 1993

Flavell, Linda and Roger, *Dictionary of word origins*, Kyle Cathie Ltd, Great Britain, 1995

Gardiner, Samuel Rawson (ed.), *The Constitutional Documents of the Puritan Revolution 1625–1660*, Clarendon Press, Oxford, 1936 (1889)

Gelber, Harry G., *The Dragon and The Foreign Devils*, Walker and Company, New York, 2007

Gillow, John, *Printed and Dyed Textiles from Africa*, The British Museum Press, 2001

Hamilton, Roy W. (ed.), *Gift of the Cotton Maiden*, Fowler Museum of Cultural History, University of California, Los Angeles, 1994

Haw, Stephen G., *A Traveller's History of China*, Interlink, New York, 2003 (1995)

Hecht, Ann, *The Art of the Loom: Weaving and Spinning Around the World*, British Museum Publishing, 1989

Hilliard, Elizabeth, *Kilims – Decorating with Tribal Rugs*, Soma Books, San Francisco, 1999

Hilton, Boyd, *A Mad, Bad, & Dangerous People?* Clarendon Press, London, 2006

Hodder, Ian, *Çatalhöyük The Leopard's Tale*, Thames and Hudson, London, 2006

Hollen Norma, and Saddler, Jane, *Textiles* 4th ed., MacMillan, New York and London, 1973 (1955)

Humphrey, Paul, *Textiles*, Wayland Publishing, Ltd, England, 1982

Inwood, Stephen, *A History of London*, Macmillan, London, 2000 (1998)

Isaacs, Jennifer, *The Gentle Arts*, Lansdowne Press, Sydney, 1987

Keep, Elizabeth, *Textiles at Work*, Oxford University Press, Melbourne, 1992

Kiewe, Heinz Edgar, (arranged), *Textile Design Anthropology 'History of Knitting' First Exhibition*, exhibition catalogue, Oxford, 1977

Legrand, Catherine, *Textiles: A World Tour*, Thames and Hudson, London, 2008

McCuin, Verity, *Chinese Textiles*, V&A Museum Press, 2005

March, Jenny, *Cassell's Dictionary of Classical Mythology*, Cassell & Co, London, 2001

Maxwell, Robyn, *Textiles of Southeast Asia,* Periplus Editions, 2003 (1990)

Moreland, W.H., *A Short History of India*, Longmans, Green and CO, London, 1958 (1936)

Moore, Heidi, *The Story Behind Cotton*, Heinemann Library, UK, 2009

Mullins, Willow G. *Felt*, Berg, Oxford, 2009

Ogg, F.A., Sharp, W.R., *Economic Development of Modern Europe*, Macmillan Company, New York, 1953 (1917)

Plumb, J. H., *England in the Eighteenth Century (1714–1815)* , Penguin Books, Middlesex, 1955 (1950)

Radice, Betty, *Who's who in the Ancient World*, Penguin Books, Middlesex, 1971

Roberts, John (ed.), *The Oxford Dictionary of the Classical World*, Oxford, University Press, Oxford, 2005

Roberts, P.E., *History of British India Under the Company and the Crown*, Oxford University Press, London, 1952 -1921)

Roberts, Stephen, and Currey, Charles, *Modern British History*, Angus & Robertson Ltd, Sydney and London, 1946

Robinson, Stella, *Textiles*, Wayland Publishing, Ltd, England, 1983

Schoeser, Mary, *World Textiles: A Concise History*, Thames and Hudson World of Publishing, 2003

Scott, Philippa, *The Book of Silk*, Thames and Hudson, London, 2001

Sears, J., *Fibres and Fabrics*, Cambridge University Press, 1985

Seeley, J.R., *The Expansion of England*, Macmillan and Co, London, New York, 1902

Spring, Chris, and Hudson, Julie, *Silk in Africa*, The British Museum Press, 2002

Spufford, Peter, *Power and Profit The Merchant in Medieval Europe*, Thames and Hudson, London, 2002

Stenton, Doris Mary, *English Society in the Early Middle Ages (1066–1307)* , Penguin books, Middlesex, 1951

Stephenson, Carl and Marcham, F.G., *Sources of English Constitutional History*, Harper, and Brothers Publishers, New York and London, 1937

Strayer, Joseph, R. and Munro, Dana Carleton, *The Middle Ages 395–1500*, Appleton-Century-Crofts, Inc., New York, 1928 (1921)

Tanner, J. R. *Tudor Constitutional Documents A.D. 1485–1603 With an Historical Commentary*, Cambridge university Press, Cambridge, 1951 (1922)

Tawney, R.H., *Religion and the Rise of Capitalism*, Penguin Books, London, 1948 (1922)

Taylor, Gordon, Rattray (consulting ed.), *The Inventions that Changed the World*, Reader's Digest, 1983

Teasdale, D.C., *The Wool Handbook*, published by author, Croydon, NSW, 2001 (1988)

Thomson, David, *England in the Eighteenth Century (1815–1914)* , Penguin books, Middlesex, 1955 (1950)

Thomson, F.P, *Tapestry – Mirror of History,* The Jacaranda Press, Australia, 1980

Trevelyan, G. M., *Illustrated English Social History: vol. I Chaucer's England and the Early Tudors*, Longmans, Green and co, London, 1958

Trevelyan, G. M., *Illustrated English Social History: vol. II the Age of Shakespeare and the Stuart Period*, Longmans, Green and co, London, 1958

Vainker, Shelagh, *Chinese Silk: A Cultural History*, The British Museum Press, London, 2004

Walsh, Penny, *The Yarn Book*, A&C Black Publishing, London, 2006

Weissman, Judith Reiter and Lavitt, Wendy, *Labours of Love*, Alfred A Knopf, Random House, US and Canada, 1987

Wilson, Verity, *Chinese Textiles*, V &A Publications, London, 2005, www.felthats.com/hats_info/making_felt.html

Whyman, Kathryn, *Textiles*, Gloucester Press, London, 1988

Yafa, Stephen, *Big Cotton*, Viking, New York, 2005

Acknowledgements

A big, big thank you to all the wonderful textile artists who so generously gave me images to illustrate this book, I'm sure that they are too good for the text:

Homer Alvarez
Bendigo Woollen Mills
Glenys Mann – textile artist, Australia, www.manmaid.com.au
Kaffe Fasset – textile artist and designer, UK, www.kaffefassett.com
Brandon Mably – textile artist and designer, UK, www.brandonmably.com
Jan Garside –Textile artist, UK, www.jangarside.com
Judy Wilford – textile artist, Australia, www.judywilford-visualartist.com
Vanessa Taylor – textile artist, Australia
Annamaria Magnus – textile artist, Australia, http://webclearnetworks.com.au/-handweaving
Vicki Taylor – textile artist, Australia
Helen Evans – textile artist, story teller, writer, Australia, www.helenevanswriter.com.au
Lisa Lichtenfels – sculptor, USA, CFM Gallery, New York, NY

And just as big a thank you to the following people who were so kind and willing to help me obtain images for the book, I can't thank any of you enough.

Neil Zukerman – gallery owner CFM Gallery, New York, NY www.cfmgallery.com
David Dunning – photography for Anohi Hand Printing Museum, Jaipur, India
Rachel Bracken-Singh – museum director Anohi Hand Printing Museum, Jaipur, India
Anokhi Hand Printing Museum, Jaipur India

And last, but never, ever least, thank you to the people behind the scenes who helped pull my messy text into the shape of a beautiful book and who waited so patiently for me to get it together:

Fiona Shoop, who gave me the commission
Lisa Hooson, who has been so lovely and not put me on the naughty seat for being so late
Pen & Sword who produced the book
My dear daughter, Beatriz Alvarez, who read and edited as much as she could of the manuscript
And my lovely, lovely agent, Isabel Atherton of Creative Authors who has stood beside me and propped me up all the way through.

Index